The Changing Middle East

The Changing Middle East

A New Look at Regional Dynamics

Edited by
Bahgat Korany

An AUC Forum for International Affairs Edition
The American University in Cairo Press
Cairo New York

About the AUC Forum for International Affairs
The AUC Forum applies respected academic standards to the analysis of policy-oriented issues.
In addition, the AUC Forum highlights issues that bridge the Middle East and the wider world.
To this end, the AUC Forum, alone or in collaboration with national, regional, and international
institutions, holds conferences, international workshops, and panels on timely topics crucial to the
region and the world in the twenty-first century.

First paperback edition published in 2011 by:
The American University in Cairo Press
113 Sharia Kasr el Aini, Cairo, Egypt
420 Fifth Avenue, New York, NY 10018
www.aucpress.com

Dar el Kutub No. 5653/11
ISBN 978 977 416 513 9

Dar el Kutub Cataloging-in-Publication Data

Korany, Bahgat
        The Changing Middle East: A New Look at Regional Dynamics / edited by Bahgat
    Korany.—Cairo: The American University in Cairo Press, 2010
        p.   cm.
        ISBN 978 977 416 513 9
        1. Social Change—Middle East
        2. Middle East—Social Condition
        I. Title
        303.4

1 2 3 4 5 6   15 14 13 12 11

Designed by Adam el-Sehemy
Printed in Egypt

For Sophie-Dalia, a gift of renewal

Contents

Contributors

Rasha A. Abdulla has a PhD from the University of Miami in Coral Gables, Florida. She is assistant professor and graduate director of journalism and mass communications at the American University in Cairo. Her research interests include the uses and effects of mass media, particularly the Internet. She is the author of three books, and several articles and book chapters. She is the recipient of the 2007 Excellence in Research Award from the School of Business, Economics, and Communication at AUC.

Ola AbouZeid holds a PhD from the University of Toronto. She won the Malcolm H. Kerr Best Dissertation Award in Humanities, MESA, in 1987. She is a professor of political thought and theory at Cairo University and director of planning and programs at the Arab Women Organization. Her research interests include issues of gender justice and Islamist movements, particularly with reference to women.

Omar Ashour is a lecturer in politics at the Institute of Arab and Islamic Studies, University of Exeter. He is a specialist on Islamist movements and ideologies, democratization, and ethnic conflict. He is the author of *The Deradicalization of Jihadists: Transforming Armed Islamist Movements* (2009), and a regular contributor to the media, including the BBC, CBC, CNN, Al Arabiya, *al-Hurra, al-Qabas, al-Sharq al-awsat,* and *Carnegie's Arab Reform Bulletin.* He specializes in democratization, ethnic/civil conflict resolution, international security and terrorism studies, and Islamist movements. His work focuses on the Middle East, the Caucasus, and Central Asia.

Julie C. Herrick holds an M.A. in international relations and is at present on the staff of the American University in Cairo. Her primary research interest is the interaction of international security, nonstate actors, political Islam, and social movements. She is currently co-authoring research exploring the economic and social roles of the Muslim Brotherhood in Egypt.

Amani Kandil has a PhD in political science from Cairo University. She pioneered studies in Arabic on Arab civil society. She has been the executive director of the Arab Network for NGOs since 1997. Her numerous books and articles on Egyptian and Arab civil society have appeared in Arabic and English.

Hazem Kandil is a PhD candidate in sociology at the University of California, Los Angeles (UCLA). He has taught at the American University in Cairo (AUC) and UCLA and has published articles on the sociology of intellectuals, military sociology, developments in warfare, and international relations. His work examines state institutions (primarily, military and security organs) and religious movements, with a special focus on Egypt, Turkey, and Iran.

Bahgat Korany is a professor of international relations and political economy at both the University of Montreal (honorary) and the American University in Cairo. He is also the director of the American University in Cairo (AUC) Forum. He has been a visiting professor at several universities in Europe and North America, including Oxford, Paris, Harvard (visiting scholar) and Princeton. He has published nine books in English or French, and some fifty-eight chapters/articles in specialized publications, some of which have been translated into Spanish, Italian, or Chinese. His first book won the Hauchman Prize in International Relations in 1976. He is the lead author of the tenth-anniversary volume of the *Arab Human Development Report*.

Preface to the 2011 Edition:
Beyond Arab Exceptionalism

Bahgat Korany

This book grew out of a desire to form a counterargument to 'Arab exceptionalism,' or the idea that while the rest of the world changes, the Arab world does not. Within a year of publication of its hardcover edition, most of the Arab Middle East had erupted. This time the explosion did not come in the form of a classic Arab–Israeli war or another round of inter-Arab skirmishes, but in the shape of massive street protests, which toppled the long-running regimes of both Tunisia and Egypt. They also ignited civil wars in countries such as Libya and Yemen, leaving other political regimes in the region increasingly on the defensive: Not long after President Hosni Mubarak's resignation, the King of Saudi Arabia offered approximately $36 billion to meet his people's demands and set up overdue reforms. Three months later, the Moroccan throne offered substantial constitutional reforms followed by debt relief for 80,000 of the county's most deprived farmers. Moreover, the ruling regimes in Bahrain and Syria, while still very far from democratic reform, now admit the necessity of change in an attempt to pacify their angry streets. Thus, the Arab Middle East seemed suddenly to have moved from a period of political sterility to one of a tsunami of protests. Traditionally perceived as stagnant and unchanging, this region is becoming part of the world in its transformation. This emphasis on change was the thesis and focus of *The Changing Middle East*, from its beginnings in 2008, as a project of the American University in Cairo (AUC) Forum, right up to its publication in the fall of 2010.The book's orientation and analysis seem, then, to have been vindicated.

Although authors want their books to have an impact, they have little control over the end result. Generally, the diligent among them conduct their research carefully and present their findings clearly, supported by the best evidence available. But this does not guarantee an impact. Have not many classics suffered from low sales and languished underutilized on library shelves?

As a student, I remember being intrigued when reading one contemporary classic, which, to the contrary, sold hundreds of thousands of copies and was translated into many languages—Thomas Kuhn's *Structure of Scientific Revolutions* (Kuhn 1970). The research of this Princeton professor was thorough, the book's main concept of 'paradigm' was well explained, and it fitted neatly into the author's overall conceptual scheme. But what intrigued me most was Kuhn's explanation of the bases of a scientific revolution: the acceptance/popularity of a scientific paradigm. For Kuhn, such popularity depended not *only* on the paradigm's scientific credentials, *but also and specially on its social context.* As a student believing in the omnipotence of science, I was sceptical of this idea and felt that Kuhn was exaggerating the impact of the social context into which scientific ideas were born. Then came the 1989 revolution in Eastern Europe, the collapse of the Eastern Bloc, the end of the Cold War, and the break-up of the Soviet Union itself in 1991. I then saw colleagues who, for years, had painstakingly researched the Cold War, or the patterns of rule in Soviet politics, only to find their manuscripts turned down by publishers who had competed for their texts just a few months earlier. Authors who had just managed to publish their books before the seismic 'Revolution in the East' found their sales dropping drastically. If these were textbooks, many students perceived them as history or even pre-history books. After all, did not an influential essay, one by Francis Fukuyama, equate the end of the Cold War and the collapse of the Soviet Union with the "end of history" (Fukuyama 1992)? For me Kuhn's emphasis on the social context of intellectual diffusion had been confirmed.

Unlike the impact the collapse of the Soviet Union had on my colleagues who specialized in the Cold War, the present 'Arab Spring' has had a beneficial impact on the hardcover edition of *The Changing Middle East*, for the book reacts against those mainstream and influential publications that singled out continuity as a central theme of Middle East politics. While it would be foolish to deny certain regional constants such as the Arab–Israeli conflict, oil politics, and patriarchal modes of thinking, *The Changing Middle East* insisted that there is no Arab stagnation. On the contrary, it emphasized the fact that, as in many societies, surface calm concealed much in the way of movement beneath. It backed up this argument by analyzing some major transformations within the region. Thus, Arab civil society organizations might be underfunded and besieged, but they are alive and even kicking, and although revolutionary feminism in the Nawal El Saadawi mold might not be the dominant pattern of Arab feminism, women's status and gender issues are increasingly becoming a part of the political agenda. Islamic movements are not only multiplying, but some—contrary to expectations—are deradicalizing. Similarly, in the all-too-present Arab–Israeli conflict, nonstate actors such as Hamas and Hezbollah are now prime contestants in an arena traditionally monopolized by states. Political thinkers, fearing the scourge of governmental authoritarianism, are venting their revolutionary ideas through different modes of expression: artistic production and cultural studies. The media have both championed and accelerated the change through Arab satellite channels such as Al Jazeera and Al Arabiya and through the much-touted new social media forms of blogging and tweeting. These are the phenomena that my colleagues and I analyzed and explored in *The Changing Middle East* and which the events of the Arab Spring brought to the fore.

For this paperback edition I debated whether, in light of these events, to make some modifications to the text itself. For instance, the long first chapter, "Looking at the Middle East Differently: An Alternative Conceptual Lens" offers an analytical model for triggers of change, and traces the evolution of the region over more than half a century: 1954–2009. This frameworks posits revolution as the second so-called trigger of change, the first one being war. As for tracing the region's evolution/transformation, I was tempted to reformulate my summary of the last phase, 1990–2009, which I designated as being one of Arab "cognitive disarray." Although the domino effect of protest/revolution may now be creating a new form of pan-Arabism at the levels of civil society and street politics, possibly leading to less disarray, it is also clear that several Middle East leaders are still facing a position of fight or flight. The transition is still in its embryonic stage and its final destination unsecured. That is why I chose to leave Chapter 1 unchanged.

I similarly debated amending this book's concluding chapter, "The Challenge of Change and the Necessity of Social Engineering," for it touches on many of the issues that were to come to the fore during the 'Arab Spring.' It explores in detail the new Arab media, and looks at their evolution across the region as emerging phenomena pushing for change. The chapter also considers the region's 'youth bulge' and contrasts it with an ailing and aging leadership, a situation that the chapter qualifies as "the volcano underneath." Again, the temptation to add to the chapter was resisted, even though the volcano has indeed erupted and its lava currently surrounds us. In short, in this still as yet tumultuous stage of the 'Arab Spring,' I chose to keep the chapters in *The Changing Middle East* unchanged. Finally, some readers might like to know that the Centre for Arab Unity Studies in Beirut is preparing an Arabic edition of this book.

In addition to my debts mentioned in the introduction to the hardcover edition, I would like to thank Morgan Roth, the AUC's director of communications, North America, who contributed to the book's promotion. Thanks are also due to media journalists from CNN and France 24, and especially to Atef Al-Ghamry, the former chief of al-Ahram's Washington bureau, who, long before the 'Arab Spring,' insightfully emphasized the book's contribution in attracting attention to change before the region was actually caught in change's throes.

Introduction

Bahgat Korany

Even before U.S. President Barack Obama emphasized the primacy of change as a driving force, globalization has meant that today there is little room for static phenomena or their analysis. Did not the end of the Cold War and the disappearance of a superpower—the Soviet Union—take the world by surprise in 1989–91, even being announced as the early beginning of the twenty-first century? Moreover, any discussion of basic issues of reform, issuing forth from the United Nations or from national societies, reflects the primacy of change in world discourse. The 2009 *Arab Human Development Report* (UNDP 2009) points to a vast number of changes occurring in that part of the world, from desertification and other environmental hazards to the evolution of 'public opinion moods.'

Mainstream vision and analysis of the Middle East seem to disregard this dynamism and to insist that the region, one of the most internationally penetrated, does not change. Is this another case of the widely held belief in 'Middle East exceptionalism'? For instance, many established books on Middle East international relations have surveyed centuries of the region's diplomatic policy in an attempt to emphasize its unchanging character. These seminal books pile up historical data to back up their thesis of unchanging Middle Eastern diplomatic behavior. On the surface, this static vision seems justified; the never-ending Arab–Israeli conflict, tribalized political processes and factionalization in Lebanon, Iraq, Sudan,

Somalia, and even wealthy Kuwait lend some support to the conventional perception of 'business as usual' in this region.

For some analysts, however, this overemphasis on continuity and the neglect of aspects of change are evidence of an inherently conservative bias in social analysis. Bias in favor of continuity also indicates an intellectual laziness, since it is easier to analyze the status quo than its counterpart, change and transformation.

The Middle East, too, has been going through the dialectics of 'modernization,' the 'crises' of development, both economic and political, the vagaries of 'humanitarian intervention,' and the contagion of globalization's 'electronic herds.' Consequently, in order to provide a proper understanding of the region, the analysis of continuity has to be balanced by the identification and analysis of elements of change. These elements do exist and are shaping the destiny of the Middle East. Elements such as the region's demographic evolution and its repercussions, new Islamic movements and 'new preachers,' the increasing salience of gender issues, literary/artistic debates, and the mushrooming of civil society organizations all come readily to mind. For instance, the 2008 *Egypt Human Development Report* (UNDP 2008) identifies more than 20,000 civil society organizations in Egypt alone. In her chapter, Amani Kandil gives the figure of 24,000 for Egypt, and Algeria, with less than half of Egypt's population, has three times as many—70,000. It is the effervescence of civil society, in more than a quantitative sense of the word.

To dissect these aspects of change, our conceptual lenses have to go beyond a single-discipline approach and aim instead at a more holistic and interdisciplinary one. Chapter 1 will develop a framework for analysis. In addition to its function as a link between the book's various chapters, the framework will offer the basic conceptualization needed for this book's approach. This conceptualization distinguishes two types of change: the sudden 'big bang' type and the steady, almost unnoticeable, but cumulative variety. Chapter 2 details three big bangs and their impact in the Middle East: war, revolution, and 'milestone events.' But since the steady process of change is the most persistent yet unnoticeable, the chapter focuses on the interaction between sudden and slow types of change over the last fifty-five years or so to present the contemporary regional political context.

The remainder of the book follows the same objective of tracking different dimensions of steady change and its interaction with the big bangs. In Chapter 2, Amani Kandil—using the findings from extensive fieldwork and surveys, most of which appear here in English for the first time—provides an overview of the emergence, consolidation, as well the obstacles of an Arab civil society. In Chapter 3 Rasha Abdulla highlights one important aspect of this society: communications media and their evolution over the last twenty years, from the impact of CNN (Cable News Network) to the emergence of Arab satellites, the Internet, and blogging. In Chapter 4, Hazem Kandil analyzes changes in Arab political thought, focusing on the reaction of Arab intellectuals of four different leanings in the face of growing political authoritarianism. Chapters 5, 6, and 7 focus on the ideas and behavior of three specific groups. In Chapter 5, Ola AbouZeid presents, from within the Arab Women Organization but with a critical perspective, an overview and an inventory of the current status of women in the Arab world. In Chapter 6, Omar Ashour investigates the ill-known phenomenon of the deradicalization of Islamist movements through a detailed comparative analysis of the cases of Egypt and Algeria. In Chapter 7, Julie Herrick makes a comparative analysis of Hamas and Hezbollah, two Islamist groups with considerable political clout, whose wars in 2006 and 2008 resulted in a change in the region's strategic landscape. Chapter 8 attempts to pull together the threads of these different aspects of the changing Middle East. The book concludes that the various chapters do demonstrate that change/transformation in many sectors is not only occurring but also, though unevenly, both accelerating and cumulative. The data appendix presents a tabulated overview of the region in the past twenty years, from data on population or urbanization to governance and political leadership.

One important caveat needs to be considered. Although all the chapters converge on the primacy of change, the book as a whole does not indicate that change is *always* good or *always* bad. Such across-the-board generalizations are neither credible nor even possible. For instance, war has proven to be a major factor of change and transformation—a midwife of History, we are told—but very few would think of its destructive and maiming effects as all positive. This, of course, is an easy case of consensus, but other cases are controversial and even divisive. The change in women's status is an example. Ola AbouZeid documents change in this area but laments its inadequacy, whereas some conservative commentators consider such change as 'cultural invasion' and an attack on Arab authenticity. They might consider the opening of the media marketplace (the impact of CNN, blogs, and the like), which Rasha Abdulla traces so systematically, as being responsible for increasing social permissiveness and cognitive disarray. Similarly, some might consider the rise of Arab civil society documented by Amani Kandil or the impact of nonstate actors discussed by Julie Herrick—especially when they count on outside support—as contributing to the erosion of state authority at a time when Arab society has to protect itself against 'somalianization' and the failed-state syndrome. (The most recent list of the world's fifty failed states, according to twenty indicators, includes no fewer than eight Arab states).[1] For Hazem Kandil, however, the evolution of the region has demonstrated the danger of increased political authoritarianism and the resulting exit of some intellectuals from costly and risky political engagement in 'cultural debates.' This could be interpreted by some as an abdication of political responsibility by 'those who know' and can 'talk truth to power.' Equally objectionable to some would be my insistence on the rise of an Arab balance of weakness—not of power—as a correlation of the decline of pan-Arabism, and favor instead my pointing to new forms of Arab social integration such as labor movements, which have proven more beneficial to the Arab population than a 'fossilized' ideology. Similarly, the instances of Islamic deradicalization, as analyzed by Omar Ashour, could be evaluated by some as another form of self-serving political expediency rather than a way of negotiating change.

These varied and often discordant interpretations of change should be accepted and even welcomed. Change and transformation are best conceived of as a challenge and the basis for a plan of action. In the Arab Economic and Social Summit (Kuwait, January 2009), Lebanon's prime minister indicated that because of demographic change and the Arab 'youth bulge,' the region will need no fewer than 51 million job opportunities by 2020 to maintain the present level of (un)employment. Rather than misleadingly assuming continuity and 'business as usual,' we could, by singling out change, identifying its underpinnings, and negotiating them, provide the region with the basis of an early-warning system and a policy of social engineering before these and other new challenges develop into unwanted or uncontrollable crises.

This is the second American University in Cairo (AUC) Forum volume published with the AUC Press. I would like to thank the Provost, Professor Lisa Anderson, who despite a heavy schedule in her first year at AUC provided effective support for the Forum's program. Randi Danforth of AUC Press was very enthusiastic from the start about this project and worked persistently for the publication to appear on time. Thanks, too, to the anonymous reviewer who presented the long list of revisions to the manuscript's first draft. Hagar Taha managed to provide much-needed data from afar. My greatest gratitude goes, naturally, to my co-authors, who accepted my deadlines so diligently, and my assistant, Shaima Ragab, who equally diligently kept things on track through continuous e-mails and telephone calls during my sabbatical. Last but not least, Margaret Korany has been, as with all my previous publications, a constant and effective support. Without such committed support, this project would not have seen the light. All these efforts will have been worthwhile if others will pursue the small step taken here by thinking about and analyzing the Middle East differently.

Notes
1   *Foreign Policy Magazine*, July–August 2009, 82–83.

1

Looking at the Middle East Differently: An Alternative Conceptual Lens

Bahgat Korany

By focusing on change in the Arab Middle East, the objective of this study is not to negate international–regional connectedness or patterns of continuity in this region. These two aspects are all too evident and it would be foolish to deny their presence.

By privileging what has been overlooked—change—this chapter aims to promote a much more comprehensive picture of how this region actually functions. Focusing on change is required academically but it could also help in the elaboration of relevant policies to cope with the evolving challenges on the ground. That is why this chapter combines conceptual and applied analyses. Dividing change into two types, sudden and evolutionary, this study elucidates four bases of change: war, revolution, milestone events, and a steady or routine but incremental and cumulative chain of events. To make the argument more concrete, the major part of the chapter is devoted to putting flesh on these conceptual factors by tracing the evolution of the region over the last fifty-five years or so, divided into five periods. As historians tell us, any periodization in the seamless web of history has its degree of arbitrariness, but periodization can here facilitate a grasp of evolutionary and revolutionary patterns over a long stretch of the region's contemporary life. Given its strategic importance even before the advent of the current petrol era, this region has been highly penetrated (S. Amin 1976; Amin 1982). The focus here is on the region's own dynamics, but in order to avoid the misperception that I have neglected the crucial external impact, I start with a note about the inside–outside connection with respect to the region.

The Middle East: An Amorphous Region with an Arab Core

A large segment of outside observers and of the proverbial Arab street reduce the region's dynamics, and even its fate, to the 'constant' of outside forces. The impacts of globalization, both economic and cultural, or the occupation of Iraq do indeed justify this emphasis on the significance of 'the outside.' But this approach can be highly reductionist and partial (in both senses of the term) if local/regional factors are not brought in to show how they interact with the outside in shaping these regional dynamics. A neologism for this inside–outside interaction is gaining credence in social analysis terminology in the twenty-first century, even among enthusiasts for the sweeping impact of globalization: glocalization (Ritzer 2007, 178–99).

This inside–outside debate was brought to the fore more than half a century ago and by no less than the University of Chicago. The famous 'Chicago School' has been, of course, well-established in economics and sociology since the early twentieth century. The school's contribution extended later to political science. David Easton, for instance, launched his *Systems Analysis of Political Life* in the 1950s (Easton 1953; 1965) and Hans Morgenthau his 'power politics' foundation in International Relations in the 1940s. Much closer to our subject is the Kaplan/Binder debate.

In 1957, Morton Kaplan published his seminal *System and Process in International Politics*. As a rebuttal to his eminent colleague's 'power politics' approach, Kaplan purported to apply scientific analysis to the evolution and functioning of the international system. We are indebted to Kaplan for his rigorous analysis of different types of international systems since antiquity, from the balance of power to bipolarity, and the popularization of such terms as 'loose' and 'tight' bipolarity. We do not need to detail the impact of such an intellectual enterprise except to mention that it was a colleague of Kaplan at the University of Chicago, and a specialist in the Middle East, Leonard Binder, who attacked the book's ethnocentrism and its reductionism of regional dynamics to reflect the rivalry and machinations of the Great

Powers. Binder's approach was to emphasize the autonomy of Middle East dynamics, their *sui generis* character, as distinct from Cold War interaction. Suffice to say that this debate led to the elaboration of an important concept relevant to our analysis of the Middle East: the region as an international subsystem. As the prefix 'sub-' shows, the region as a set or system is conceived of as part of a wider international environment but without the negation of the characteristics proper to its own dynamics (see Thompson 1973 for a good conceptual analysis; Acharya 2007 for an extension to the whole architecture of world politics). So we can have our cake and eat it too! But this happy solution was not applied to the region itself.

One of the early manifestations of this steady change is the debate from within on the *definition of the region* and the emphasis on a distinct Arab identity. Veteran Egyptian journalist Muhammad Hassanein Heikal distinguished between a specifically Arab regional identity and a wider Middle Eastern one in clear-cut terms. Even though his reasoning is related to the Cold War era and its alliance-making in the 1950s, it is worth quoting in detail his distinction between the two frames of reference. Heikal defined the Middle East system as:

First advocated by Britain, France, the United States and Turkey, the real architect of the system was, in fact, the United States, backed by Great Britain. This system saw the Middle East in geographical terms, as a vulnerable land mass lying close to the Soviet Union. Wholly preoccupied with the Soviet threat, the architects of the system held that the countries of the area must organize themselves against this threat by joining in an alliance with others who were concerned for the region's security. This alliance would have to coordinate its defense with other countries exposed to the "Red Peril" (i.e., communism) in Europe and Asia. A Middle Eastern alliance would be the final link in a chain of alliances (including NATO and SEATO) encircling the southern frontiers of the Soviet Union. In the logic of this system, the Arab countries were expected to join in an alliance with Turkey, Iran, Pakistan, even Israel—that is, the Middle Eastern countries directly concerned with the region, as well as with the United States, Britain, and France, the international parties concerned with the region's security as well as being the major participants in NATO and SEATO.

But as a counter frame of reference, there was

the Arab System. Based on a different outlook toward the region, this system saw the Middle East not as a hinterland lying between Europe and Asia—a simple geographical expansion—but as one nation having common interests and security priorities distinct from those of the West. According to this logic, the countries of the area, which enjoyed unity of language, religion, history and culture should—indeed could—create their own system to counter any threat from whatever source. And the main threat, as the advocates of this system saw it, came from Israel, not only because it cut across the African-Asian land bridge but also because, with its seizure of the Auja area demilitarized under the Rhodes armistice agreement, it was clear that it harbored expansionist aims. At the same time, while admittedly the Soviet Union did represent a threat, it was felt that there was not immediate or direct danger from that source. Many people in the area, including Gamal Abdel Nasser, held that the lack of common borders between the Arab nation and the Soviet Union would deter the Soviets from undertaking any military act against it. And in any case, Nasser felt that the answer to communist infiltration did not lie in joining Western-sponsored alliances with their imperialist overtones, but rather in promoting internal economic and social development and in affirming the spirit of nationalism and independence. (Heikal 1978a, 714–16)

As we will see below in dealing with the first phase of the region's evolution, the 1954–55 debate over the Baghdad Pact brought to the fore the collision between these two frames of reference (Korany 1976, 198–300).

The emphasis here is on the Arab subsystem, composed of the twenty-three members of the Arab League, whereas the Middle East 'environment' includes, in addition to this Arab core, the three countries of Iran, Israel, and Turkey (see Noble 2008 for a recent detailed application; Hilal and Matter 1980 for a pioneering attempt in Arabic; Sa'id 1994 and Abu-Taleb 1994 for more recent analyses; and Idris 2001 for application to the Gulf sub-region only. Tables in the appendix provide data on both sets of countries). One important evolution of the last sixty years is that the period began, following the affirmation of Arab nationalism, with a strong political demarcation line between the Arab world and the rest of the Middle East and ended with this line becoming increasingly blurred. How and why this change occurred is what this chapter aims to elucidate

Focus on Change: A Suggested Framework

If the relationship between global and regional levels of analysis appeared to find a happy solution with the elaboration of the international subsystem concept, the problem of analyzing change remained marginalized. Most analyses of the Middle East emphasized continuity, if not stagnation. Consequently, the objective here is to balance out this one-sided conventional wisdom in order to present a comprehensive view of politics and society in the region. To achieve this objective we need to move beyond the generalities of a counter-paradigm, or a counter-general worldview, and present an operational research program. To be operational and applicable, such a research program has to go beyond being satisfied with a pure juxtaposition of disciplines if it is to be interdisciplinary and focused. The suggested method of attaining this objective is to emphasize interdisciplinary concepts such as change and transformation.

This interdisciplinary focus on transformation can help us better understand the present context of the Middle East and its dilemmas. The dilemmas are manifold: the growing pressures of demographics; the change in media politics, from satellite TV channels to growing numbers of bloggers; the debates on education and its privatization; issues of identity and the secularization/theocracy polarization; the impact of aging governing elites versus the youthfulness of the population. If well analyzed, an understanding of these dilemmas can help in policy planning and social engineering.

A prerequisite to reorienting our conceptual lens toward emphasis on change is the presence of an analytical framework. Such a framework would help us sort out data into different fields, classify findings, and link the various chapters into a coherent book, as opposed to the several 'readers' that flood the study of the region.

This framework is based on dividing change/transformation into two basic types: the sudden and/or noticeable variety, and steady or slow but cumulative processes. The former is triggered by any of three 'big bangs': war, revolution, and milestone events. The latter is more of an evolutionary process that can be associated with daily life and normal patterns, such as the evolution of ideas, demographics, environmental hazards, or the impact of unemployment. For instance, in 1970, 41 percent of the population in Arab countries was urban. By 2005, this had grown to 57 percent, and it is likely to surpass 70 percent by 2020, with dire consequences if this urbanization surge is not properly planned (UNDP 2009, 3). It should be emphasized, however, that this distinction between big bangs and steady change is an analytical one and that the two types are not mutually exclusive. Indeed, they are very interactive: a steady process can swell and blow up to become a big bang, and a big bang can by definition accelerate (or hinder) the steady process.

War

From historians to anthropologists, there is consensus on the impact of war on the evolution of societies, to the extent that titles of books talk about the war system and its social process. In his seminal survey of the five-hundred-year period between 1500 and 2000, Paul Kennedy (1988) convincingly shows that interstate war determined both the rise and fall of the Great Powers, the controllers and shapers of the world system. As another authority confirms, "war historically has been the basic mechanism of [international] systemic change. It has always been thus and always will be, until men either destroy themselves or learn to develop an effective mechanism of peaceful change" (Gilpin 1981, 209–10).

The present Middle East state system was itself shaped by the First World War and its repercussions. The war saw the collapse of the Ottoman Empire, the flowering of the Arab nationalist movement, and the rise of 'succession states,' with their incessant problems of 'national sovereignty' and border demarcation (Rogan 2005; Fromkin 2000).

In the contemporary period, the impact of wars has not changed, from the first Arab–Israeli War in 1948, the 1956 Suez War, the 1967 Six Day War, the October 1973 War, the 1982 Lebanon War, the 1980–88 Iraq–Iran War (the First Gulf War), the 1990–91 Second Gulf War, the 2003 Third Gulf War, or the 2006 Israel–Hezbollah and the 2008 Israel–Hamas wars. Many of these wars are so recent that their effect is still unfolding. The old ones also continue to shape history and even daily life.

Witness the first Arab–Israeli War, which saw the birth of Israel, and the numerous armistice agreements with various neighbors that followed (Egypt, 24 February 1949; Lebanon, 23 March 1949; Trans Jordan, 3 April 1949; Syria, 20 July 1949). These armistice agreements bestowed on Israel, *de facto* if not *de jure*, 78 percent of mandatory Palestine. Roughly 750,000 Palestinians were expelled from some four hundred villages—a refugee crisis that has since mushroomed. In the three years following this war, 700,000 Jews, mainly from the displaced in Europe, settled in Israel (Morris 2001). A Europeanized settler-state was to shape the politics of the region.

This close connection between Europe and the region is manifest also in the 1956 Suez War, known in Arab discourse as the 'Tripartite Aggression.' It was based on a covert scheme between Israel and the two colonial powers of Britain and France to punish an emerging anti-status quo Egypt after its nationalization of the Suez Canal Company in July 1956.

This invasion resulted in a restructuring of the Middle East. The political defeat of Britain and France led to the decline of their respective empires and their replacement in the region by two superpowers: the U.S. and the Union of Soviet Socialist Republics (USSR). The Suez War also saw the consolidation of militant Arab nationalism under Nasser's charismatic leadership, Nasser becoming a role model for national liberation movements from Algeria to South Yemen and beyond. But the region became even more internationally penetrated with the stationing (on Egyptian territory only) of United Nations emergency or peacekeeping forces in Sinai as a buffer between the Egyptian army and the Israel Defense Forces (IDF). Even though budgetary cutbacks and changing needs shrank this force to 3,378 persons by 1967, the IDF's withdrawal in May of that year brought about the military confrontation that became known as the Six Day War, resulting in Israel's occupation of Sinai, the Golan Heights, and the West Bank (Love 1969; Kissinger 1994).

Although the emphasis in this chapter is on war and regional dynamics, war also has what economists call a "multiplier effect"—that is, its impact can go beyond the manifestly external dimension to influence domestic societies. The destruction of so many factories, bridges, and other elements of basic infrastructure means that a country's development is pushed back years. Even its very survival can be called into question. For instance, as we shall see later in the chapter, post-1967 Egypt witnessed its Sinai occupied, its oil fields exploited by Israel, and its Suez Canal revenues lost. 'Revolutionary' Egypt had to accept subsidies from its erstwhile enemies—the conservative oil-producing countries—to survive. Syria and Jordan had to do the same. The quadrupling of oil prices in 1973–74 was a direct result of the October/Yom Kippur War. Yezid Sayegh shows how war bestows on the Palestinians international recognition and statehood before the fact (Sayegh 2000, 200–39), and Michel Camus does the same for Algeria (Flory et al. 1991, 387–450). Although not our focus here, civil wars—with their attendant warlords and militias—in Lebanon, Iraq, Somalia, or Sudan can have an even more direct effect on social structure.

The death or maiming of so many thousands of young males—the famous war victims—meant not only the loss of basic economic potential but also of the formation of new families and the renewal of society. An ensuing demographic imbalance is bound to shape the evolution of war-torn societies, in the Middle East as elsewhere. Given the history of European states and the multidimensional analyses of their ruinous world wars, European studies—contrary to the Arab Middle East—are abundant in this respect (Tilly 1975 is a pioneering collective effort). The graduation of recent female police officers in Algeria, although still controversial ("Algeria's Women Police Defy Danger and Stereotypes," 2009), cannot be dissociated from the impact of the country's savage eight-year Liberation War. But with few exceptions (Jerbawi 2008; Sayegh 2000, 200–449; Owen 2000, 325–34; Saad 2000, 240–57), systematic analyses have not yet taken over from anecdotal references on this subject.

What has been elucidated more, however, is the relationship between defeat in war and certain domestic big bangs, such as sociopolitical convulsions in the form of revolutions or coups d'état.

Coup d'État/Revolution

The contemporary global system could not be what it is today without the anti-colonial 'national liberation' revolution that tripled U.N. membership or the scientific and/or technological revolution that made this planet 'one world.' What we are concerned with here, however, are the 'national liberation' movements that changed the Middle East's political system and indeed the region as a whole. Some upheavals were purely military coups and quickly evaporated. Syria witnessed three of these in 1949 alone, after the return of its armed forces from the military defeat in Palestine. An army takeover is to be expected—justifiably or not—after a military defeat, as the case of Ataturk in post-Ottoman Turkey illustrates.

Inspired partially by Ataturk, the 1952 Egyptian coup d'état by the Free Officers movement occupies a special place in this respect. Under the leadership of Gamal Abdel Nasser, it graduated, so to speak, from a pure coup to a socioeconomic revolution. After sending King Farouk and his immediate entourage into exile, it changed the political system from monarchy to republic. From its early years, it adopted radical social measures such as agrarian reform, welfare policies in support of the very poor, and Egyptianization/nationalization policies with respect to the economy. Most important, it became a model to many of the coups d'état and/or revolutions that shook the region afterward. For instance, the 1958 Iraqi revolution, the 1962 Yemeni revolution, and the 1969 Libyan revolution were all directly inspired by this 'new Egypt' and began by abolishing the monarchy and establishing a republic in its stead. Even when not army-based, as these three cases were, a Middle Eastern revolution could still associate itself with the Nasserist revolutionary ethos. The most relevant example is the 1979 Islamic Revolution in Iran.

Although some might argue that the Iranian revolution is still ongoing, it began in early 1978 with the first major demonstration to overthrow the Shah, and formally concluded with the instatement of the new theocratic constitution in December 1979 whereby Ayatollah Khomeini (who had returned in February 1979 from exile in Paris) became Iran's supreme leader. In the interim, the military rallied to the revolution, the ruling Pahlavi dynasty collapsed and fled, and a national referendum on 1 April 1979 overwhelmingly approved Iran as an Islamic republic.

In many respects, the Iranian Revolution is unique. It lacked several customary causes of revolution: defeat in war, a financial crisis, a peasant rebellion, or a disgruntled military. But, as is to be expected from revolutions, it produced profound change at great speed: the overthrow of a regime thought to be heavily protected by a lavishly financed army and security service, and the replacement of an ancient monarchy with a theocracy based on the Guardianship of the Islamic Jurists (*wilayat al-faqih*).

Depending on the observer's perception, the domestic impact of the revolution has been mixed. The broadening of education and healthcare for the poor, the governmental promotion of Islamic values, and the elimination of excessive westernization and American influence in government have met with great success. However, political freedom, the role of women, and the treatment of religious minorities have been controversial issues, ones where the revolution is accused of not fulfilling its promises. But overall, Iran's Human Development Index rating has climbed significantly from 0.569 in 1980 to 0.732 in 2002, which is on par with neighboring Turkey.

Internationally, and long before the controversy over revolutionary Iran becoming nuclear arose, the revolution's impact has been immense. In the non-Muslim world, it has changed the image of Islam and generated interest in revolutionary Islamic politics. In the region and the wider Muslim world, particularly in the early years, it triggered enormous enthusiasm and boosted opposition to western interventionism and 'cultural invasion.' Islamist insurgents were on the go from orthodox Saudi Arabia (Fandi 2001) to secular Syria (the Muslim Brotherhood rebellion in Hamas) to westernized Lebanon (the 1983 bombing of the American embassy and of American/French peacekeeping troops). Indeed, one indicator of the influence of a revolution is when it extends beyond its borders, as both Egypt's and Iran's did, triggering other revolutions or at least milestone events.

Milestone Events
Before such occurrences as the end of the Cold War, the disappearance of the Soviet Union, and, more recently, the devastating 2008 world economic crisis, mention of milestone events as triggers of change might have required some convincing. Whereas wars and revolutions are easily identifiable, and hence their impact more easily measured, the milestone aspect of some events is less immediately evident. Milestone events are distinguished here from political earthquakes such as wars and revolutions, but are also conceived as definitional and consequential, separating 'before' and 'after.' They can exist at different levels; for example, marriage or birth in a family's life, development in an individual's career, or the death of a charismatic leader or icon in a national society (Nasser's death in 1970, Princess Diana's fatal car accident in 1997).

The First World War saw several milestone events for the Middle East. These included, for instance, the 1917 Balfour Declaration, which laid the groundwork for the establishment of the State of Israel, and the 1916 Sykes–Picot Agreement, that is, the secret exchange of notes among the chief allies, Britain, France, and Russia, on inheriting possessions of the then-ailing Ottoman Empire. But there are also instances of milestone events in more recent history. The 1958 establishment of the United Arab Republic (U.A.R.) between Egypt and Syria is such an example at the regional level. Arabs had talked for so long of the 'inevitability' of Arab unity that both Arab thinkers and the Arab street tended to accept it as a necessary and natural evolution. On 22 February 1958, it became a reality amid popular euphoria that stretched beyond the borders of Syria and

Egypt. When Nasser arrived in Syria after it became the 'northern' region of the U.A.R., the Syrian masses literally attempted to lift his car in the street. Rival regimes in Jordan and Iraq felt the threat and immediately declared a federation between the two monarchies governed by two wings of the same Hashemite family.

In retrospect, the emotional enthusiasm for the establishment of the U.A.R. was not matched by either steady preparation or careful planning. Consequently, the makeshift nature of this first experiment in Arab unity brought about its downfall. A military coup in Damascus on 28 September 1961 led to Syria's secession from Egypt. Thus, the demise of the U.A.R. was also a surprise milestone event that dealt a fatal blow to the conventional wisdom of the necessity for Arab unity. The U.A.R.—a complete and almost spontaneous amalgamation between two states—remained a childless experience in the annals of Arab unity and continued to shape the Arab agenda at both the state and the civil society level (al-Sayed 1999).

There is an example, however, of a milestone event that had a very different impact. In November 1977, Egypt's President Anwar Sadat surprised his own people and indeed the whole world by declaring his intention to visit Israel. At the time, Egypt and Israel were still theoretically in a state of war (despite the 1975 agreement on the separation of forces). Consequently, Sadat's declaration was perceived by many as either verbal exaggeration or an unintended slip of the tongue (interview with Herman Eilts, U.S. ambassador to Egypt, November 1979). But Sadat was adamant and chided *al-Ahram*'s editor-in-chief when the latter did not include Sadat's statement as a headline in the newspaper's first edition.

After receiving an invitation from the then-Israeli prime minister, Menachem Begin, Sadat addressed the Knesset in Jerusalem on how to achieve a comprehensive peace in the Arab–Israeli conflict. A series of meetings between Egypt and Israel, facilitated by U.S. President Jimmy Carter, led to the Camp David Accords (September 1978) and the Egyptian–Israeli Peace Treaty (March 1979). The treaty established full normal relations between the two countries, including the exchange of ambassadors, economic collaboration, and the free passage of Israeli ships through the Suez Canal. Notably, the treaty made Egypt the first Arab country officially to recognize Israel. Given Egypt's weight in the Arab world, its 'defection' led to the exclusion of an Arab war against the Jewish state at a time when some Arab lands were still occupied and the Palestine problem unsolved.

While Begin and Sadat shared the Nobel Peace Prize in 1979, the treaty was very unpopular on the Arab street. Most Arabs believed that Sadat had reneged on Egypt's Arab role and destroyed the possibility of a united Arab front. The Arab League suspended Egypt's membership and moved its headquarters from Cairo to Tunis. It was not until ten years later that Egypt returned to the League and the League returned to its headquarters in Cairo—all this while Egypt maintained its peace treaty with Israel.

Sadat's surprise visit and later Egypt's return to the Arab League heralded an important transformation: a new regional order that can be labeled the Camp David Order. This order is based on the integration of Israel into a new Middle East (Korany 1997, 98–113), a state system based on full diplomatic and economic relations. The 1979 Egyptian–Israeli Peace Treaty was soon duplicated in the 1993 Oslo Accords between the Palestinians and the Israelis and in the 1994 Jordanian–Israeli Peace Treaty, and is at present the basis of Syrian–Israeli bilateral negotiations. This chain of milestone events led to, but was also influenced by, a steady process of change.

The Steady Process of Change

The linkage between the big bang and steady change processes is not immediately apparent because the latter is by definition initially and relatively unnoticeable. Yet steady change is not only cumulative, but can also easily engender many of the big bangs.

For these two reasons—its initial lack of visibility and its cumulative character—the chapters of this book focus on this process of steady change. By presenting the political context as a steady process of change in the region over the last fifty-five years, this chapter faces the task of demonstrating this interaction between big bangs and the evolutionary chain of events.

To facilitate a grasp of this evolving political context, its development is traced in five stages, whose patterns are here synthesized, followed by a detailed presentation in the rest of the chapter. This chapter began with an exposition of the clear clash of ideas over the different conceptions of the region: the Middle East versus the Arab world. This clash is not only about a geographical definition, but is also identity-based and highly political. To concretize these different dimensions of this clash of conceptions about the region, I dwell here on a milestone event: the 1954–55 debate about the Baghdad Pact.

The defeat of the Baghdad Pact and the victory of those emphasizing an 'Arab core' as distinct from the wider Middle East led to the primacy of pan-Arabism's most enthusiastic advocate: Egypt. As a first stage in this political evolution of regional politics, Egypt's hegemony (1954–67) is traced and its bases are emphasized. This hegemony was not fully accepted by all and was contested by some in what can be called the Arab Cold War in the 1960s. Ultimately, Egypt overstretched as a base (for example, Egypt's military intervention in Yemen 1962–67) and became exhausted. It bled to defeat in the 1967 Six Day War.

In principle, a move toward a multipolar pattern of politics is usually healthier as it is more democratic, encouraging multilateral collaboration and 'additivity.' Initially, there were the germs of Arab complementarity (stage two: 1967–73). It saw the rise of oil-producing countries, which brought exceptional wealth to the region in an extremely short time. And since these rich countries lacked both basic infrastructure and the labor force to build it, they counted on neighboring labor-intensive countries (such as Egypt, Jordan, Lebanon, Morocco, Palestine, Sudan, and Syria). But this logical complementarity did not lead to higher forms of institutionalized regional integration or even negate Arab power diffusion. In stage three (1973–79), the Arab handicap remained, even after the limited victory of the 1973 October War. This 'Arab crisis' manifested itself starkly when the most populous Arab member, Egypt, chose to defect (in 1977–79) and join the adversary, Israel (stage four: institutionalizing state-centrism or the Camp David Order, 1979–90).

Although Egypt returned to the Arab system ten years later, the process of erosion of Arab integration was not stopped. It came to the fore (stage five: 1990–2009) when the various Arab skirmishes were overshadowed by the 1990 invasion of one member of the Arab League, Kuwait, by another, Iraq. An anti-Iraq international military coalition (that included Syria side by side with the U.S.) was mounted to remove Saddam Hussein's forces from Kuwait. Sanctions and even Anglo-American attacks continued against Saddam's Iraq until this country was finally invaded in 2003. The 150,000 or so American forces stationed in Iraq make of the U.S. a real—and no longer a merely virtual—Middle East power. Even before Jihadism's spillover in the 2001 attacks against the 'distant enemy' in Washington and New York, or the rise of a potentially nuclear Iran, the Gulf area was increasingly becoming a primary conflict cluster.

Although the Arab–Israeli conflict remains at the center of the regional political order/disorder, even at this level there is a change. Israel's latest wars, in 2006 against Hezbollah and in 2008–2009 against Hamas, indicate a new type of war: war against nonstate actors. Even though states are present (for example, Iran or Syria), the direct adversary on the ground vis-à-vis the IDF is an elusive nonstate actor and not a professional state army.

Thus the overall strategic context of even this central conflict is changing with the presence of formal peace treaties and the emergence of new actors, including Arab civil society. Indeed, Arab civil society (and Arab satellite channels) has become a new factor in this region. Profiting increasingly from Information and Communication Technologies (ICT), it has placed its concerns on national agendas, from the status of women to the thorny issue of Islam in politics.

Let us then see the pattern of this evolution in more detail by tracing the region's political evolution, divided here into five stages (updated from Korany 1997; 1999).

Regional Transformation, 1954–2009: The Interaction between Big Bangs and Steady Factors of Change

As stated above, one of the earliest manifestations of this steady change has been the debate on the *definition of the region* and the emphasis on an Arab identity as distinct from the overall Middle East one. The 1954–55 debate over the Baghdad Pact brought to the fore the collision between these two frames of reference, these two conceptions of regional identity (Korany 1976, 198–300).

The Baghdad Pact project (a milestone event) officially went into force with the Turko-Pakistani Treaty on 4 April 1953 to complete the chain of western 'containment' alliances to encircle the Soviet Union. As Turkey was already a member of the North Atlantic Treaty Organization (NATO) and Pakistan of the Southeast Asia Treaty Organization (SEATO), Anglo-Saxon attempts to incorporate Iraq and Iran into the new 'anticommunist' organization were destined to stretch the encirclement chain from the Bosphorus to the Indus. Britain was enthusiastic in welcoming this arrangement because it promised a new treaty instead of the existing Anglo-Iraqi one that was to expire by 1957. Thus, on 24 February 1955, Turkey and Iraq signed their mutual assistance pact.

Britain joined on 5 April 1955, followed in September by Pakistan and in November by Iran.

Egypt's Nasser reacted violently to Iraq's 'defection.' The issue dominated policies in Arab interstate society for almost that entire year. Nasser's arguments were diffused through the widely heard Cairo Radio, Sawt al-'Arab ('Voice of the Arabs'), which gave them added weight. He also contacted Arab nationalists throughout the region, explaining that Iraq had violated the solidarity of the League in committing itself to outside obligations. He threatened to withdraw Egypt from the League, a move that would have brought about the institution's demise. Nasser's line of attack was simple. He emphasized pan-Arabism against "imperialism and Zionism" and argued that the Baghdad Pact was not aimed at the "real" enemy of the Arabs—Israel—but was instead an alliance with those who had created and still supported this "imperialist base" against the Arabs, in other words, the West.

Not only was the pact unrelated to the Arabs' defense against their 'real' enemies, according to Nasser, but it was also an imperialist formula permitting imperialist forces into the Arab world through the back door. The appeal of this argument to formerly colonial people was strengthened when 'material evidence' was cited to 'prove' its truth. According to the agreement governing British accession to the Turko-Iraqi pact, "the airfields in Iraq occupied by Great Britain in accordance with the 1932 treaty were to pass under Iraqi sovereignty; but the existing facilities of overflying, landing and servicing British aircraft in Iraq were to be maintained and British military personnel would remain in Iraq, under British command, for this purpose, and would enjoy appropriate amenities. Furthermore, the installations on the airfields retained for British use were to remain 'British property'" (Barraclough and Wall 1955–56, 28). Two British analysts summarized the pact as follows: "The effects of the new agreement were therefore juridical rather than practical; in other words, although sovereignty and legal ownership passed to Iraq, effective use by Great Britain remained largely undisturbed" (Barraclough and Wall 1955–56, 28).

Thus, Nasser insisted, as far as the relationship between the Arabs and the western powers and their "regional stooges" was concerned, Iraq's step meant a return to the old treaty relationships, which brought the newly independent state back into the "imperialist sphere of influence." Instead, he maintained, an alternative Arab strategy could achieve the Arab nationalist aim of independence by creating Arab solidarity on the basis of the

1950 Arab League Collective Security Pact. In practice, as the Free Officer and Egyptian Minister Salah Salem put it, efforts had to be focused on arranging and organizing the 'Arab house': consolidating Arab military and economic capabilities and coordinating Arab efforts and plans. At this stage, no commitments should be concluded with foreign states, which was why Arab states should not participate in the Turko-Pakistani alliance or any other defense arrangements outside the 'Arab homeland.' This "unification of an Arab policy," as Turkish newspapers labeled it, would put an end to the dispersion of Arab capabilities and the "wasting of energy" through disunity. Moreover, a "unified Arab stand" would make of the Arab states a "weighty" interlocutor and give them an elevated status in the international system.

Nasser also emphasized why such an "Arab strategy" would appeal to the "masses" psychologically: "The Arabs have been colonized for a long time and they are always afraid of falling back under western domination." That is why "defense of the area . . . has to spring from the area itself," otherwise the Arabs would not feel that "they are defending their own families, their own children, their own property . . . [but] British or American interest[s]" (Nasser 1960, 66–67).

Consequently, if the western powers were really interested in having independent states that would provide a Middle East defense against "communist danger," Nasser thought they should supply the Arabs with weapons without pressure and without requiring political commitments. The west should not insist on retaining the power of command in this field, as the Arabs themselves were capable of providing it without any political alignment.

The Baghdad Pact controversy is significant in at least two respects. According to Nasser, he was speaking not only for Egypt but also in the name of a unified Arab strategy. What is characteristic of his speeches at that time is his identification with nationalist Arab aspirations and the transcendence of the interests of individual states and governments.

Second, the controversy between the supporters of pro-western alignment and those of nonalignment was depicted as synonymous with the battle of "imperialism, Zionism and their stooges" against the forces of independence and Arab nationalism. If anyone questioned this equation, Israel's 28 February 1955 attack on the Egyptian-controlled territory of Gaza (killing thirty-eight people and wounding thirty-one) was held up as evidence for the fact that Egypt was paying the price for its opposition to 'imperialist' alliances. This confirmed that Nasser—an Arab champion—was the 'target of the Arabs' enemies' and this strengthened his position in the Arab world enormously. Of course, power struggles were not only limited to relations between Arabs and non-Arabs but also permeated inter-Arab relations.

As milestone events, the Baghdad Pact and especially the controversy that followed were so potent as to determine the pattern of inter-Arab and Middle Eastern relations for more than a decade, essentially until the 1967 Six Day War. It was a period of Egyptian regional hegemony consolidated by Nasserism's charismatic leadership, but also its contestation and decline.

Egypt's Hegemony, 1954–67

The controversy over the Baghdad Pact was crowned with Egypt's success in establishing its regional supremacy. This preeminence rested on important bases of power, both tangible and intangible. Egypt's population at the time constituted no less than a third of the entire Arab population. (In fact, at the height of their petro-power in 1975, the six countries that coalesced into the Gulf Cooperation Council accounted for not more than one quarter of the population of Egypt.) Historically, al-Azhar University radiated enlightenment all over the Arab and Islamic worlds; Egypt's many prominent authors, poets, and journalists set the literary and intellectual pace; and Egypt's teachers flocked to other parts of the Arab world to assist in the creation of future Arab elites. Admission into Egyptian universities was the goal of promising Arab intellectuals, and many Arab high school students felt compelled to work hard and earn high grades in order to gain admission to Cairo University; otherwise they would be 'forced' to go to Oxford or Cambridge!

Egypt's multifaceted predominance in the region was already reflected in the Arab League. In Alexandria in 1944, a meeting was convened to establish the League and approve a protocol. The minutes of this meeting are full of speeches affirming Egypt's regional preeminence, and it was in Cairo that the new organization located its headquarters. Until the late 1950s, Egypt's share in the League's budgets ran between 40 and 50 percent, and until as late as 1974, of the 253 permanent and nonpermanent staff members of the League, 162 were Egyptians. Until the League was forced to move from Cairo to Tunis after Egypt's separate peace treaty with Israel, the three secretary generals were all Egyptians, as is the current secretary general.

Various quantitative indicators that span a long period in the evolution of the Arab regional system confirm Egypt's centrality in Arab affairs. For instance, the pattern of official visits between 1946 and 1975 confirms Egypt's preeminence among Arab and other third world countries (Korany 1988, 164–78). Similarly, at the civil society level, in the mid-fifties when Jordanian leaders seemed inclined to join the Baghdad Pact with their Hashemite cousin, Iraq, huge demonstrations erupted in Jordan and other Arab countries at the instigation of Egypt and her Arab supporters. Consequently, Arab membership in the Pact was limited to Nuri's Iraq, and when this regime was overthrown in 1958, one of the first measures of Iraq's Free Officers was to withdraw from this military alliance (which had then to change its official name to the Central Treaty Organization, or CENTO).

Egypt's prestige grew and its leadership confirmed this when it managed to nationalize the Suez Canal Company in 1956 and politically defeat the "Tripartite Aggression of Britain, France and Israel." This rising political hegemony was reinforced when Cairo was explicitly solicited to lead the union with Syria in the United Arab Republic (Flory and Korany 1991; Riad 1986, 193–222). Not only were two prominent states combining their capabilities, but two pan-Arab ideologies—Ba'thism and Nasserism—were joining forces to establish an imposing influential pole mapping the future blueprint of Arab society.

Even though the U.A.R.'s existence came to an end after only three and a half years, Nasserism survived. It manifested its tangible power by sending troops across the Red Sea to ensure the survival of a revolutionary regime in one of the most inhospitable areas for revolutionary change in the Arab world: Yemen. Egyptian troops were thus amassed in the backyard of the leader of Arab conservatism and traditionalism: Saudi Arabia. More than once these troops crossed Saudi frontiers in hot pursuit of Yemeni royalist forces. Increasingly, Arab interactions were polarized. With the main western powers actively involved on the Saudi side, the Arab world echoed the global bipolar structure. As at the global level, bipolarity did not mean complete parity between the camps. Algeria's independence in 1962 and the 1963 coups in Syria and Iraq, followed by tripartite unity talks in the spring and summer of that year, were evidence that Nasserism still represented the region's dominant pole, both at the state and the civil society level. Cracks within the Saudi regime, such as the defection of some Saudi pilots, the activities of 'liberal princes,' and the departure of King Saud himself for asylum in Egypt, confirmed Egypt's apparent hegemony. Yet, in contradiction to the theory of hegemonic stability (Gilpin 1987, 86–92), Egypt's hegemony did not last long. Egyptian supremacy was overstretched and eventually exhausted. The humiliating defeat in the third war with Israel, the so-called Six Day War, confirmed this exhaustion (Korany 1988, 164–78).

Arab Power Diffusion and the Attempt at Complementarity amid Israel's Military Hegemony, 1967–73

Nasser's declaration in November 1967 is still valid: "After this great catastrophe, we were like a man who had gone out into the street to be hit by a tram or a car and lay both motionless and senseless on the ground." Six months later, on 25 April 1968, he described himself as "a man walking in a desert surrounded by moving sands not knowing whether, if he moved, he would be swallowed up by the sands or would find the right path." Indeed, on 23 November 1967, Nasser admitted that his country's direct losses at the hands of a state with one-tenth of Egypt's population were 11,500 killed, 5,500 captured, and 80 percent of Egypt's artillery and 286 of its 340 combat aircraft destroyed. The chaotic collision between two divisions of the Egyptian army in their disorganized race to withdraw to the mountain passes showed that the army as an effective military corps had ceased to exist. To add insult to injury, Israel's casualties were comparable proportionally to yearly road accidents in any industrialized country, or even in Israel itself.

Worse still, there was no diplomatic victory (as in the 1956 Suez War, for instance) to compensate for this military disaster. On the contrary, to this Arab military defeat was added political humiliation. As one observer noted:

> The pre-war picture of Israel as a beleaguered fortress ... had earned the Israelis wide international sympathy. . . . By the discrepancies between their threats and their performance, the Arabs had invited the world's derision. This had been skillfully encouraged by Israeli psychological warfare and propaganda which stressed the cowardice rather than the lack of skills of the Arabs and took every opportunity of showing the Arab and especially the Egyptian armies in a humiliating light—for

example, by photographing Egyptian prisoners stripped to their underwear or other unheroic situations. (Stephens 1971, 497)

Arab speeches of the time are full of themes of the "ordeal," the "cruelty of our situation," "our great pains," "the greatest test and crisis of our modern history." These expressions are in fact reminiscent of the first wave of writings by Constantine Zurayk and others after the first "catastrophe," that of 1948. The "setback" in 1967 led to a second wave of lamentation literature (Korany 1988, 164–78; Maddi 1978; Shukri 1970).

What is important about the Six Day War in this respect is that it showed a yawning gap between Nasserism as a sociopolitical vision and its capacity to deliver on its promise. Nasserism was consequently perceived as wanting and discredited. The market of ideas to replace it was wide open. Marxists insisted that the defeat was not that of the 'proletariat' or even of the people as a whole but of the exploiting bourgeoisie, as Marxism had predicted all along. Liberals reiterated that the defeat was the outcome of a closed and repressive political system, far behind world evolution in science and technology. As for Islamists, they reminded their adherents of what they had been preaching all along: you cannot win if you depart from "the straight path" of God. This market of ideas remains, even though Marxist ideas declined somewhat with the end of the Cold War, the disappearance of the Soviet Union, and the rise of privatization in China. But the fight for liberalization, democratization, and human rights, as well as the prevalence of different patterns of religiopolitics (Korany 2005), is still very much with us.

The opening of the post-Nasserism market of ideas was paralleled by a post-Egypt hegemony pattern of power. Instead of being concentrated around Cairo, regional power became much more diffused.

Nasser's personal popularity notwithstanding, the demise of the Egyptian pole was confirmed and even legitimized during the August 1967 Khartoum Arab Summit. Nasser's Egypt and the radical Arab order was to become subservient to what we can dub 'political petrolism.' Two immediate indications of the retreat of the radical order were the hurried withdrawal of Egyptian forces from Yemen and Egypt's growing financial dependency on subsidies from the oil-rich states. Neither the emergence of a fervent Mu'ammar al-Qadhafi (1969) in his fragile state nor the stateless Palestinian revolution could provide an alternative base for the radical order. The power vacuum (to use the language of balance of power adherents) was to be filled by 'petro-powers,' at least by default (Korany 1988, 164–78).

The end result was not, then, another cycle of hegemony but rather, power diffusion. Within this pattern there were attempts at collaboration. Although issue-specific and consequently short-lived, they still went beyond axis building. A well-known example of such a collaboration was the Egyptian–Syrian–Saudi coordination for the launch of the 1973 October War with Israel.

The preparation for (rather than the performance of) the October War was based on minute planning, systematic information-gathering and analysis, and detailed discussion and bargaining among the different participants, notably between Syria and Egypt. These two countries' negotiations and discussions resulted on 31 January 1973 in the organization of a unified command for their armed forces (Korany 1986, 87–112). Continuous and intense coordination at the top political and military levels fixed the specific day and hour of the attack on the ceasefire lines with Israel: Yom Kippur, Saturday, 6 October 1973, 2:00pm, Middle Eastern time.

Along with this politicomilitary coordination, the war had a wide impact on the global economy because of the accompanying decision to impose an oil embargo. This move was actually a cluster of decisions including the announcement on 17 October 1973 by the oil ministers of the Organization of the Petroleum Exporting Countries (OPEC) of a monthly 5 percent cut in the flow of oil to the United States and other countries supporting Israel against the Arabs. It also included Saudi Arabia's 18 October decision to cut oil production by 10 percent at a time when the United States in particular was pressing oil-producing countries to increase their production to meet the demand of an increasingly oil-thirsty world. Another part of the embargo was Saudi Arabia's 20 October announcement that it would stop all oil exports to the United States following President Richard Nixon's 19 October demand to Congress for $2.2 billion in emergency security assistance to Israel and the continuation of a massive U.S. airlift beginning 13 October to compensate for Israel's war losses.

Continuing Arab Complementarity without Pan-Arab Power Additivity, 1973–79

Several quantitative indicators for this period confirm the primacy of the oil-rich states in inter-Arab politics, leading to a "new Arab social order"

(Ibrahim 1982; Dessouki 1982, 326–47). By 1979, 55 percent of the capital of inter-Arab economic joint ventures was contributed by oil-rich Saudi Arabia, Kuwait, the United Arab Emirates (U.A.E.), Qatar, and Libya. Usually the country that contributed the most capital became the host country for any new project headquarters. In this way, the oil-rich states were becoming the locale for an increasing number of new Arab organizations. In 1970, Cairo was host to twenty-nine, or 65 percent, of these organizations; Iraq hosted none and Saudi Arabia only one. Eight years later, Baghdad had become the locale for twelve organizations, thus occupying second place after Egypt, and Saudi Arabia was in third place with eight organizations.

Fewer Arab League meetings were held in Egypt and more in the oil-rich states. The proportion of meetings held in Cairo decreased from 70.5 percent in 1977 (the year of Sadat's visit to Jerusalem) to 42.2 percent in 1978 (the year of the Camp David Accords). Egypt's share in the Arab League budget dropped. That share was above 40 percent until the late 1950s but continued to decline. By 1978 (the year the Arab League moved to Tunis) it was only 13.7 percent, equivalent to Kuwait's contribution.

Yet the rise of oil-rich states created a golden opportunity for a balanced, less monocentric Arab interstate community to develop. For instance, basic shortages of the newly rich powers were offset by labor surpluses of the old declining powers, enabling some measure of income redistribution (see Figure 1.1).

Figure 1.1

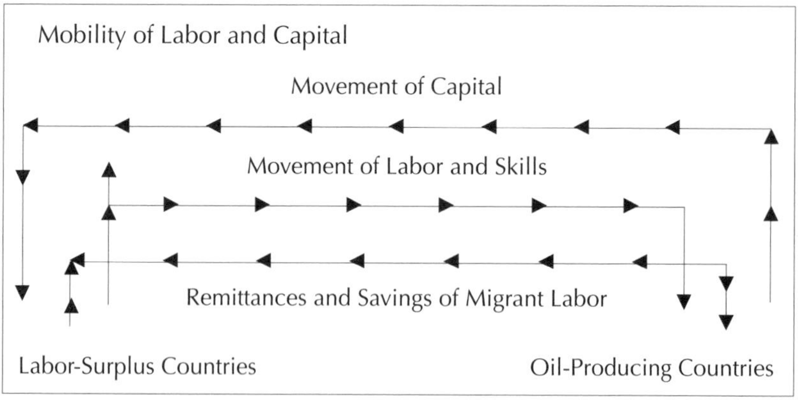

Figure 1.1

Mobility of Labor and Capital

Movement of Capital

Movement of Labor and Skills

Remittances and Savings of Migrant Labor

Labor-Surplus Countries   Oil-Producing Countries

Source: Abdel-Fadil 1979, 161.

Table 1.1: Remittances in select labor-exporting and importing countries (millions $US)*

Country	1973	1974	1975	1976	1977	1978
Export Labor: LaboLaLabo						
Sudan	6.3	4.9	1.5	36.8	37.0	66.1
Egypt	123.0	310.0	455.0	842.0	988.0	1824.0
N. Yemen	N/A	135.5	270.2	675.9	987.1	910.1
S. Yemen	32.9	42.8	58.8	119.3	187.3	254.8
Jordan	55.4	82.0	172.0	401.8	420.8	468.0
Country	1973	1974	1975	1976	1977	1978
Import Labor:						
S. Arabia	-391.0	-518.0	-554.0	-989.0	-1506.0	-2844.0
Bahrain	N/A	N/A	-227.6	-252.8	-300.3	-387.7
Oman	N/A	-111.0	-208.0	-220.0	-222.0	-212.0
Libya	-273.0	-350.0	-260.0	-257.0	-856.0	-557.0
Kuwait	N/A	N/A	-276.0	-315.0	-370.0	-433.0
Country	1979	1980	1981	1982	1983	1984
Export Labor:						
Sudan	115.7	209.0	322.7	107.1	245.8	275.3
Egypt	2269.0	2791.0	2230.0	2116.0	3315.0	3611.0
N. Yemen	936.7	1069.5	777.4	911.4	1084.4	995.5
S. Yemen	311.5	347.1	406.2	429.7	436.3	479.3
Jordan	509.0	666.5	921.9	932.9	923.9	105.3
Import Labor:						
S. Arabia	-3365.0	-4064.0	-4100.0	-5211.0	-5236.0	-5284.0
Bahrain	-278.8	-282.8	-317.6	-311.4	-300.0	-345.7
Oman	-249.0	-326.0	-452.0	-684.0	-692.0	-819.0
Libya	-371.0	-622.0	-1314.0	-1597.0	-2098.0	-1544.0
Kuwait	-532.0	-692.0	-689.0	-702.0	-906.0	-855.4

Source: International Monetary Fund, *International Financial Statistics Yearbook*, December 1980, February 1983, December 1985 (adapted from Choucri 1986).

Moreover, the huge oil revenues were partially redistributed through remittances to the poor labor-exporting countries, with the result of more equally widespread benefits to the region. In 1975, workers' remittances were $1.13 billion, reaching $15.36 billion in 2004, with the main recipients being Lebanon ($5.1 billion), Egypt ($3.3 billion), and Jordan ($2 billion) (Noble 2008, 94).

What better basis for an integrated Arab regional system could there be? But power diffusion continued as the oil-rich states failed to provide a power base equivalent to the former Egyptian one, a base that could maintain the unity of an Arab entity.

With the exception of Algeria and Iraq, the so-called rich countries were lacking—at least initially—in everything from food to arms. There were huge deficiencies in infrastructure and in established bureaucracy, as well as in personnel. Once development projects were envisaged, both skilled and unskilled labor were urgently needed, and importing it was beneficial to the Arab interstate society since the problem for most Arab countries was one of labor surplus.

Thus, the complementarity among the factors of production, labor, and capital provided an excellent basis for integration and thus a higher level of resource exploitation. Moreover, the acceleration of the laborers' movement across state frontiers showed the fragility of legal state barriers and made the different strata of Arab society aware of their interdependence.

So why did this integrative process stop halfway despite the factors in its favor? This question touches on one of the most persistent issues of recent social analysis: the transformation of political systems. Although some studies have successfully addressed the transformation of nation-state systems (Goldstone 1989; Moore 1966), analysis of the transformation of interstate or international systems is still in an embryonic stage (Armstrong 1993). Consequently, the ups and downs in Arab interstate society can shed light on the conceptual issues of international system transformation as a whole, while also providing information on important regional dynamics in this part of the world.

Two preliminary reasons why the Arab integrative process failed in mid-effort were the inability (even if willingness existed) of the oil-rich states to act as an alternative regional base and the absence of a pan-social project to give normative direction and hold the interstate society together. The result of this fragility of a petro-based hub would not be a shift to another hegemony but, rather, power diffusion.

The oil-rich states were not powers in the conventional sense of the concept. If they were powers at all, it was purely in the financial sense. They lacked almost all other attributes of power: sizable populations, solid administrative structures, well-trained effective military manpower, and pan-Arab political organizations. For example, even though Saudi per capita income was sixteen times that of Egypt, Saudi Arabia was basically poor in most indices of development. In 1975, the Saudi petroleum minister, Ahmed Zaki Yamani, described his country in the following way:

We are still a poor country . . . we lack industry, agriculture . . . man-power. We have to import engineers, technicians, specialized workers that we don't know where to house because we lack hotels. To build hotels we need contractors, but the contractors themselves need hotels to live in. It is a vicious circle that exhausts us. Among other things we lack cement. We lack harbors because we lack cement to build them. Last, but by no means least, we lack water. We haven't a single river, a single lake. We depend on rainfall alone. For one hundred years, it has rained less and less frequently, for the last twenty-five years hardly at all. (Ayubi 1982, 23–24)

Even in purely financial terms, Saudi per capita income was comparable to that of Finland, which is not a particularly rich country and has lent its name to the political term 'Finlandization,' indicating almost total marginality and dependence. Until the gigantic projects at Jubayl and Yanbu' managed to give an industrial base to the Saudi kingdom, it would remain dependent on the outside world. In fact, in all of the oil-rich states, infrastructure is still consolidated thanks to foreign labor. For instance, in 1975, foreign workers constituted 81 percent of the labor force in Qatar and 85 percent in the U.A.E.

Another reason for the fragility of the petro-based hub lies with historical patterns of social organization. The process of state formation rendered those countries family-states rather than nation-states. As economist Hazem el-Beblawi writes:

Though oil wealth has transformed [the Gulf states] into advanced welfare states, they still remain patriarchal in a distinctly familial way. The Sauds, the Sabahs, the al-Thanis, the Qasimis, the al-Nahayans, the al-Maktums, the al-Khalifas are not only the ruling families: they embody the legitimacy of the existing regimes. (El-Beblawi 1982, 210–11)

Pan-Arabism retreated in the face of *raison d'état*, which was indiscriminately mixed with *raison de famille*. Two outcomes resulted from this situation. First, the leadership was characterized by a limited time horizon and an extremely personalized perception of national and international events. Second, inter-Arab relations were fraught with a long history of interfamily feuds. In short, family frictions imposed extreme limitations on political coordination. Unfortunately, the rising technocratic elite has not been able to change this situation to any great extent. Consequently, Arab finance has not been complementary to pan-Arabism. The oil-rich states have been unable or unwilling to devise an Arab strategy. If they seemed in control, it was not so much that their achievements had won out, but that the outcome had been determined by the failure and exhaustion of the so-called radicals. Thus, these states' primacy in Arab interstate society represented victory by default.

This is not a strong base for an integration process, let alone unity. Even if Saudi Arabia, the birthplace of Islam, became armed with oil and was increasingly the site of secular as well as religious pilgrimage, it would not be able to keep a regional system together. As has been said, "the hegemony of mere money unsupported by manpower, cultural attainments, military strength or industrial development may be something of a mirage" (Kerr and Yassin 1982, 11).

Growing labor–capital complementarity was not correlated, as the functionalist theory of integration insists, with equivalent political integration. All that could be achieved from 1971 to 1977 was a Cairo–Riyadh axis, based on a tradeoff of Egyptian capabilities and Saudi money. A predominant characteristic of a relationship based on money is constant haggling, which can destroy that relationship at any time. A general mood of 'affairism' rivaled nationalist commitment and penetrated the highest echelons of society, even trickling down to the masses in former revolutionary centers such as Egypt and Syria. Muhammad Hassanein Heikal summarized the change in both elites and social mood:

> For a generation the men who directed the course of events in the Arab world had been ideologists or officers from the armed forces—or sometimes officers who turned into ideologists or ideologists who tried to behave as if they were officers . . . (for example, Sadat, Assad, Boumedienne, Qadhafi, Michel Aflaq, Saddam Hussein). . . . Many of these were still there, but they were now being joined by the first

installment of a new breed of power brokers, the middlemen, the arms dealers, the wealthy merchants who flitted between East and West, between royal palaces and the offices of royal companies . . . (for example, Kamal Adham, Mahdi Tajir, Adnan Khashoggi) . . . and by royalty itself, for who in the Arab world now exercised more power than Prince Fahd or Prince Sultan of Saudi Arabia? Could not individuals such as these, it was argued, achieve more for the Arab world than mass movements and radical revolutions? It is not surprising if in this changed atmosphere men and women in Egypt and Syria felt that the time had come for them, too, to see some improvement in their material circumstances. They had known hardship; now they looked for their reward—for more to eat and for better houses to live in. Of course, money would have to be found to pay for this. But who would dare to suggest that the Arabs were short of money? It was being said that the Arabs possessed the power to bring the rest of the world to starvation; surely they must have the power to feed themselves? So eyes turned to the oil-producing countries. Oil fields began to loom far [larger] in the public mind than battlefields; *tharwa* [riches], it was said, had begun to take over from *thawra* [revolution]. (Heikal 1978b, 261–62)

Power Diffusion Institutionalized: The Camp David Order, 1979–90

The Camp David order denotes, of course, an Egyptian–Israeli partnership legally codified in the 1979 Egyptian–Israeli peace treaty, with the direct participation of the U.S. Administration at the highest level—that of the U.S. president, Jimmy Carter. It is not only the rationale behind and conception of this regional order that has been emphasized but also the *way* it has been planned and executed. Camp David is thus not only a milestone event but also a projected paradigm for managing Arab–Israeli relations and a norm of regional organization.

In September 1975, Egypt formally initialed its go-it-alone diplomacy with Israel by signing its second disengagement agreement with a political clause amounting to a state of nonbelligerency. The rift between Egypt and Syria was patched up temporarily in a 1976 tripartite summit in Riyadh. Saudi mediation facilitated Egyptian–Syrian reconciliation where Syria agreed to tone down its critique of the Egyptian move and Egypt accepted the presence of Syrian troops in Lebanon. Egypt's go-it-alone diplomacy with Israel was confirmed and consolidated on the occasion of Sadat's 1977 "sacred mission" to Jerusalem.

In a nutshell, the Camp David Accords mark an important watershed in Middle Eastern politics because they witnessed, in 1979, a separate peace agreement between the Arab system's arch enemy, Israel, and its base, Egypt. An American scholar-participant in the Camp David negotiations elucidated the significance of the event:

> Events of historic significance can give new meanings to words. This was the case with 'Camp David', words that for many years meant nothing other than the name of a private presidential retreat located in the hills of Maryland. On Sept. 17, 1978, after twelve arduous days of negotiation, the president of Egypt, Anwar Sadat, and the Prime Minister of Israel, Menachem Begin, finally informed President Jimmy Carter that they were prepared to sign two 'framework agreements'. One spelled out an approach to an overall Arab–Israeli peace settlement. The other specified principles that should govern the negotiation of an Egyptian-Israeli peace treaty. Henceforth, in the language of diplomacy, Camp David was synonymous with the process that led to Egyptian-Israeli peace and with the particular formula for trying to deal with the Palestinian question. *Camp David, in short, was redefined by events to connote a set of principles and processes.* (Quandt 1986, 1, emphasis added)

The impact of this set of principles and processes would have been less substantial, or its realization less assured, if the reconciliation had been with an adversary other than Israel (the main regional threat and analyzed by some as even the raison d'être of Arab togetherness), or if Israel's acceptance had been formalized by a peripheral member of the system, not the central one. Even more basic was the symbolic and normative impact of Egypt's go-it-alone diplomacy on a vital and all-Arab issue, the granting of a *carte blanche* to the territorial state to practice its own real politik separate from pan-Arabism, and even at its expense:

> States are building up their own curricula, and a national university, even in Qatar or in Oman, has become an utmost corollary of national sovereignty. Meanwhile this inward-looking perspective (as opposed to a pan-Arab one) is leading to the production of school textbooks reflecting each state's particularism. (Salame 1988, 350)

This rise in realpolitik and narrow *raison d'etat* has become even *raison de famille*. Indeed, many Gulf states are still family states, and this political organization seems to be spreading. Moreover, this realpolitik was reinforced by the continuous blurring of the Arab/non-Arab distinction and the emerging institutionalization of an alternative Middle Eastern system. The ideological vision and political blueprint was confirmed by Israel's ex-prime minister and current president, Shimon Peres:

> Peace between Israel and its Arab neighbors will create the environment for a basic reorganization of Middle Eastern institutions. . . . Our ultimate goal is the creation of a regional community of nations, with a common market and elected centralized bodies, modeled on the European community. (Peres 1993, 62)

Thus, after the 1991 general Arab–Israeli peace conference in Madrid, four different economic integration conferences were convened: Casablanca 1994, Amman 1995, Cairo 1996, and Doha 1997 (for details, see Korany 2005, 59–76). The objective was to set the basis for a new Middle Eastern system and to replace a balance-of-power approach with what I have elsewhere called a "balance of benefits" and "warfare by welfare" (Korany 1997; 1999).

By the late 1980s the suspension of Egypt's membership in the Arab League was coming to an end and the League returned from Tunis to its headquarters in Cairo. However, the pattern of Arab polarization did not cease; it simply changed protagonists.

From Arab Balance of Weakness to Cognitive Disarray, 1990–2009

While the region's main conflict (Arab–Israeli) was changing military components and structure, another conflict cluster was brewing in the Gulf area, specifically around Iraq. As early as 1980, Saddam's Iraq, perceiving revolutionary and disrupted Iran as easy prey, invaded its neighbor, thereby launching the longest war since the Second World War, the eight-year First Gulf War. Although the direct protagonists were Iraq and revolutionary Islamic Iran, most Arab countries, including all the Gulf countries, supported Iraq politically, economically, and militarily. The objective was not only to defeat revolutionary Islam but also its Persian incarnation and Shi'i imprint (Louer 2009). Baghdad's war propaganda and the Gulf media (to the great chagrin of Ba'thist Syria) depicted the war as being one of Arabs versus non-Arabs. This was certainly not the case in 1990 when Saddam Hussein turned his guns toward Kuwait, heralding the beginning of the Second Gulf War.

Iraq's invasion of Kuwait was enormously consequential, marking a demarcation line in time in the region's annals and beyond. Initially, as the emergency meeting of the Arab League in August 1990 shows, Arab states were divided over the proper response to Baghdad's blitzkrieg. Even more divided were the various segments of Arab civil society, especially when Saddam dubbed his invasion a step toward Arab unity. Arguments were heated for or against rich tribal sheiks and their quasi-welfare states; trans-state labor movements were disturbed; remittances so essential to many countries from Sudan to Pakistan were interrupted or ceased altogether; and even families were split. Amid this political and cognitive disarray, it was the U.S.-led international coalition (with many Arab countries, including Syria) that decided the 'proper' response: the military ousting of Iraq from Kuwait and the defeat/humiliation of Iraqi forces.

Iraq's Kuwait fiasco and its abortive attempt at hegemony made it impossible to return to the *status quo ante*, divisive as it was, and thus made an already bad Arab situation worse. Saddam's Iraq had violated a taboo. It not only initiated inter-Arab warfare on a large scale but also sought to eradicate an Arab League member. Moreover, it justified its action by appeals that were attractive to the majority of the Arab population: correcting colonial border demarcation, achieving Arab unity, and redressing flagrant inter-Arab inequalities.

Consequently, the end of the military confrontation did not mean the end of all forms of inter-Arab political warfare, either between states or within their respective societies. Mutual recriminations of 'stoogism,' 'treason,' and 'adventurism,' as well as vendettas, lingered on both sides. Data of intra-Arab visits demonstrates a pattern of rival coalitions: the anti-Iraq and the pro-Iraq groups confronted each other in 1992. The first group exchanged 131 visits among themselves as compared to 38 visits with the nine-country pro-Iraq partnership (*al-Taqrir al-stratiji al-'arabi al-sanawi* 1992, 192–96). In short, Arab society had bruise marks that were likely to remain for a long time. This was hardly a political or psychological context conducive to partnerships. Moreover, a series of 'international sanctions' were set in motion to destroy Saddam's regime economically and restrict Iraq's sovereignty and freedom of action. Even before the

U.S.-led invasion of Iraq in 2003, a major Arab actor was reduced to fighting for its own survival, let alone acting as a regional power.

Thus at the beginning of the twenty-first century the Arab international subsystem presents a pattern not only of power diffusion but also of weakness diffusion. The minimal inter-Arab coordination has not only declined but in many cases also been replaced by narrow state interests and interstate competition even in relation to core Arab issues such as the Arab–Israeli conflict. A prevailing atmosphere of mistrust among many Arab leaders—especially between the Palestine Liberation Organization (PLO) and Jordan or Syria—has been diligently exploited by Israel's negotiators to emphasize the diversity of Arab state interests (*al-Taqrir al-stratiji al-'arabi al-sanawi* 1992, 211–31; 2000, 321–99). Hot-button Arab issues, such as Somalia's disintegration or the civil wars in Yemen and Sudan, have emphasized the glaring absence of any Arab mechanism of conflict resolution or even conflict management.

In this context, it is more appropriate to talk of an Arab balance of weakness, rather than balance of power. This becomes clear when we return to the distinction of Arab versus non-Arab clusters in the region. As early as the 1980s, Iran had threatened the Arab status quo—especially in the Gulf—by virtue not only of its physical size and strength but also its revolutionary Islamist ideology. The support extended by Arab Gulf states and other Arab regimes to Iraq during its eight-year war against Iran stemmed specifically from the hope of undermining the credibility of revolutionary Islam. But then Iraq, with its 1990 invasion of Kuwait, carried out a complete *volte-face*. Consequently, during this second Gulf War, Iraq found it necessary to rebuild bridges with its erstwhile enemy. In a desperate bid to minimize the destruction of its military corps, Iraq sent part of its air force—23 planes according to Iran, 135 according to Baghdad—to the safety of Iranian airfields. Tehran's Islamic Republic, long considered a pariah state, seemed to have been rehabilitated in the wake of the Second Gulf War at Iraq's expense. With Iraq in disarray, Iran's potential for future regional hegemony was on the rise.

The Second Gulf War further consolidated Israel's military predominance in the region. Conventional indicators establishing Israel's military superiority over the Arab world are too well known and numerous to be repeated here. It suffices to point out that Iraq's defeat and decline obviously tilted the balance even more in Israel's favor. More important, however, is the degree to which this Gulf War furthered Israel's political integration within the region. A few years ago, hardly anyone could have imagined the signing of formal agreements or even the convening of multilateral Arab–Israeli talks. Visions of Omani delegates speaking publicly with Israeli counterparts in Moscow corridors would have seemed far-fetched, as would suggestions that Saudi Arabia's Prince Bandar might coordinate moves with U.S. Jewish leaders, or that his country would host visiting Jewish delegates. These events have occurred, and the ongoing Middle East peace talks have moved from discussions of military and political matters to technical and cultural issues. The fact that all of this has transpired with no radical transformation of Israel's approach to some basic conflict issues, such as the return of the refugees and the status of Jerusalem, is a stark indication of how far the balance of power has tilted in Israel's favor.

Either as a result of a power vacuum or because Turkey represents a different pattern of 'Islamic politics,' Turkey has been invited to be more active in both Arab–Israeli and inter-Arab regional politics. Turkey was, for example, the formal mediator and headquarters of Israeli–Syrian negotiations, and it mediated intra-Palestinian and intra-Arab divisions following the Hamas–Israel 2008–2009 Gaza war. A major strategic restructuring was taking place as the political distinction between an Arab regional subsystem and a wider Middle Eastern one was losing its erstwhile political demarcation line and significance (Noble 2008).

A spillover of this political and cognitive disarray was al-Qaeda's 2001 attacks on New York and Washington. The attacks indicated that Jihadism was going global to get at the "distant enemy" (Gerges 2005; Brachman 2009). They also reflected the rise of '(un)civil society' and the active participation of nonstate actors in a sector usually monopolized by states—globalized war (Ould Mohmedou 2007). In relation to the Middle East the language of international relations at the beginning of the twenty-first century was littered with terms such as 'axis of evil' and 'Islamic fascism.' In addition, restrictive rules at airports, instances of ethnic profiling, and the mounting censorship of financial transfers and of the work of charity organizations created a sense of siege in the region. The spiraling sense of threat for some, and the resort to suicide attacks by others increasingly dominated the regional/ global debate (Achou and Drucker 2007). Suicide attacks were on the rise. With the exception of 1985, the average number of suicide attacks per year during the 1980s and 1990s was seven. But between 2000 and 2007, with the wars in Iraq and Afghanistan continuing, the number of such attacks rose constantly: 54 in 2001, 71 in 2002, 81 in 2003, 104 in 2004, 348 in 2005, 353 in 2006, and 535 in 2007 (Moghadam 2008/2009; Shay 2007).

While some of these suicide bombers think of the act as the shortest road to paradise, fatwas—after some hesitation on the part of sheikhs—are starting to dissociate the violent slaughter of civilians from martyrdom (for example, Sheikh Ansari's fatwa, Al Arabiya, 2 September 2009). Similarly, the rise of the phenomenon of new preachers (Benzine 2004; Lotfi 2005) as well as the political fratricide within the Palestinian national movement (Chehab 2007; Gunning 2008) show that divisions go beyond the conventional Arab cold war. This sense of political and cognitive disarray is reflected in literary and artistic works, for instance, the film *Beirut I Love You* (2009), in which Zena Khalil portrays a city often on the brink of war whose inhabitants work hard and party even harder.

Within this situation of division and power diffusion, there were passing partnerships, shifting alliances, and even some subregional institutionalized coalition-building. The most notable examples are the subregional organizations. These were three on the eve of the Second Gulf War: the Arab Cooperation Council (Egypt, Iraq, Jordan, and Yemen); the Union du Maghreb Arabe, or UMA, comprising Algeria, Libya, Mauritania, Morocco, and Tunisia); and the Gulf Cooperation Council, or GCC (Bahrain, Kuwait, Oman, Qatar, U.A.E., and Saudi Arabia). The fifteen Arab countries involved in these different organizations represented two-thirds of all the Arab population, hosted the highest number of universities and research centers, and controlled 90 percent of traditional energy resources and 75 percent of water and agricultural resources. These power bases did not translate, however, into a unified or even coordinated *Arab* capability. The UMA is in serious limbo, divided by the conflict between Morocco and Algeria, notably over the status of the Western Sahara. The Arab Cooperation Council—which held no fewer than nine meetings in less than two years—was not informed of Iraq's decision to invade Kuwait, and its members finally supported the international coalition against their erstwhile convenor, Baghdad. These solemn institutions, which paid lip service to an Arab unity that rapidly evaporated, could only feed the cognitive disarray.

The GCC demonstrates a different pattern. At the end of August 2009, the GCC held its 112th ministerial meeting—an indicator of the continuation of some semblance of Arab togetherness. It is also continuing with plans for a customs union and even a unified currency for the group. But the projects do not seem to materialize. On 30 December 2001, just over twenty years after the GCC's establishment, the then crown prince of Saudi Arabia, Abdulla remarked:

> "We have not yet set up a unified military force that deters enemies and supports friends. We have not reached a common market, nor formulated a unified political position on political crises. . . . We are still moving at a slow pace that does not conform with the modern one."
> (Legrenzi 2008, 107)

Although established in 1981 to protect its members against encroachments by their larger neighbors, Iraq and Iran (who were busy in their destructive military confrontation, launched a year earlier), the GCC could not even prevent one of its founding members, Kuwait, from being overrun by Iraq. While the GCC members still maintain their sub-regional organization, this is generally perceived as a measure to protect their wealth rather than a demonstration of the will to act as the center of a regional Arab system. Indeed, the GCC's functioning has been perceived by outsiders as an expression of an exclusive *Khaliji*, or Gulfian, identity and a club by and for the wealthy. In the wider Arab region, the GCC reflects the division between the 'have-nots' and the 'have-lots.' Among the leading thirty banks in the region, twenty-eight are based in the Gulf subregion (Chatham House 2009). Similarly "desert capitalists" dominate the list of the wealthiest Arab personalities (Rivlin 2007). Undeniably, this petro-wealth is an important element of soft power, but unless backed up by other dimensions of power, it suffers from the "vulnerability of the rich" (Ayubi 1982). The recent global financial crisis demonstrated just how true this is (Davidson 2008).

Conclusion

Those who continue to reduce the region to interstate conflicts, particularly the Arab–Israeli conflict, now realize that conflict clusters are propagating in the Gulf. Even before the heated dispute over the rise of a potentially nuclearized Iran, three destructive Gulf wars occurred. War has certainly been a primary factor of regional restructuring and social transformation. But change has taken place even within conflict clusters, including the primary Arab–Israeli one. We can no longer ignore that at this level the strategic environment has changed noticeably. Contact with Israel is no longer confined to the military front, as peace treaties now link this country with Egypt, the Palestinian National Authority, and Jordan. Moreover there were direct and also ongoing negotiations between Syria and Israel, and Israel deals commercially with some Gulf countries. When Israeli–Arab military confrontation does take place, the IDF faces non-state actors—Hezbollah in 2006, Hamas in 2008—with no Arab state jumping into the military fray.

The impact of these latter two confrontations on the 'Arab Street' shows, however, that at the beginning of the twenty-first century Arab countries continue to resemble a large sound chamber where currents of thought and information circulate and resonate widely. But the character of present-day togetherness is different from that of the pan-Arab days of the 1950s and 1960s. Today's togetherness is based to a much larger extent on civil society networks and such phenomena as labor movements, satellite channel diffusion, and cultural affinities.

Compared to the pan-Arabism of Nasserism and Ba'thism in the 1950s–1960s, the Arab Middle East today is a different region. It is much more explicitly state-centric, where the concept of *dawla*, or territorial state, and its 'national interest' supersede that of the *umma*, or community (Ghalioun 1997; Barghouti 2008). Inter-state rivalry is growing and leading to deeper divisions of basic political orientation, as witnessed in Syria's alliance with Iran against most Arab countries during the First Gulf War, or Egypt's unilateral peace treaty with Israel. I dubbed this state-centric orientation the Camp David order, a quasi-reenactment of the Westphalian order of 1648 in Europe that codified the national state's sovereignty as separate from the (supranational) authority of the Roman Catholic Church.

Alongside this explicitly state-based order there are increasingly deep political divisions and mutual underminings, leading to what I referred to in this chapter as the Arab balance of weakness. In addition, some Arab states are coalescing with non-Arab states, making the demarcation line between the Arab world and the Middle East increasingly blurred. For instance, at the beginning of September 2009 press reports published an official invitation by Damascus for the formation of a coalition among Syria, Iraq, Iran, and Turkey for regional coordination (*al-Hayat*, 10 September 2009). This declaration was followed by Syria contracting "a strategic agreement" with Turkey, including mutual abolition of entry visas and initiation of a policy of "open borders."

A new element is the rise of civil society in Arab countries. Despite difficulties in organization and financing, its ranks are vibrant with debates on ethnic/religious issues, or secularism/Jihadism, or women's status and dress code. The new Arab media certainly embody Arab togetherness in the geolinguistic marketplace within the region and beyond, in the diaspora (Al-Azmeh and Fokas 2008). Although the content of lively debates in this unifying media attests to Arabs' linguistic affinities, it is not a substitute for their present balance of weakness or cognitive disarray.

The reference to the rise of Arab satellite channels attests to the growing impact of technology, especially ICT, in the region, as some of the data in the annexed tables show. We will pursue some of these issues in the concluding chapter after considering other aspects of change in more detail in the following chapters.

2

An Attempt to Evaluate the Development of Arab Civil Society

Amani Kandil

One way to gauge the size and type of changes occurring in the Arab region is to investigate developments in Arab civil society—the characteristics of the changes related to this sector, as well as the features predicting its sustainability.

Arab civil society exists, and is sustained through, an interactive relationship with its surrounding socioeconomic and political environment. As such, it is necessary to examine the changes that have taken place within civil society on the one hand, and the developments in the relationship between the organizations belonging to this sector and the state on the other.

An attempt to identify the changes in and interaction of Arab civil society and developments in the Arab region reveals several important issues. While many believe that the Arab region does not undergo major changes in its existing political and democratic systems, there are in fact not only changes and interactions but also lively political dynamics within Arab civil society, dynamics that began in the 1980s and continue to be felt today.

The relationship between civil society and the state is characterized by varying levels of distrust, conflict, and tension. This relationship witnessed a turning point during the third millennium as an outcome of the unprecedented pressures on civil society organizations (mainly human rights and advocacy organizations), together with variables related to globalization and foreign pressures, to achieve political reform and reinforce democracy, freedoms, and human rights. I refer to the change that occurred at the level of formal political discourse, and to the trend toward amending legislation regulating civil society (in seven Arab countries), combined with the continuing pressures toward additional improvements in legislation.

Furthermore, a study of Arab civil society indicates important changes in terms of the players, not only from the perspective of global civil society, as some contemporary studies tend to consider, but also from a national perspective, at the level of each Arab country and, from a local perspective, within each country. The year 2008 saw the rise of 'the activists of the civil society,' new elements of the Arab male and female elite, hailing from diverse social backgrounds and differing age groups, and working in various human rights and developmental fields. The vast majority are not directly active in the political arena (through political parties, or in political circles) and are not merely based in the capital—Cairo or Rabat, for instance—as was the case in the past. These new elites exercise pressure to achieve political and economic reform and eradicate corruption. Some of them are important pillars of protest movements (as in Egypt and Morocco), as well as the center of activity among groups of young bloggers (Kuwait being a prominent example, alongside Egypt and Morocco). The social changes in traditional elites highlight new, unprecedented forms of interaction between actors at the levels of society and state, reinforced by rapid developments in the field of technology linked to the era of globalization.

Civil society organizations are naturally part and parcel of society at large. The challenges facing civil society are similar to those facing the majority of Arab societies, whether at the level of human development (poverty and limited efficiency in the allocation of resources), the political system (good governance and democratic practices), or political culture (acceptance of diversity and difference, dialogue among state and civil society actors, adherence to the principle of rotation in office). As such, adopting civil society as an entry point through which to identify changes in the Arab region will demonstrate that effectiveness, or lack thereof, in this sector mirrors obstacles in Arab society as a whole. Thus, not only are civil society organizations a microcosm of the wider society at large but their methods of provoking social and political change are also influenced by the same pathological symptoms, such as a lack of democracy and a limited culture of dialogue and tolerance, found in society as a whole.

Map of Arab Civil Society: Change and Continuity

Concepts Used in This Study

The first concept used here is that of 'civil society,' widely disseminated worldwide as well as in the Arab region, especially since the 1980s (see the basic elements agreed upon in the definition of civil society in Kandil 2008a, 61–67).

Civil society is composed of "the overall voluntary, autonomous, and freely formed organizations that fall between the family and the state. They are not profit-oriented and aim at contributing to the public benefit, to some marginalized sectors, or at achieving benefits for their members. They are committed to values and standards of respect, tolerance, and acceptance of the other, as well as the peaceful resolution of conflicts" (Kandil 2008a, 21).

This definition summarizes the majority of attributes agreed upon by the literature concerned with civil society today. The components of the definition point to the challenges and limitations facing Arab civil society in the following respects:

- The free, intentional, and voluntary act
- Civil society as an organized sector of society
- The nonprofit aspect
- The public benefit as target
- Autonomy and self-governance
- The activities of civil society being directed by 'civic culture,' characterized mainly by tolerance, acceptance of diversity and difference, the practice of democracy, and the peaceful resolution of conflict based on mutual consent.
- The sector seeking formal political power (this is an important criterion that distinguishes civil society organizations from political parties).

The study, *Kharitat al-mujtama' al-madani al-'arabi* (Kandil 2008a), uses the concept of 'mapping,' or elaborating a (conceptual) map, a term that describes a specific methodology useful in the marshalling of data and their accumulation in the context of the information society (Yassine and Kandil 2008, 22–38). This concept implies the analysis of the main dimensions of a given topic from a quantitative and qualitative perspective to identify a civil society's profile and its capacities and activities at the current historical moment, as well as opportunities for the future.

In this context, the concept of mapping goes beyond the analysis of statistics and data related to civil society. It aims to achieve a comprehensive understanding of a sociocultural phenomenon (civil society) that is affected not only by values, ideas, and beliefs but also by the socioeconomic and political milieu. Drawing a cognitive map of civil society allows the identification of the players in this sector and their capacity to make an impact. It also enables the classification of civil society, either at the Arab level or within each country, as a coherent entity. Within this coherent entity are various parties, with different levels of effectiveness, which are often in direct competition and conflict with each other. While some adopt a traditional, religious discourse, others are more open, and still others further a secular or more liberal discourse. In this instance, mapping succeeds in highlighting the dissimilarities in the philosophy of functioning, and consequently in the features of change or continuity (namely the traditional philanthropic, empowerment-driven and developmental, or human rights and advocacy approaches). It also distinguishes independent organizations from dependent ones or those opposed to the government (for more on civil society in the Arab region, see Kandil 2008a).

As such, mapping facilitates the integration of various elements of the analysis, thus guaranteeing a holistic approach to the topic, the components of which are often nonhomogeneous and constantly evolving.

Features of the Current Map of Arab Civil Society
This section attempts to give an outline of the features of the civil society map of the region on the basis of quantitative and qualitative indicators, highlighting the changes affecting the map as of 2008, in comparison with the data available from the last two decades of the twentieth century. Before detailing the transformations affecting Arab civil society today, some preliminary remarks are in order.

Attempts to study civil society organizations in the region began only in the 1990s, with scientific and organized accumulation of knowledge conducted by researchers specialized in political science and sociology. Later, this focus on the study of civil society organizations featured prominently in the field of information technology. Undoubtedly, the Arab Network for NGOs was the initiator and leader in this domain, enriching the Arab canon with thirty publications since the 1990s.[1] In parallel, a core academic community was developed in various Arab countries to conduct scientific research in the area of civil society. Since civil society is characterized by the multiplicity of its components, its study requires a multidisciplinary approach.

Furthermore, the Arab region lacks a developed and up-to-date database of civil society organization listings and their fields of activity, let alone one that includes indicators of their expenses, sources of funding, the nature of their work, and the social background of their members (gender, education, income, and so on). Researchers therefore have to make intensive efforts to obtain accurate data. Adding to the difficulty is the absence of an accurate classification of civil society organizations, as most Arab countries rely on the traditional system of dividing organizations into social care units—including charity organizations as well as service delivery entities—and developmental organizations. The classification of organizations thus mainly becomes the responsibility of researchers. It is worth mentioning that Johns Hopkins University has, since the 1990s, conducted a comparative project at the international level (with contributions by the author at all its stages). The project developed a classification, which relies on twelve principal and subgroup indicators, that has since met with global consensus. Arab countries have yet to adopt this new classification.[2]

Nevertheless, a tangible change has occurred in the map of scientific research in this field recently, through various developments. The first development relates to the growing number of Arab publications on this topic. Another is that the study of civil society has been included in the curricula of several Arab universities (for example, Cairo and Ain Shams universities in Egypt, the University of Jordan, and the United Arab Emirates University). Also worth mentioning is the growing number of conferences and scientific meetings dealing with this topic. Last but not least, it is important to note the increased participation of Arab researchers in global research projects.

The Map of Arab Civil Society from a Quantitative Perspective

The overall number of volunteer organizations registered according to Arab legislation amounted in 2007 to 250,000 in seventeen Arab countries (wherever data is available). Based on the growing number of registered organizations, we can estimate that they will have reached 300,000 by 2008 (Kandil et al. 2008).

One of the first comprehensive Arab studies conducted by the author, and published in 1995, indicates that the number of NGOs at that time was just 120,000. The rapid rise in that figure is a significant indication of the process of political change occurring in the Arab region, as well as of an emerging trend among Arab citizens to participate and influence this process.

Average growth rates vary from one country to another, and the over-all distribution in the number of associations varies depending on several factors. The most important of these factors is the nature of the political system and the extent of legal tolerance for citizens' desire to establish such organizations; this is related to democracy indicators. The next consideration is the inclination of citizens—especially in elite circles—toward social and political participation; this is related to awareness, education, and culture indicators. Third is the openness of political discourse in some Arab countries, especially those that grant their citizens some margin of freedom (mainly Morocco, Egypt, Lebanon, and Jordan), and which are simultanesously exposed to economic pressures. Previous studies reveal that countries that have adopted structural adjustment and market policies have tended to witness the highest level of growth of civil society organizations (Kandil et al. 1998, 261–79), mainly in the fields of alleviating poverty, female empowerment, and health services. Finally, there are factors linked to globalization and interaction with other civilizations, as well as the flow of funding to specific sectors of civil society (human rights, women's empowerment, and so on). Table 2.1 illustrates this quantitative aspect of NGOs in Arab countries.

Qualitative Indicators of the Arab Civil Society Map
The quantitative indicators illustrate important changes in the map of Arab civil society. These changes reflect the rapid rates of growth for this sector between 1995 and 2007, with all that this implies of a changing relationship between civil society and the state. There are also qualitative indicators that complement the picture of change in the Arab region.

An examination of the map of the fields of activities of civil society organizations highlights major changes, particularly in the widening gap between the third and fourth generations of NGOs. Although the first

Table 2.1: Number of non-governmental organizations (NGOs) in Arab countries

Country	Overall number of NGOs
Egypt	24,600
Lebanon	3,360
Tunisia	9,065
Algeria	70,000
Morocco	37,000
Saudi Arabia	329
Oman	62
Jordan	1,189
Iraq	5,669
Bahrain	450
United Arab Emirates	175
Kuwait	66
Qatar	17
Yemen	5,300
Sudan	1,785
Syria	1,225
Palestine	1,495

Source: Official data from relevant ministries for the year 2007.

generation (philanthropic organizations based on a direct relationship between donor and recipient) continues to occupy the first place (around 60 percent of the overall number of organizations at the Arab level), and although service delivery organizations have a prominent place in most Arab countries (with the exception of the Gulf area, where governments are responsible for providing education and health services), the work of these traditional first generation organizations should not lead us to underestimate the process of political change in Arab countries. In civil society terms, this process is reflected through two aspects.

First, there is a noticeable growth in the size of developmental organizations seeking to empower citizens and include them in the process of development. This is achieved through the provision of opportunities in the fields of education, work, and other training, combined with attempts to raise awareness and encourage involvement. These organizations now comprise almost 25 percent of the overall number at the Arab level (with diverse percentages in different countries), whereas they were quite limited at the beginning of the 1980s.

In this context, a number of trends on the Arab civil society map can be noted, the first of which is the unprecedented increase in the number of developmental organizations (besides human rights organizations) in the field of female empowerment (Kandil 2005). In 2008 the number of these organizations tripled that of 1995 (the year of the Beijing Conference on women). This important growth occurred mainly in Egypt, Lebanon, Jordan, Yemen, and Morocco. Another unprecedented change took place in the fight against poverty and in the provision of microcredit projects, and there is also a new trend to establish organizations concerned with youth, led by youth, and expressing the younger generation's concerns. The Arab country that witnessed this phenomenon the most is Egypt, as shown in field research conducted in 2007, which indicates that these organizations came into existence with the start of the new millennium (Kandil 2006, 27–30).

In addition to developmental organizations, an analysis of the qualitative indicators reveals the emergence of a fourth generation of civil society organizations, consisting of human rights and advocacy organizations. Usually, these do not provide services, focusing instead on human rights issues and advocacy. These human rights issues cover a wide range of topics in the fields of political and civil rights on the one hand and of socioeconomic and economic, social, and cultural rights on the other.[3]

The first human rights organization, the Arab Organization for Human Rights (AOHR), was born in 1983. At the time, all Arab countries refused to host its founding conference, which was finally held in Cyprus. Just a decade later, a series of human rights organizations had emerged in Egypt, Palestine, Jordan, Lebanon, Morocco, Algeria, and Yemen. In 2008, there were sixty-seven human rights organizations in Egypt and sixty in Morocco. This trend extended further afield to several Arab Gulf countries (Bahrain, Qatar, Kuwait, and the United Arab Emirates) (Kandil 2006, 22–30). Human rights organizations in the Arab world are increasingly aware of the importance of fighting for socioeconomic and political rights (Kandil 2006, 38–40). Today there are new patterns of human rights organizations working on citizens' entitlement to education, health, housing, knowledge, and access to information, as well as organizations working on transparency and the fight against corruption (among them regional Arab organizations such as the Anti-Corruption Arab Organization, and organizations with branches in several Arab countries). Recently, an organization was established in Egypt claiming the freedom of faith and belief, and another one championing the rights of the inhabitants of slums.

A further development worth noting is a growing interest in human rights perspectives, as opposed to service delivery and social care perspectives. There are numerous examples of this, mainly campaigns for the rights of people with special needs and for their social inclusion (the Nass, or 'People,' organization in Egypt), as well as for Arab children's rights and their protection from all forms of violence (the Arab Council for Childhood and Development and the Egyptian Network for Child's Rights) (Kandil 2008c). What is more, Arab women are progressively adopting a human rights approach with new trends, including the protection of women from violence, their right to occupy all posts and positions, their right to legal inheritance (as is the case in Upper Egypt), and the rights of female heads of households, who represent between 17 and 23 percent of all household heads in Egypt, Morocco, Lebanon, and Algeria.

Continuity amid Creeping Change

General trends in the Arab region can also be noted, with dissimilarities among Arab countries, reflecting diversity in the political and economic context on the one hand, and in social and culturally constructed values on the other. In this part of the study, we will focus on those attributes of civil society linking it to the emergence of the first non-governmental associations in 1821 and leading to the spread of the phenomenon in Arab countries over almost two centuries.

A primary feature of continuity has been the weight of religious or faith-based organizations. According to a field survey undertaken by the author in the 1990s, these can be defined as "organizations relying on religious values to mobilize members of the society and encourage their participation and the adoption of their principles on the basis of religious incentive" (Kandil 1997, 32–45). These organizations are still significant and reflect characteristics that are specific to the Arab region. For one thing, the vast majority adopt a name that has a religious connotation; thus, the name might refer to the religion (the Islamic Association, the Christian Association, the Orthodox Association, and so on), or rely on symbols implying its religious affiliation (this applies specifically to Lebanon, Iraq, and Bahrain, which are home to several sects belonging to the same religion).

Since the establishment of the Islamic Association (Egypt, 1868) and the Coptic Association (Egypt, 1875), however, most of these organizations do not merely adopt objectives relating to religious teaching, but are also active in providing social services such as education, healthcare, and social care. A significant number of these organizations have moved, since the 1990s in particular, into developmental activities such as the alleviation of poverty and unemployment, training, professional habilitation, and female empowerment (the cases of Egypt, Lebanon, and Jordan). However, philanthropic activities focused on supporting the poor remain the main feature of the majority of these organizations (Kandil 2008a).

The field survey of the 1990s mentioned above indicates that nearly 32 percent of the total number of organizations that existed in 1997 were compatible with this definition, that is, of faith-based organizations combining charity activities and preaching. Around 8 percent of these represent Christian organizations. The same phenomenon can be noted in Lebanon, but with a higher proportion of faith-based organizations. This is due to the existence of eighteen religious sects owning associations and schools. A recent study of Iraq refers to the same phenomenon, where the number of associations was estimated in 2007 to be 4,500 (Taher in Kandil 2008c, 227–53) and where almost 50 percent of the registered organizations have a religious sectarian nature. This religious characteristic of a wide sector of active civic organizations in some Arab countries, especially in those characterized by sectarian differences, raises several questions requiring additional research: What capacity do these organizations have in terms of initiating dialogue, tolerance, peaceful resolution of conflicts, and acceptance of the other? Do these religious organizations contribute to social and political change, whether in the sense of melding together or of aggravating sectarian fault lines? Finally, are they compatible with the agreed-upon definition of civil society? These questions are important given that the most prominent continuous feature from the first quarter of the nineteenth century to this day is the weight of Arab associations based on religious affiliation.

The second feature of continuity is represented by the attempt to improve philanthropic and care activities, in comparison with developmental and human rights activities. Arab civil society is generally overwhelmed by philanthropic and social care initiatives, which tend to dominate in the number and activities of Arab civil society organizations—from 85 percent (in Arab Gulf countries) (Kandil 2008b) to 50 percent or less in non-Gulf Arab countries. There are several reasons for this predominance, one of which is the strength of the religious incentive to practice charity. While the perception of the Arab citizen is that national development is the responsibility of governments, the prevailing culture of charity in Arab countries makes of philanthropic actions a sustained tradition. (This explains why politically oriented human rights organizations in all Arab countries are funded by foreign donors.) Activity in the philanthropic and social care fields is 'secure,' in as much as it does not conflict with Arab governments' domestic policy trends and does not lead to tension or confrontation.

A third aspect of continuity in the Arab region, with negative impact on civil society organizations, is the mutual mistrust between governments and civil society. This latent and chronic tension is reflected in the various laws restricting freedoms and granting the right of monitoring and inspection to the bureaucratic system (mainly represented by the ministries of social affairs in most Arab countries, the Ministry of Interior in the case of Tunisia, or the Council of Ministers in some Arab Gulf countries). The mistrust manifests itself through the interventions of the security apparatus, which are effectively capable of refusing to grant these organizations official registration (especially in the case of human rights organizations) or of objecting to the inclusion of certain persons as members of their boards.

Mistrust between government and civil society highlights the fact that there are legislative tendencies in the Arab region that contradict contemporary global trends and human rights conventions (Kandil et al. 2003). The following indicators illustrate this situation:

- The right of the government (the Ministry of Social Affairs) to approve or reject the establishment of an organization.
- The right of this same administrative body (and not the judiciary) to dissolve or liquidate an organization (except in the cases of Morocco and Yemen).
- The right of the organization to appeal against a governmental decision—including dissolution—takes place with the same governmental body, which in effect plays the double role of judge and referee (Khalil 2006, 31–53).

Determinants of the Future of Arab Civil Society

These determinants can be summarized in a single concept: capacity. Widely used in the civil society literature, this concept refers to actions, practices, and processes capable of achieving efficiency and effectiveness and enhancing the impact of civil society (Mathison 2005).

These capacities, which represent the key to change, have four dimensions.

The first is a political and legislative environment conducive to the promotion of a civil society that includes a series of factors related to the political will on one hand, and to legislation that seeks to liberate Arab civil society from the hegemony of the state on the other. These are respect for the autonomy of civil society organizations; transparency practiced by state and civil society; placing power with the judiciary, not the executive/administrative branch of government, for resolving conflicts between government and civil society; simplifying registration procedures for the creation of civil society organizations; and monitoring the performance of civil society according to clear rules.

It is worth mentioning that all the empirical research carried out in the Arab region from the late 1990s up to 2009 has proved that the legislative and political environments related to civil society in particular need essential changes. An opinion poll conducted in Egypt in 2009 surveyed activists in civil society (working in development and human rights). It concluded that the perceived main priorities for facilitating these activists' role in enhancing development and having an impact on human rights were as follows:

- Legislation to guarantee equal opportunities (40 percent of respondents)
- Restricting the impact of the Emergency Law (36 percent of respondents)
- Introducing new civil society legislation (24 percent of respondents). (Kandil 2009b)

A survey in Gulf Arab countries (the sample was made up of 486 voluntary associations) revealed that one of the main demands of associations was legislation to lessen the dominance of governmental bureaucracy over civil societies. Forty-five percent of surveyed associations in Bahrain voiced this demand, as did 50 percent in Kuwait and lower percentages in Saudi Arabia, Qatar, and Oman (Kandil 2008b).

Second, governmental and other so-called environmental obstacles notwithstanding, capacity-building efforts of civil society organizations themselves are equally crucial, almost a prerequisite for their effectiveness. Among changes that could foster such effectiveness are good internal governance, including respect for institutionalism and its impersonal rules, collective or teamwork, rotation of office, democratic practices, rule of law, widening the scope of participation, and so on. Recent comparative studies in several Arab countries highlight the lack of some of these basic factors, especially regarding teamwork and democracy. This is related to the prevailing political culture and some socialization patterns that are not conducive to the civic culture that civil society organizations should promote and pioneer (dialogue, respecting the ideas of others, collective work, rule of law, and so on) (Leila and Kandil 2007).

In this context, it is important to mention that when we raise the problem of collective work, we mean basic practices of teamwork (institutionalized) within civil society organizations, and not 'social solidarity.'[4] The absence of democratic practices and teamwork, where consensus-building and respect for specific roles and responsibilities in an organization are required, constitutes one of the main obstacles to the development of credible and effective civil society organizations. A recent study of five Arab countries (Egypt, Lebanon, Morocco, the Emirates, and Yemen) indicated a lack of ability to work as a team and to reach consensus in 40 percent of the six hundred civil society organizations (all working in development) surveyed (Kandil et al. 2010).

The third dimension is the lack of availability of both material and human resources for civil society organizations. Studies indicate limited skills, especially in the human rights and developmental fields. The scarcity of material resources, meanwhile, has a negative impact on the stability and sustainability of the programs conducted by several kinds of civil society organizations. While human rights organizations and programs concerned with the empowerment of women rely mainly on foreign funding, some important activities (such as promoting education and the eradication of illiteracy) are not granted the same level of support.

Finally, several factors affecting the efficiency of civil society organizations can be identified. According to a wide study conducted in fifteen Arab countries by the Arab Network for NGOs in 2007 (Kandil 2007), these are abstention from participation in public life, the regression of Arab women's role in volunteer activities, and the low level of youth (aged under thirty-five) participation in the vast majority of voluntary organizations. The main reason for the last factor is that youth do not find support and encouragement inside organizations, or opportunities to gain experience and to influence their programs.

Thus, the first obstacle encountered is the limited (or even absent) culture of volunteerism, in addition to the marginalization of certain categories (women and youth in particular). The second obstacle lies in the need to make a code of ethics within the work of civil society mainstream. This should include a series of principles and values, the most important of which are transparency, the free flow of information, the eradication of corruption, the avoidance of conflicts of interest, the initiation and sustenance of collective work, and respect for different ideas and opinions (United Nations University 1999).

Crucial to capacity-building is the achievement of sustainability, a vital concept with the following prerequisites:

- Clarity of roles and responsibilities
- Accountability
- Rule of law
- Collective participation in decision-making and programs
- Democratic practices and rotation of position-holders
- Inclusion versus exclusion or marginalization
- Transparency and the free flow of information
- The building of strong relations between organizations' boards and those organizations' general assembly members
- Strategic planning for projects and programs according to a vision statement catering to the community's needs

Sustainability promotes capacity-building in at least three ways. First, sustainability promotes credibility vis-à-vis public opinion as well as governments, thus increasing the appeal of voluntary work and the mobilization of serious volunteers on the one hand, and raising funds from the private sector and donor agencies on the other. Credibility means "validity and trust in evaluating the performance of the organization by the various parties."

Second, the achievement of sustainability partially implies that the institutionalization achieved is linked to a process of accurate monitoring. This concept refers to an "organized process to follow up the implementation of plans and programs since the beginning of the project, allowing and ensuring the compatibility of each step with the targets declared, the responsibilities and roles, and the resources allocated." This concept is open to adjustments that seek to improve efficiency and effectiveness (Mathison 2005).

Third, volunteer work relies mainly on a collective initiative, therefore sustainability is linked to the practice of democracy and collective work. The lack of a collective spirit, which we refer to as the lack of teamwork in institutions, represents one of the main negative aspects of Arab volunteer work, as pointed out in recent field studies and research. It also explains the multiplicity of internal divisions within organizations and the trend to establish other, independent ones.

Empirical research indicates that sustainability is one of the main challenges facing Arab civil society. Sustainability in this context refers to the ability of civil society organizations to raise funds and develop effective projects, and to increase their impact on society, in turn raising that organization's capacity (recruiting volunteers, improving the skills of paid staff, and fostering good governance and strategic planning). A survey of five Arab countries revealed that 40 percent of the civil society organizations surveyed have doubts about their future, mainly due to a lack of funds, 25 percent believe that they face problems in attracting skilled people to work in civil society, and 20 percent have limited capacity to mobilize volunteers (Kandil et al. 2010).

It is worth mentioning that the global financial crisis also affected civil society organizations. Field research carried out on fifty-one companies in Gulf countries, well known for their contributions to voluntary organizations, indicated that they have been affected by the financial crisis, and that 60 percent of these private commercial companies believe that their support for associations will be negatively affected. Thirty percent of companies surveyed pointed to the value of monitoring and evaluating the impact of voluntary associations on society in order that support for them can be sustained (Kandil 2009a).

Finally, all the factors mentioned above make up the various facets of a healthy civic culture. Thus, the absence of, or lack of respect for, any one of those factors takes away from an organization's quality of being a 'civil society' institution.

This study confirms that a focus on civil society is of paramount importance in understanding change in the Arab region. This approach reveals social, political, and cultural dynamics, as well as mechanisms of interaction between the various parties attempting either to affect and operate change or, conversely, to preserve the status quo. Compared to the the beginning of the new millennium, there is, at present, a new degree of vitality in the arena of Arab civil society that seeks to bring about change, reinforced by the social movements taking place in some Arab countries together with the movement led by young bloggers.

Notes

1 Refer to the publications of the Arab Network for NGOs (1997–2008) on the organization's website: http://www.shabakaegypt.org.
2 For additional information about Johns Hopkins University's project of classification, refer to Salamon and Anheier 1997; Salamon 2004.
3 Regarding the concept of human rights and advocacy organizations, see Kandil 2008, 119–28.
4 Social solidarity describes the belief in, and practice of, helping the poor. Social solidarity is rooted in religion, culture, and alms-giving traditions, but is not necessarily institutionalized. One of the best examples of individual trends in social solidarity, proven by recent empirical research in Egypt (Information and Decision Support Center, Egyptian Cabinet, 2009) is the fact that two million citizens, in urban areas alone, benefit from *Mawa'id al-Rahman* (al-Rahman Tables), a term used to refer to the daily open buffets in streets, parks, and open areas organized and paid for by the wealthy as a means of feeding the poor. Empirical research carried out by the Information and Decision Support Center shows providers as being wealthy individuals for the most part, with only 13 percent of contributions coming from associations. Indeed, social solidarity is practiced all over the Arab world, particularly the practice of supporting the poor during Ramadan (Arabs call it a generous month).

3

Arab Media over the Past Twenty Years: Opportunities and Challenges

Rasha A. Abdulla

Introduction

No discussion of the political, economic, democratic, or developmental arena of a country or region is complete without a discussion of its media system. The cliché of the media institution as being the supposed watchdog of political systems is long known, but the relationship actually runs deeper than that, particularly with the emergence of new media, starting with satellite television and ending with the Internet and Web 2.0 applications. The ideal relationship is a symbiotic one, where political systems provide freedom of expression and access to information while the resulting healthy environment and participatory civic society help fuel democracy and development.

In a volume on the changing Middle East, therefore, there has to be a chapter on the media systems in the Middle East, and how much change they have undergone in the last twenty years or so. I would like to begin by clarifying a few important semantic and operational issues. The first relates to the definition of 'Middle East.' This term sometimes is used interchangeably with 'Arab world,' and, at other times, more accurately in my point of view, is used to encompass Egypt, the Gulf area, plus Iran, Turkey, Cyprus, and Israel. Media systems are complex enough when we address one country, and certainly a major challenge when we address the 'Middle East' in the larger sense of including non-Arab countries. The reason for this is that media systems in the Arab world share certain characteristics, including ownership patterns and the main language of content dissemination, which allows for major program swapping. However, the media systems of these countries and those of Iran, Turkey, Afghanistan, or Israel have little in common, and these non-Arab countries themselves have very different media systems from each other. For these reasons, I focus my attention in this chapter on the media systems of the Arab countries of the Middle East.

The second semantic issue worth raising is the fact that although the media systems of the Arab Middle East share a few characteristics, these countries also have differences, some of them significant, in their programming and presentation styles, governing policies, and the amount of freedom they can afford. Therefore, to the extent possible, I will try to present examples from the Arab Middle East that shed light on these differences.

Third, this chapter focuses on the electronic media systems of the Arab Middle East, and addresses print journalism only in so far as it has been affected by the Internet in terms of interactivity and the new trend of blogging, or civic journalism. Although the traditional press is no less important, I believe it is electronic media systems that have been the active agents of change during the last twenty years, principally because the main factors involved are satellite television and new media, particularly the Internet. These media were almost forced to develop as a result of the global media convergence trends that have made our world a true global village. New media and new media trends, including certain aspects of programming content and format for television, have forced a level of civic participation that is unprecedented in the Arab Middle East. Such participation has led to new levels of awareness of and involvement in the political and social affairs of these countries, whose development, I believe, has been directly related to the extent to which they have fostered and encouraged, rather than hampered and inhibited, the civic participation that was brought about in part by the developments of new media and new media trends.

Chapter 1 identified two types of change: a sudden, 'big bang' type and a slow, steady, incremental type. It may be true that in the larger scheme of things, any changes within media systems would be classified as incremental. In other words, we cannot speak of changes in media systems in the same way we do of wars, revolutions, or changes in political systems. The latter have more immediate and dramatic effects. However, the changes that have occurred within media systems in the Arab Middle East have themselves undergone both types of change: the big bang type and the incremental type. The two types, together with a few setbacks, have resulted in a third type of change: the two-steps-forward, one-step-back change.

This chapter addresses some of the major big bang and incremental changes that have occurred within the media systems of the Arab Middle East over the last twenty years. I start with a background of historical developments from before that time frame, and then proceed to the changes. I focus on Egypt in many ways because Egypt has been known to be the media leader in the Arab world and the Arab Middle East (although the extent of that leadership may be changing). The reader will see how most major changes were introduced to the region through Egypt and then transported to the rest of the Arab Middle East. I focus on a few developments that I think were big bang media change agents, namely, the introduction of Cable News Network (CNN), the launch of Al Jazeera, and the introduction of the Internet. Please note that the changes associated with each of these factors will differ in impact, time, and scope depending on the penetration rate of each factor in a particular country. But, overall, it is my belief that these three factors were big bang media changes in terms of the effect size each has eventually created in the Arab Middle East. The steady, incremental changes will then be the effects of the (sometimes slow) penetration of each of these factors, along with other political and socioeconomic factors, on the fabric of society. I also address a few setbacks that are slowing the progress of Arab Middle Eastern media, foremost among them, ownership patterns and challenges to freedom of expression and information dissemination. The overall result is change and progress in Arab Middle Eastern media, but at a much slower pace than is hoped for by media experts and scholars.

Arab Middle Eastern Media before the Nineties

Most Arab media systems are government-owned and controlled. Although there are now exceptions to the rule, particularly in Egypt, Saudi Arabia, and Lebanon, this was certainly the norm before the 1990s. Hussein Amin states that "Radio and television broadcasting in the Arab World are absolute monopolies and under direct government supervision. Most Arab states' governments own, operate, and control the broadcast institutions. . . . Most Arab radio and television systems are subsidized by governments and partially financed by advertising revenues" (Amin 1996, 124). Schleifer argues that the Arab media were not only state-owned but also actually "extensions of the ministries of information" (Schleifer 1998).

In terms of the broad functions that Arab media serve, they are the same as those of media elsewhere, although the political systems and socioeconomic realities of the Arab world dictate certain differences in the way these functions are carried out. William Rugh (1979; 2004) identifies these functions as conveying news and information, interpreting news and providing commentary, reinforcing cultural norms, advertising, and entertainment. Rugh states that with the exception of some of the new, post-1990, television channels, "Arab media rarely meet the ideal expressed for American journalism, of providing 'a forum for the exchange of comment and criticism'" (Rugh 2004, 16). He argues that the politics and culture of any particular Arab country deeply influence the news and commentary of that country.

Indeed, a look at any news bulletin (or newspaper for that matter) in the Arab world prior to 1990 (the year in which CNN was introduced to the Arab region) illustrates Rugh's point. In most democratic countries, the news bulletin is structured according to newsworthiness, with the most important national or international news stories coming first, followed by the less important stories. In Arab countries prior to 1990 (and sometimes to this day), the news bulletin had to first feature news of the head of state, followed by that of the senior officials of state, with no regard as to the story's newsworthiness. In other words, the routine daily meetings of the head of state would necessarily precede news of an international conflict breaking out or a natural disaster killing hundreds of people. The news item would be just footage of the head of state during his meetings or while escorting a world leader, while the announcer read copy that had been written by official or at best semi-official media agencies. The news, therefore, was not prioritized according to universal journalism standards but rather according to a political protocol that could not be circumvented.

Historically, the Arab Middle East has reacted positively to any 'new' media, although series developments in media systems were almost nonexistent and were more often confined to the introduction of a single new medium. Egyptian leaders since the 1952 revolution (Gamal Abdel Nasser, Anwar Sadat, and Hosni Mubarak) realized the importance of the media to the nation's development and to advancing Egypt's position as a political and cultural leader of the Arab world. Gamal Abdel Nasser was quick to realize the importance of the media in reinforcing values and so cleverly used radio, and later television, to disseminate his socialist pan-Arab messages. al-Sharq al-Awsat (The Middle East) and Sawt al-'Arab (Voice of the Arabs), both originating in Egypt, became landmark radio stations for Arab audiences. But while Arabs would tune in to these stations for their daily dose of news and entertainment, in times of crises, they resorted to different outlets. The only available outlets at those times were the Voice of America (VOA), the British Broadcasting Corporation (BBC), and the French Radio Monte Carlo Middle East (Abdulla 2007b; Boyd 1975; 1999).

There are no clear boundaries between national and transnational radio broadcasting in the Arab world. Arab countries have historically acquired powerful medium-wave and short-wave transmitters to attempt to reach out to audiences all over the Arab world. Historically, countries with the strongest radio transmissions, mainly Egypt, but also Syria and Iraq (pre-1990), had the strongest propaganda effects on those other Arab countries that possessed less sophisticated systems. Egyptian radio continued to be the most popular broadcasting service throughout the Arab world, reaching sophisticated levels of programming content and format (Boyd 1977; 1999; Rugh 1979; 2004).

Mainly through Sawt al-'Arab, Nasser broadcast his pan-Arabist messages to the Arab world, at a time when it was mostly still under British and French occupation. Nasser put the station to strategic use, helping Arab nations gain their independence and serving other 'nationalist' causes. The station was so successful that it became a "household name" (Boyd 1999, 325), drawing in Arabs to listen to its news, commentary, drama, and entertainment.

Television, once introduced to the Arab Middle East, followed the same trajectory and usage patterns of radio. According to Boyd, Arab countries' national television, particularly Egypt's, is usually received and followed in neighboring Arab countries. "The tall antenna towers on apartment houses and private residences in Jeddah (Saudi Arabia) are not necessary to receive Saudi Arabian television; they are needed to receive Egyptian television from across the Red Sea" (Boyd 1999, 6).

The Egyptian national television signal before the 1990s was also regularly seen in Lebanon, Syria, the Palestinian territories, and in some Gulf states. Like radio, television was used by the Egyptian regime to spread appropriate political and cultural messages to the rest of the Arab world. Soon, Cairo became known as the 'Hollywood of the Middle East,' and Egyptian colloquial Arabic became (and remains) the most widely understood dialect in the Arab world, as a direct result of Arabs growing up with Egyptian programs, music, and drama. It is common knowledge that Arab countries continued to be heavy consumers of Egyptian radio and television productions even during the Arab boycott of Egypt that took place after the Egyptian–Israeli Peace Treaty was signed.

Rugh classifies the Arab media prior to 1990 into three main categories: "strict-control" or "mobilization" systems; "loyalist" systems; and "diverse" systems. The mobilization media systems describe those of Egypt, Algeria, Iraq, Syria, Libya, South Yemen, and Sudan (Rugh 1979; 2004). These regimes believed in the importance of the media to a country's development, and therefore gave special attention to their media systems. Despite very tight control, these regimes were quick to adopt radio and later television and to help subsidize the cost of radio and television sets because it meant that government messages would reach a higher percentage of the Arab population, which had high illiteracy rates. Rugh emphasizes that these governments used the media to propagate their political messages and mobilize the masses.

The loyalist media systems pre-1990 were to be found in Morocco, Tunisia, Jordan, Saudi Arabia, Bahrain, Qatar, and the United Arab Emirates. According to Rugh, these countries were not as eager to adopt new media technologies as were the strict-control countries. Overall, the media systems in these countries developed more slowly, and programming was less politically motivated. The governments of these countries were not interested in social mass mobilization or in using the media to propagate particular political messages. They therefore exercised slightly less control over the media than the strict-control countries, although ownership and control remained mostly in the hands of governments (Rugh 1979; 2004).

The diverse media systems were to be found in Lebanon first and foremost and, to a lesser degree, in Morocco and Kuwait. Lebanon, according to Rugh's pre-1990 classification, amounted to a special case of diversity, largely due to its internal political strife. Rugh believes that Lebanon does not fit into any of the third world or western media systems. Due to its political diversity and the civil war that deeply affected the country for more than a decade, there did not exist a clear, unified political agenda or message for dissemination by the country's media. Media outlets were divided among different political and/or sectarian factions, which led to a great deal of diversity in the messages relayed. Rugh notes, however, that this diversity came at the price of greater bias on the part of each individual broadcasting entity (Rugh 1979; 2004).

In this chapter I argue that three main big bang-type factors have prompted change in the Arab media systems. The electronic media scene in the Arab Middle East changed after 1990 as a result of these factors, which were the introduction of CNN, the creation of Al Jazeera, and the introduction of the Internet and its applications to the region.

The Satellite Revolution in the Arab World
The satellite revolution in the Arab world began with the introduction of CNN to the region in 1990 and expanded with the creation of Al Jazeera in 1996. I will next look at the impact of each of these two factors, then give an overall view of the satellite media scene in the Arab Middle East today.

The Introduction of CNN
This is the first factor that revolutionized the Arab media scene at the beginning of the 1990s. CNN was first introduced to Egypt around the end of 1990, but really became a phenomenon in the Arab world during the 1991 Gulf War, which was the first war to be broadcast live on television, by CNN. With the resounding slogan, "history as it happens," CNN found its way straight into Arab homes, as the station was broadcast through a deal with Cable News Egypt (CNE).[1] At that time, satellite dishes were scarce in the Arab world, but some Arab governments, foremost among which were Egypt and Saudi Arabia, realized that it would be beneficial for them to air the CNN coverage on their terrestrial television stations to combat Iraqi propaganda entering their air waves through Iraq's radio transmitters, which were quite strong at the time. And so it happened that suddenly, after years of watching state-controlled official news that was composed mainly of head of states' meetings, Arabs were watching live war beamed straight into their living rooms twenty-four hours a day on CNN.[2]

The event caused a media culture shock of sorts, not only to viewers but to media personnel and governments as well. For the first time ever, Arabs had access to good-quality television journalism, in a sense that they had never known existed. They no longer had to turn to the BBC, VOA, or Radio Monte Carlo to get some version of credible news; the news was unfolding right before their eyes in full color from the battlefield, complete with American news-style graphics, music and sound effects, maps, and statistics. After the war was over, CNE continued to beam CNN on terrestrial television for a while for marketing purposes before the company decided it was time to make it subscription-based.

The introduction of CNN to the Arab Middle East, coupled with a major regional political event (the Iraqi invasion of Kuwait followed by the U.S.-led war against Iraq) meant that Arab television broadcasters simply had to change their old ways to be able to compete with the new style of journalism beamed into Arabs' living rooms via CNN. Even though the CNN broadcasts were in English, Arabs simply turned away from their own national broadcasters, who in turn realized that they had to change, and fast, in terms of both content and format. The first reaction on the part of Arab broadcasters was to try to imitate CNN in any way they could, including the introduction of actual professional news reporting (in inverted pyramid style),[3] relatively objective analysis, better presentation of news items in terms of its newsworthiness (although the news of the head of state still weighed very heavily in most news broadcasts), as well as the introduction of maps, graphics, statistics, and even music and sound effects, which had been viewed until then as inappropriate for a 'serious' news bulletin.

I have argued elsewhere that Arab news bulletins at the time tried as best as they could to mimic everything CNN was doing. Soon, graphic banners similar to CNN's began to appear on Egyptian news bulletins, coupled with sound effects very similar to those on CNN. The graphics and sound effects on Egyptian television would change every time CNN's changed, and in a very similar manner. When CNN had an imposed super that read "The Gulf War,"[4] the Egyptian news had the same slogan, with similar graphics, translated into Arabic *(Harb al-Khalij)*. For the sake of variety, CNN soon changed its slogan to read, "War in the Gulf," and the Egyptian news producers changed their translation to the same *(al-Harb fi-l-Khalij)*. Whether acts like these were coincidental or not, the fact remains that CNN became the standard and every Arab news bulletin attempted to imitate it (Abdulla 1991; 2005c).

Perhaps the greatest impact of CNN on the news bulletins of the Arab Middle East came in the form of a realization on the part of those responsible for these bulletins that the days of 'concealing' news from their people were over. Arab governments could no longer hide information from their publics, since the skies were by then virtually open, and the publics could receive the news via satellite from anywhere around the world (Abdulla 2006). No longer was it easy just to ignore a news item, sometimes as major as a war, and rely on the fact that if your national news media did not report it, then your population had a dismal chance of finding out about it. One striking example took place when Saudi Arabian television failed to report the Iraqi invasion of Kuwait for almost three whole days. Saudis first found out about the conflict from CNN, as well as from United States Armed Forces Television, which was beaming to U.S. forces stationed in the Gulf. Such incidents would be unthinkable today after the proliferation of satellite television networks in the Arab Middle East (Boyd 1998; Sakr 2001; Schleifer 2005).

CNN has therefore helped enforce a radical change in terms of freedom of expression and access to information in the Arab Middle East and was the catalyst that brought about the concept of around-the-clock news to the region. That effect would later manifest itself in the many new Arab satellite channels that would try to adopt the fast-paced and exciting format of CNN. This phenomenon offered alternative paths for Arab audiences around government-owned and controlled programming, and forced these governments to rethink their own broadcasting policies in an effort to retain viewers.

The Arab Broadcasting Scene after 1990

By the time the 1991 Gulf War had ended, CNN had established an excellent reputation for itself in the Arab Middle East. As direct broadcast satellite (DBS) technology was introduced to the Arab world, satellite dishes began to penetrate Arab markets as satellite transmissions grew stronger and the cost of satellite dishes declined. Thus, a huge new market for media consumption opened up for investors. Satellite adoption skyrocketed within three to five years, particularly in the affluent Gulf area, where videocassette recorders were also abundant. The most popular programming on video tapes and DBS has been Egyptian dramas, movies, and serials. Arab countries had already launched their own satellite system, ARABSAT, in 1985. The first Arab satellite station that came into existence was the Egyptian Space Channel in 1990,[5] which started as a daily, thirteen-hour transmission in Arabic to the Middle East, North Africa, Europe, and parts of Asia. This was followed by the introduction of Nile TV International, broadcasting both in English and French (and now in Hebrew), and a second Egyptian satellite channel.

In Saudi Arabia, by the time the Gulf War ended, investors related to or closely associated with the monarchy had realized the importance of satellite channels as a powerful political, economic, and development tool. They reacted quickly by establishing three major satellite networks, the first of which was the Middle East Broadcasting Centre (MBC). MBC started in September 1991 and was based in London to make use of Arab expatriate journalists or at least BBC training programs to train its staff. MBC strived to produce CNN-style news bulletins, in addition to drama and entertainment for the Arab family. The channel's news reporting was a welcome addition to the Arab world because, in striving to follow in the footsteps of CNN, it resorted to the universal values of newsworthiness instead of the traditional Arab emphasis on political protocols. Eventually, the channel developed a well-trained and highly professional staff who were stationed as foreign correspondents in major cities around the world, giving the channel the added advantage of having access to first-hand accounts of breaking news. The channel's credibility in terms of news production soon earned it a solid reputation in the Arab world.

A few years later, in 1994, Saudi investors, headed by Sheikh Saleh Kamel, established Arab Radio and Television (ART), a private network composed of over twenty specialized entertainment channels, now mostly operating on a subscription basis. Since the majority of its channels are in Arabic, ART has gained popularity in the Arab world as well as with Arab expatriates around the world. The channels specialize in Arabic movies, Arabic series and entertainment, western movies, music, and sports. Transmitted from a huge state-of-the-art production center in Italy, ART now also has a large production center in Cairo's Media Production City as well as in several Arab cities. ART does not offer a news service on any of its channels.

In the same year, 1994, the third Saudi media investment was launched, that of the Orbit network. Also operating from Italy, the subscription-based Orbit packages carry a variety of over sixty channels, most of which carry English-language programming. The packages include a melange of western movies and entertainment, Arabic movies and entertainment, news, sports, documentaries, music, children's programs, and even Filipino channels. Orbit's production center in Cairo broadcasts one of the most successful Egyptian and Arab talk shows in the region, *al-Qahira al-yawm* (Cairo Today).

Amid this heavy competition, the need for each Arab country to have at least one satellite channel was a logical consequence. A satellite channel was the way to showcase the country to the rest of the Arab world (and the world at large), and to confront any messages that may be deemed inappropriate—politically, culturally, or otherwise—by a regime. The first country to feel such a need (outside of big investors Egypt and Saudi Arabia) was Kuwait. Shortly after the 1991 Gulf War, the country launched its own satellite channel to present its case to the world and mount international pressure on the Iraqi government to release Kuwaiti prisoners of war (Amin and Gher 2000).

The Space Network of Dubai followed in October 1992 with twenty-four-hours-a-day transmission that covered the Arab world and Africa as well as major parts of Europe and Asia. Then Jordan launched its channel in 1993 with a daily broadcast that reached sixteen hours after eleven months and covered the Arab world and parts of Europe. Oman, Lebanon, Bahrain, and Qatar also launched their own satellite channels or otherwise placed their national broadcasts on ARABSAT for the rest of the Arab world to see (Amin and Gher 2000). Of these, the Lebanese channels, in particular the Lebanese Broadcasting Company (LBC) and Future Television, proved quite popular with audiences.

The Launch of Al Jazeera

In 1996, the second major communication and media revolution in the Arab world took place with the launch of Al Jazeera channel. The main figure behind Al Jazeera was the then newly installed amir of Qatar, Shaikh Hamad bin Khalifa al-Thani, who had overthrown his father less than a year before. The amir saw an opportunity after an attempt by Orbit to install and maintain BBC Arabic as one of its main news channels fell through because of differences between the BBC and the Saudi regime. The amir realized that there were scores of BBC-trained Arab reporters and television journalists who had just been laid off by BBC Arabic. He hired them and launched Al Jazeera, the first around-the-clock Arab news channel.

The amir gave Al Jazeera $137 million to pay for start-up costs, supposedly to cover the first five years of the channel's operations, as it was expected that by that time the channel would be self-sustaining. This has never happened, however, and the channel is still largely financed by the

Qatari government. In terms of ownership, the channel is an independent public institution, with the Qatari government owning a majority of shares (Pintak 2006; Schleifer 1998; 2001). In 1998, the amir closed down the Qatari Ministry of Information, whose office had frequently monitored and censored the media. The move was welcomed by journalists and media observers in the Arab world as it gave the Qatari media, including Al Jazeera, greater access to information and freedom of expression. Mamoun Fandy points out that Al Jazeera still receives over $300 million annually from the Qatari government, and that the channel has some royal family members and senior government administrators among its highest ranks. Therefore, he argues, "it is very difficult to claim that Al Jazeera is independent" (Fandy 2007, 47). However, Fandy states that "Al Jazeera has been known for its willingness to flirt with contentious issues that break longstanding taboos" and that the station has "contributed to raising the ceiling of what can and cannot be said on pan-Arab television" (Fandy 2007, 47). This includes openly criticizing *some* Arab heads of state, although never Qatari officials, and featuring controversial figures on the screen ranging from opposition leaders to Osama bin Laden to Israeli officials.

It is this controversy over the channel's policies, coupled with its CNN-style journalism, which gives priority to newsworthiness over political protocol, that made Al Jazeera the talk of the Arab world and, in many instances, the whole world. Even Al Jazeera's critics will admit to the technical professionalism of its reports, while still questioning their objectivity. The BBC-trained journalists of Al Jazeera have known how to gauge the Arab viewer since the station's first days on the air. It was the first time that Arabs had access to an Arab twenty-four-hour news channel that spoke their language and adhered to the professional standards of western television journalism. The closest thing that resembled this style before Al Jazeera was MBC, but the latter only broadcast two half-hour news bulletins a day, which do not compare with Al Jazeera's twenty-four-hour coverage.

Middle East media observes such as Naomi Sakr said the channel "astound[ed] viewers with uncensored political coverage quite different from any Arabic-language television programming previously seen" (Sakr 2001, 13). Al Jazeera reporters resembled "agents of democratic change in a region trapped with the grids of autocracies" (Pintak 2006, 70). The channel has frequently been dubbed "the CNN of the Arab world," and has even at times been referred to as "one of the most important de facto 'Arab political parties'" (Hafez 2005). Rugh has called it "the most unique, controversial, and influential" Arab satellite channel (Rugh 2004, 214). Philip Seib has called it "the best known international satellite TV channel . . . in terms of brand recognition" (Seib 2007, xii). White House officials in the Clinton administration called the channel a "beacon of light" (Hilton 2005) and Israeli minister Gideon Ezra told the *Jerusalem Post*, "I wish all Arab media were like Al Jazeera" (Neslen 2004).

Quotes like that of the Israeli minister are the cause of criticism of Al Jazeera by some who see it as serving a political agenda of its (or rather, of Qatar's) own. Examining Qatar's political relations with the rest of the Arab world as well as with the United States and Israel, Fandy concludes that the station is a "Qatari government enterprise," utilizing the tools of western media to serve its political gains (Fandy 2007, 52). He contends that the political tensions between Qatar and Saudi Arabia and between Qatar and Egypt are reflected in the relationship between Al Jazeera and the media systems of Saudi Arabia and Egypt, including Al Jazeera's now fierce competitor, Saudi Arabia's Al Arabiya. Al Jazeera's reports against the Saudi royal family and against the Egyptian president, government, and policies, particularly as they relate to the Palestinian issue, illustrate this point. Fandy adds that the favorable light in which the United States is portrayed on Al Jazeera as well as the channel's lack of hostility toward Israel and the frequent appearance of Israeli officials on its programs are necessary as Qatar has tied itself economically, politically, and militarily to the United States. He contends that, as such, Al Jazeera may well be following glamorous western-style journalism but that does not mean the channel is editorially independent. Instead, he says, "Al Jazeera is simply Qatar's Information Ministry with a new name and a new agenda" (Fandy 2007, 52). Fandy points to the fact that Qatari politics and internal affairs are off-limits to Al Jazeera, and contends that the day the channel reports critically on Qatar as it does on Egypt or Saudi Arabia will be the day we can call it free and editorially independent. Indeed, Abdallah Schleifer has maintained that the channel "seems at times as much devoted to embarrassing Saudi Arabia as it is to free discussion that never manages to touch upon Qatari sensitivities" (Schleifer 1998).

Al Jazeera's coverage of Palestinian–Israeli events, particularly since the three-week Israeli assault on Gaza in December 2008–January 2009, only added to the controversy over the channel. Many were upset that the channel openly accused Egypt of not doing enough to help the Palestinian cause and for giving Israeli officials more airtime than Arab officials. Since then, the channel's popularly in some parts of the Arab world, and particularly in Egypt, has sharply declined. Biased coverage of critical events such as these together with the fact that Al Jazeera never criticizes any aspects of its own Qatari society or regime reduce the amount of credibility that the channel could enjoy in the Arab world.

However, the fact remains that Al Jazeera had a major effect on the media scene in the Arab Middle East. Shortly after Al Jazeera was introduced, the MBC group launched Al Arabiya, another twenty-four-hour news channel that uses CNN-style journalism. Arab News Network (ANN) was launched in 1997 by former Syrian vice-president Rif'at al-Asad, and within a year the channel was also broadcasting high-quality news twenty-four hours a day. More than anything, the presence of Al Jazeera convinced every Arab government that it needed at least one satellite television channel to speak for it and represent its politics, society, and culture. More important, it dealt a strong blow to terrestrial television censorship, since Arab citizens now had regular access to relatively credible news in Arabic twenty-four hours a day, thereby transcending the barriers of illiteracy and language. Hiding facts from one's citizens no longer seems viable; in fact, it seems quite embarrassing in light of the plethora of satellite channels now available, not that some Arab governments do not still try to conceal information every once in a while.

The other phenomenon that Al Jazeera has introduced to the Arab world is talk shows, particularly those modeled on CNN's *Crossfire*, and complete with citizen participation through telephone calls, faxes, and e-mails. The idea of live debate held great appel to the Arab world, an area that for too long had been exposed to only one voice, that of the governing regime. The idea of citizen participation, a form of democracy in which the average citizen feels that his or her voice is being heard, adds much-needed democratic value to the people of the region. Some scholars credit the station for creating an unprecedented sense of involvement in news affairs on the part of the Arab viewer: "One of Al Jazeera's strengths has been its introduction of energetic and sometimes contentious debate into an Arab news business that was previously known for its drab docility" (Seib 2007, xii). Although some accuse Al Jazeera's talk shows of becoming a mere "shouting match" (Schleifer 2005), the format itself was adopted by many other channels that followed Al Jazeera's lead, resulting in a new favorite program genre for the Arab masses. Today, talk shows are a main source of news for Arab citizens, and presenters of popular talk shows are nothing short of major celebrities in the Arab world.

The Broadcasting Scene in the Arab World Today

In 1999, Naomi Sakr predicted that satellite broadcasting would bring an end to the era of censorship in the Arab world, noting that if Arab terrestrial media continued to present heavily controlled news and entertainment, Arab audiences would simply seek better content from the many channels of transnational media that are beamed into their living rooms (Sakr 1999). Indeed, Jordan's ex-information minister, Nasser Judeh, reportedly referred to satellite television as "offshore democracy" (Sakr 2001, 4). Satellite television was especially welcomed by those who could afford it in the affluent Gulf, since it offered an uncensored alternative to otherwise government-owned and regulated media. In Saudi Arabia, for example, there is an official ban on satellite dishes, yet the ban has never been enforced. One can purchase a satellite dish and receiver at any local technology store, and numerous satellite dishes commonly appear on building rooftops. In 1997, it was estimated that almost two-thirds of the Saudi population had access to satellite television (International Telecommunication Union 2001; Marghalani, Palmgreen, and Boyd 1998).

Today, there are over five hundred satellite free-to-air channels in the Arab world, and over 150 pay TV channels, a true explosion of transnational broadcasting by any means. In addition to ARABSAT, Egypt launched Nilesat 101 in 1998, and thus became the only Arab country individually to own a satellite system. This was followed by Nilesat 102 in 2000. Egypt has been trying to match the strong and heavily financed Saudi news and entertainment satellite networks. Since 2007, ten years after their first launch, the country has relaunched several satellite channels, including the digital Nile Television Network, encompassing Nile Drama, Nile Life, Nile Sports, Nile Cinema, Nile Culture, Nile Comedy, and Nile News. Egypt also owns the only Arab satellite channel that broadcasts in English, French, and Hebrew: Nile TV International. Launched in 1993, Nile TV International targets foreign viewers in Europe, North America, Asia, and Africa, aiming at promoting Arab culture and literature, as well as expressing Arab political viewpoints.

In an important development, Egypt has also allowed for several private satellite channels, starting with Dream Television (two channels) in 2001 and El Mehwar in 2002. More recently, in 2008, Al Hayat (three channels), OTV, and OneTV, also started broadcasting to Arab viewers. Dream, Al Mehwar, and Al Hayat now broadcast three of the most popular Arabic evening talk shows in the Arab world, presenting a mixture of news, interviews, and audience participation. The other two major talk shows are presented by Orbit and Al Masriya. Egypt therefore has a monopoly over the five most popular talk shows in the Arab world. Four of these talk shows are produced and beamed via private, independent satellite channels, and the fifth via the government-owned Al Masriya. It is very common for Arabs to zap through the five talk shows with their remote controls on any given evening to get the day's news, analysis, and interviews.

Egypt also owns a Media Production City (MPC), located in Sixth of October City, southwest of Cairo. The city features 114 state-of-the-art studio complexes and numerous temporary and permanent location sets, aims at achieving an annual 3,500 hours of indoor studio production, and 5,000 hours of programs and outdoor production. The studio complexes were fully occupied months before the city was officially inaugurated in 2001.

Access to satellite television varies from one country to another in the Arab world, depending on how affluent the residents of the country are and the relative cost of the service. A lack of scientific audience research leaves us with estimates of such access. Syria, for example, was estimated in 1999 to have a television penetration of 30 percent of households. Lebanon had an estimated 42.5 percent for the same year. Algeria was estimated at 80 percent. A 1995 survey of students in the United Arab Emirates showed that 81 percent of households in the sample had access to satellite television. The average figure for ten Arab states was estimated at 27.2 percent. In comparison, Western European states were estimated to have an average of 48.5 percent home television penetration rate (Sakr 2001). In Egypt, satellite penetration was estimated at 28 percent in 2005 (Media Monitor 2005). More recent figures estimate satellite penetration in Egypt to have reached 45 percent in 2008, but that does not take into account the *wasla* (illegal connection), which is estimated to account for another 30–35 percent. It was also reported that about 98.9 percent of television viewers in Bahrain have a satellite dish. That percentage is 94 percent for Saudi and for Kuwaiti citizens (AAG 2008).

At the beginning of this chapter, I discussed William Rugh's classification of the Arab media systems before 1990, which he divided into "strict-control" or "mobilization" systems, "loyalist" systems, and "diverse" systems (Rugh 1979). Twenty-five years later, Rugh revisited his categories and documented a few changes. Most prominently, Egypt and Algeria were removed from the mobilization category, and Jordan and Tunisia were removed from the loyalist category. Together the four countries formed a new category of "transitional" media systems. Rugh also included Yemen and Iraq, with Lebanon, Morocco, and Kuwait in the diverse media systems category. Rugh concluded that since satellite broadcasting bypasses illiteracy and government control, it has had a major effect on the Arab world. Satellite channels enjoy much more freedom to present news and information than terrestrial channels, and they also act as a voice for the average citizen, in turn reflecting Arab public opinion (Rugh 2004).

Although the satellite broadcasting revolution is definitely the most significant change that the Arab Middle East has undergone in the last twenty years, I cannot end this chapter without discussing the Internet revolution and what it meant for the Arab world.

The Internet and the Changing Arab Middle East

The Internet was introduced to the Arab Middle East around the same time that satellite broadcasting was beginning to boom. The first Arab country to have Internet access was Egypt, in October 1993 (Abdulla 1995; 2005a). All other Arab countries followed suit between 1993 and 2000 (Abdulla 2005b; 2007b).[6] The Arab world, with the exception of the United Arab Emirates, Bahrain, Kuwait, and Qatar, is still on the low end of the digital divide, with relatively low Internet penetration rates.

However, if satellite television was regarded as a form of 'offshore democracy' to the Arab world by virtue of the many choices it afforded its viewers, the Internet is an onshore democratic agent in the region. To start with, the unlimited supply of information afforded by the Internet about virtually anything, political or otherwise, is an unprecedented phenomenon. Satellite television increased the viewing options of Arab citizens from their own limited, and often censored terrestrial stations to a multitude of Arab and international television stations. However, ownership of these stations, particularly the Arab ones, was still concentrated in the hands of a privileged few. The Internet took this issue to a whole new level, giving its users access to any news source they wanted, anywhere on the planet. These news sources range from credible, brand-name news organizations (CNN, BBC, Reuters, and so on) to news items written by individual citizens (blogs). The mere presence of the Internet as a source of information therefore helps open up a freer space for public debate, and makes it much more difficult for governments to censor information since the same information will appear in a multitude of other sources in or out of the jurisdiction of the censoring country. For example, there have been many instances where an Arab government has censored an article in a magazine or an issue of a newspaper only to find that article or newspaper in its entirety on the Internet and in people's e-mail in-boxes (Abdulla 2009). It is true that Internet access is still relatively limited in the Arab world, but the mere fact that the information is available somewhere to some people makes it much harder, if not impossible, for governments to attempt to hide information.

By its nature, the Internet is a democratic medium, at least in the sense that anyone who has Internet access can immediately become a publisher of information. Of course, credibility is a different issue, but at least the average person, who may not have a chance to publish a newspaper article or even a letter to the editor and may not have a chance to appear on television or to call a program (sometimes due to high call volume) can readily have a website, publish a blog, or have a page on the numerous social networking sites, whereby he or she can make his or her views public.

Indeed, the introduction of Web 2.0 applications in recent years has made the Internet more democratic than ever. Web 2.0 applications are those based on interactivity and audience participation. They include the famous Wiki sites such as Wikipedia, Wikibooks, Wikitionary, Wikiquotes, Wikinews, and Wikiversity, where anyone can post content, edit it, and/or review it. They also include YouTube, where people can post videos, and social networking sites such as Facebook, MySpace, and LinkedIn, where people can have a personal page to post information about themselves, their work, their friends, communities, and so on. Most important, Web 2.0 applications also encompass the new Internet revolution of blogging.

A blog, short for 'Web log,' is a personalized space on the Internet where a person can 'blog' or write about anything he or she pleases. The new phenomenon has exploded in the Arab world during the last few years, with the number of bloggers approaching half a million at the beginning of 2009 (Abdulla 2009; IDSC 2008). Although this number is still about

0.5 percent of the total blogs available online, Arab bloggers have already shown that they can act as agents of change in their societies. Blogs constitute "a populist approach to information dissemination that signals a significantly altered balance of media power" (Seib 2007, xiii). Indeed, Bahraini blogger Chan'ad Bahraini says that bloggers in his country have managed to break "the government's news monopoly," adding that "a space has been created where a wide range of topics are discussed with honesty" (RSF 2006). The popularity of blogging is aided by the fact that, on the Internet, a user can remain anonymous if he or she so chooses. Although most blogging and social networking sites require users to register, users do not have to register with their real names—any nickname or pseudonym will do. This phenomenon is widespread in some of the Gulf countries where governments hit hard at Internet activists. Still, the concern of the governments is itself evidence of the potential impact of the blogging phenomenon.

Blogs have certainly allowed an alternative platform for voices in the Arab Middle East that had previously gone unheard. In Bahrain, blogging has created a public sphere far less restrained than any other. Some Bahraini blogging sites have served to provide citizens with such forums, for example, in 2002, when many people were anxious about a government scandal concerning the national pension fund, a critical issue, the most sensitive aspects of which the mainstream media could not address. In Lebanon, after the assassination of Prime Minister Rafiq al-Hariri in 2005, blogs and public bulletin boards provided a much-needed open forum for discussing the political aftermath of the incident, and email was used to organize anti-Syrian demonstrations. Bulletin boards were also vital for Arabs in the aftermath of 9/11 when they took to the Internet to discuss openly what the attacks meant for the United States, Arabs, and Islam (Abdulla 2005d; 2007a).

Some Arab bloggers, whether or not they use their real names, have actually become stars in their roles as Internet activists, Internet dissidents, or supporters of political reform and civic engagement. One of them, Egyptian blogger Wael Abbas, recently received the prestigious Knight International Journalism Award of the International Center for Journalists (ICFJ). According to the ICFJ/Knight International website, Abbas received the award because he "raised the standards of media excellence" in his country (ICJ Website 2008). This was the first time that a blogger, not a traditional journalist, won this prestigious journalism award, a testament to the important work such bloggers are doing.

However, Internet penetration remains relatively low in the Arab world, estimated at only about 13–15 percent of the Arab population in 2009. Arab Internet users face many obstacles, not the least of which is illiteracy. Other obstacles include language and computer illiteracy and cost. Arab users also suffer from a relative lack of Arabic-language content on the Internet, such content having been estimated at less than 1 percent of the total content on the Internet (Abdulla 2007b; 2008).

Due to these factors, the effect of the Internet on the Arab Middle East cannot yet be determined accurately, although the potential is unlimited. Some effect has already started to show though, and I argue that it manifests itself for the most part in two forms. First, by providing a space to publish news, commentary, videos, or whatever content that gets repressed by a government, and, second, by shedding light on important societal or political issues that are first reported by bloggers and then picked up by the mainstream media in the Arab world. The latter phenomenon is almost the reverse of part of the two-step flow of communication theory, whereby information goes from the mass media to opinion leaders to the masses. Through blogging, information flows from bloggers (opinion leaders) to the mainstream media to the masses. Some examples of this phenomenon could be observed in the sexual harassment case in downtown Cairo in 2006, as well as with some police brutality cases. These cases were brought to the attention of the mainstream media (satellite channels and newspapers) a few days after they were reported by bloggers. One famous police brutality case in Egypt, brought to light through the videos posted by blogger Wael Abbas, resulted in the police officers involved receiving three-year prison sentences, marking the first judicial condemnation of police officers in a brutality case in Egypt—a powerful testament to the effect of blogging and of new technologies.

Social networking sites also afford users some new interesting features, not the least of which is gaining supporters and followers of a user's screen page. Social networking sites such as Facebook allow users to post events, invite people to these events, form groups for various political or societal interests, advertise public causes, and so on. Perhaps the most striking example of the use of Facebook for political activism in the Arab Middle East came from Esraa Abdel Fattah, a twenty-eight-year-old woman who formed a group called the "April 6 Youth Movement" to rally support for workers in the Egyptian city of al-Mahalla al-Kubra, who were planning a demonstration on 6 April 2008. Abdel Fattah asked people simply to stay at home that day, not to go to work, and not to engage in any monetary transactions such as buying or selling. To her own surprise, Abdel Fattah's group attracted some 73,000 members and caused much havoc among national security forces on the 6th of April. She was dubbed "the Facebook girl" and "the president of the Facebook Republic." Such examples as the sexual harassment incident, the April 6 strike, and the police brutality case illustrate the major impact of new technologies, when issues are brought to light by bloggers and then brought to the attention of the masses through the mainstream media, especially satellite channels. Such an impact is only expected to grow as technologies become cheaper and easier to use, and as Internet penetration increases in the Arab Middle East.

Challenges and Conclusions

As I have illustrated in this chapter, quite a few major developments have occurred in the Arab Middle Eastern media over the last twenty years. I have referred to this pattern of change in my introduction as two-steps-forward, one-step-back change. The reason for this is that the development of a robust media system in the Arab world is held back by a number of factors, including the general climate of lack of democracy in the region. While political reform (or the lack thereof) is outside the scope of this chapter, it has to be borne in mind as a significant hindrance to the development of informative, well-integrated, and independent media systems in the Arab world. It must also be noted that a relatively participatory media system cannot by itself be taken to mean a democratic society. Call-in shows do not mean equal opportunities for citizens, unless those citizens have a chance to vote in truly democratic elections without fearing for their safety and without doubting the credibility and transparency of the election process. Bloggers and Internet activists cannot demonstrate their full potential as long as activists such as Esraa Abdel Fattah have to spend weeks (or months) in detention as a price for their Internet activism.

In fact, one could go a step further and argue that there is a potential danger that democracy-hungry Arab audiences would be satisfied with their dose of television and Internet democracy as a virtual alternative to real institutional democracy. Television call-in shows and debates thus become a virtual alternative to the tough game of real political participation. So far, Arab audiences seem happy to receive their virtual dose of mediated democracy while keeping themselves (physically) safe in the security of this out-of-range democracy. One would surely hope that the media and political institutions can pull each other up on the democracy scale. The media alone cannot make societies more democratic without a positive response from the political systems involved.

There are other media-related factors that contribute to the two-steps-forward, one-step-back development style and these are worth discussing in these concluding remarks. The media-related factors include media ownership patterns and the challenges imposed by governments to freedom of speech and expression in the Arab world. Arab media are still mostly government-owned and controlled. Although the past twenty years have ushered in some significant changes, the pace of change and development has not been as fast as is desired under the circumstances. Arab satellite stations are for the most part still dependent on the state (or a close relative or associate of those in power) for their financial well-being, the result being a space that, while it has come a long way in terms of freedom of expression, still cannot be deemed free or independent. Al Jazeera is a striking example of this. Despite its well-trained staff and high-budgeted programming, the channel never touches on any subject related to Qatari politics or even Qatari society, let alone those in power. The same pattern is followed by MBC, Orbit, and Al Arabiya in relation to Saudi Arabian politics and the monarchy; ANN in relation to Syrian politics and government; Al Masriya in relation to Egyptian politics and government; and so on. This is a major obstacle to the credibility of these stations among Arab and international audiences. In countries where residents do not have much by way of a public sphere in which to voice their concerns and opinions, satellite television and call-in shows may be useful, but freedom from government control is an important prerequisite for the well-being of that sphere.

Freedom of expression is still a much-stifled right in the Arab world. Whether through media laws and broadcasting regulations or through a deeply ingrained culture of self-censorship, few people can voice their opinions freely in the Arab world. There is a, sometimes unwritten, code whereby residents of each country know their red lines, and those who dare cross know they will have to bear the consequences. Not a year passes by in the Arab world without several major court cases involving journalists, writers, and broadcasters. Prisoners of opinion unfortunately still abound in the Arab world. On 31 January 2009, news sources reported that an Egyptian appeals court had overturned one-year jail sentences given in 2007 to four editors of independent newspapers for defaming senior members of the ruling National Democratic Party, including the president and his son. Still, the editors each had to pay a fine of LE 20,000[7] (Egypt court 2009). This case is not unique in the Arab Middle East. In fact, some newspaper editors take pride in the number of court cases filed against them by governments or government-affiliated individuals because it raises the credibility of the journalist and the newspaper involved in the issue.

Arab governments also pay special attention to bloggers who bring sensitive issues to light, thus crossing their boundaries to become "cyber dissidents." Abdulla (2009) documents many cases of Internet activists being detained or jailed for their opinions. In its 2010 report, Reporters Sans Frontières listed four Arab countries on its list of Internet enemies (Egypt, Saudi Arabia, Tunisia, and Syria), and another two (Bahrain and the United Arab Emirates) to its list of countries under surveillance. Most of these countries have engaged in massive website blocking and jailing of cyber dissidents. Egypt's Facebook girl, Esraa Abdel Fattah, was detained for two weeks after her "April 6 Youth Movement" group on Facebook gathered 73,000 members. Fouad al-Farhan, a Saudi blogger, was detained for 137 days for "violating security regulations in the Kingdom." He had been blogging about democratic reforms in Saudi Arabia. Karim Amer, an Egyptian blogger, is serving a four-year sentence for defaming Islam and the president of Egypt. Bloggers and cyber activists have also been jailed in Syria and Jordan.

While transnational satellite broadcasting and the Internet sometimes make it difficult to prosecute "dissidents," particularly if they happen to be outside a government's borders, Arab governments have not given up. In 2008, a gathering of Arab information ministers adopted a Satellite Broadcasting Charter that is seen by many as a means "to control satellite broadcasters" (Nelson 2008). Arab countries, with the exception of Qatar and Lebanon, agreed to adopt the charter as a basis for new information and media laws that will be drafted in each individual country covering satellite broadcasting and the Internet. The charter begins with a call for broadcasters to "abide by freedom of expression as the cornerstone of Arab media," but then continues, "provided that such freedoms are practiced with full responsibility, for the protection of the supreme interests of Arab countries and the Arab world. The entities shall respect the rights of others and the commitment to media professionalism and ethics." The problems arise in the vague terminology of the charter, dubbed the "charter of contradictions" by Munroe Price (2008), and by Daoud Kuttab as "satellite censorship Arab League style" (2008). The key question is who decides what does or does not constitute "the supreme interests of Arab countries and the Arab world"? Kuttab contends that the charter is not an innocent attempt to ban pornography or create an Arab Federal Communications Commission (FCC). Rather, he notes, "it is nothing short of an attempt to control the minds and thoughts of Arab viewers, mostly on political issues."

There are several other clauses in the charter that stand out for their vagueness, which therefore carry the implicit threat of being interpreted according to the whims of those in power. Among these clauses is the statement: "Abstaining from broadcasting anything that would contradict with or jeopardize Arab solidarity and [promoting] pan-Arab cooperation and integration." It was the following particular phrase, however, that caught media observers' attention the most, namely where the charter calls for media entities to abide by "objectivity, honesty and respect of the dignity and national sovereignty of states and their people, and refrain from insulting their leaders or national and religious symbols." Human rights and freedom of speech advocates and organizations worldwide voiced their concern over this statement, which essentially prohibits any criticism or discussion of the affairs of Arab rulers, as well as of anyone deemed by those rulers to be a "national symbol" or a "religious symbol."

The charter was adopted during the same week that Saudi Arabia decided to cancel live call-in programs, after a caller openly criticized a change in the salary system of Saudi civil servants, which was interpreted as criticism of the monarchy. That same week, Egypt banned two channels from its satellite network, Nilesat. The charter gives governments the power to suspend or revoke the broadcasting license of 'offending' broadcasters. Egypt is currently working on establishing an agency that would be responsible for 'regulating' broadcast media issues, including the Internet. A law based on the charter is yet to be passed by the parliament.

So, has there been change in the Arab Middle Eastern media over the past twenty years? The answer is a definite yes. Has it been to the better? The answer, again, is a definite yes. Is it happening at a good enough pace? No, not exactly. There are times when big-bang changes occur, such as the introduction of satellite broadcasting led by CNN, the launch of Al Jazeera, or the advent of the Internet, and these changes are usually followed by slower but sure developments. The setbacks take place in the form of a general climate of a lack of democracy, a predominance of government-owned and controlled media, and, at times, relentless efforts on the part of governments to restrain freedom of expression.

Seib (2007) notes that it is remarkable how during the 1991 Gulf War, the Arab world obtained most of its news from CNN (which in itself was a major development, as this chapter illustrates), while during the 2003 U.S.-led invasion of Iraq, the whole world got the news from Al Jazeera, Al Arabiya, and other Arab satellite news networks (Seib 2007). These Arab satellite news channels inform the Arab masses about what is happening in their own backyards, as well as educate them by parading democratic practices all over the world and encouraging a new political culture that is based on facts and empowered by credible journalism.

There is no question that new media technologies, from broadcast technologies to the Internet, offer the Arab world a chance for a more democratic, less restricted flow of information and a chance for a stronger and more robust civic society. It is becoming increasingly difficult, by the day, for governments to distort facts or conceal information from their citizens. New technologies in the form of the Internet and Web 2.0 applications mean that every citizen can now become a publisher of information, not just a consumer of information. Media convergence means that as a citizen journalist (or a civic journalist), a video you shoot of a police officer harassing a citizen or preventing one from voting can be not only uploaded onto the Internet immediately for the world of Internet users to see, but also downloaded by mainstream media channels worldwide, literally for the whole world to see. The prospects are magnificent, but they require an overall concomitant change in the prevailing political climate. Media technology developments have certainly opened up the skies in the Arab Middle East over the past twenty years, but they cannot on their own transform autocratic nations into democracies. They need, at the very least, the support of mass audiences to pressure their governments. Governments feel the potential of the media and sometimes try to stifle it, which is in effect a testament to the power of such media. It remains up to the Arab citizen to decide how to use these new media to try and force more institutional democracy in every aspect. Media laws and broadcasting regulations ought eventually to give much more power to the media if we are to hope for a truly global Arab society. There are many variables at play, and too much at stake, but the potential for development and for advancing debate in every aspect of life in the Arab Middle East has never been greater.

Notes

1   Cable News Egypt later changed its name to Cable Network Egypt.
2   It is interesting to note that while Egypt broadcast the CNN signal unedited, Saudi Arabia recorded the signal and aired it several hours later after censoring what it deemed inappropriate (Schleifer 1998). This came to an end soon after, once the signal became available on Arabsat and on other European satellites for anyone to see.
3   Inverted pyramid style is a style of news reporting that is concerned with covering the most important elements of a story first. It starts with the who, what, where, when, why, and how of a story, then moves on to less important details.
4   A 'super' is imposed typeface over an image, commonly used in television broadcasts.
5   ESC was later renamed the Egyptian Satellite Channel, and most recently in 2009 again renamed al-Masriya, or 'the Egyptian.'
6   For a detailed account of the Internet in the Arab world, see: Abdulla 2005b; Abdulla 2007b.
7   The equivalent of about $3,610.

4

On the Margins of Defeat: A Sociology of Arab Intellectuals under Authoritarianism

Hazem Kandil

State repression, under authoritarianism, is so frequently taken for granted that its deeper ramifications are rarely studied. In this chapter, I examine one of the less-studied impacts of repression on intellectual life. I do not document the number of detentions and executions, the restrictions on dialogue and interaction in the public sphere, or the obstacles facing the production and dissemination of thought. My goal is to expose how repression influences the way intellectuals actually think: which topics they choose to tackle, and how they do so. The main argument here is that we can best understand the development of contemporary Arab thought by tracing how repression—or, more accurately, the constant awareness of repression—has pushed Arab intellectuals toward the less confrontational domain of culture and away from the domain of politics (properly understood as the contestation of state power).

By comparing the historical development of the four main schools of Arab thought (Islamist, leftist, liberal, and nationalist) in the second half of the twentieth century in parallel to the rise of authoritarianism in the region, I detect a clear relationship between these two trends: the more authoritarian Arab states become, the more Arab intellectuals, across the board, shift their work from the domain of politics to that of culture.

This comparative take is missing in the English-language literature on contemporary Arab thought. Compared to the comprehensive studies of nineteenth and early twentieth century modern Arab thought (see, for example, Adam 1933; Gibb 1947; Kerr 1966; Hourani 1970; Binder 1988), the few works that have touched on contemporary thought are either polemic or edited stacks of Arab intellectual contributions (such as Laroui 1976; Karpat 1982; Salvatore 1997; Kurzman 1998; Esposito and Voll 2001; Tamimi 2001; Arkoun 2002). It may be that scholars like to "call the world into question" far more than they like to "call the intellectual world into question," as Pierre Bourdieu once remarked (Bourdieu 2007, 23), but the fact that the current Arab intellectual scene has fallen into disarray may be part of the problem as well, for intellectual developments have been "confused and confusing" (Abu-Rabi' 2004, 62), and Arab thinkers have become the world's intellectual lumpenproletariat (Said 1995, 229).

In this chapter, I explore how contemporary Arab thought has developed in response to authoritarianism. Clive Thomas claimed that the "degeneration of political activity that accompanies the rise of the authoritarian state must be placed in the wider context of the degeneration of culture" (Thomas 1984, 123). I turn this supposition on its head. By analyzing the cycles of exclusion and inclusion of various intellectual trends from and in the dominant political order, I contend that the development of the main intellectual trends in the Arab world has been determined by the extent of toleration and/or repression of its political rulers. As the regimes' capacity for repression increased, Arab intellectuals refashioned their thought to avoid political confrontation. They did so by either rearranging their ideological priorities to fit the rulers' agendas or reorienting their thought toward apolitical cultural themes. In other words, far from "speaking the truth to power," as Said prescribed (Said 1994, 102), the prevailing tendency in Arab thought has been acquiescence in the face of repression.

I base my argument on two premises. The first is that ideas do not evolve in a vacuum, but within particular socioeconomic and political structures. Because intellectuals are, as Said noted, necessarily "*of* their time" (Said 1994, 21), ideological shifts can only be explained in relation to structural changes. Michel Foucault stressed the same point: intellectual production is "too profoundly enmeshed in social structures" to be studied separately from social and political developments (Foucault 2000, 111–12). Political thought, in particular, is neither the "reward of free spirits, the child of protracted solitude, nor the privilege of those who have succeeded in liberating themselves" (Foucault 2000, 131), but rather the product of an identifiable political world. The second premise is that under authoritarian regimes, such as those that exist in the Arab world today, political repression defines and limits the contours of intellectual development. Intellectuals in highly repressive environments tend to be less intransigent, less forward in their political demands, and less defiant toward political authority. To uncover the underlying causes for change in Arab thought, we must therefore review the structural shifts that have taken place in Arab politics and society.

The analysis in this chapter covers the second half of the twentieth century. Following the framework of analysis outlined by Bahgat Korany in Chapter 1, I trace both sudden changes and slow, cumulative ones. The sudden disruptions I highlight are the coups of the 1950s and 1960s, which marked the beginning of the nationalist phase in Arab politics, and the 1967 and 1973 wars that marked its decline. The more pertinent change for my analysis, however, is the cumulative process that began in the 1950s and continues still, that is, the consolidation of authoritarianism in the Arab world as a result of the degeneration of modernizing nationalist states into repressive personalist regimes. It is this latter process that has influenced contemporary Arab thought greatly.

The nationalist military coups of the 1950s and 1960s divided the Arab world into nationalist progressive republics (such as Egypt, Syria, Iraq, and Algeria) and nationalist conservative monarchies (such as Saudi Arabia, Kuwait, Jordan, and Morocco). Progressive regimes incorporated loyal nationalist and leftist intellectuals into state institutions, persecuted Islamists, and undermined liberals by destroying their social bases (the commercial landowning and nascent bourgeois classes). Conservative regimes, for their part, supported pro-monarchy nationalist and Islamist thinkers, while targeting liberals and leftists. As a result, intellectuals who could secure political support (nationalists and leftists in progressive republics, and nationalists and Islamists in conservative monarchies) tempered their ideological goals to maintain that support, while repressed intellectuals (liberals and Islamists under progressive regimes, and liberals and leftists in conservative monarchies) turned to cultural reform as a safe detour from political opposition.

With the disintegration of the nationalist project in the late 1970s, a single political model rose to dominance in the Arab world, namely, the authoritarian neoliberal model. This regional development was reinforced by sea changes on the global level. Three trends stand out: first, the expansion of the global neoliberal institutions associated with late capitalism (transnational corporations, global banking and insurance companies, and international monetary and financial institutions); second, the demise of communism following the collapse of the Soviet Union and the Eastern Bloc, as well as China's integration into the global market; and third, the global war on Islamist militancy that was launched in the late 1990s and escalated considerably following the September 11 attacks. The net effect of these regional and global changes was to bolster neoliberal thought, while keeping nationalists, leftists, and Islamists on the defensive. The new authoritarian regimes, which drew heavily on the support of both domestic and global capitalists, embraced the advocates of neoliberal thought and repressed all other intellectual tendencies to varying degrees (Islamists were more harshly repressed than nationalists and leftists, whose political force was spent following the defeat of Arab nationalism and international communism).

The transformation from the nationalist to the authoritarian neoliberal crystallization reconfigured Arab thought in several ways: (1) liberals, now reincarnated as neoliberals, shifted their emphasis from political to economic freedoms; (2) nationalists accepted the infeasibility of Arab political unity and explored the potential for cultural unity instead; (3) leftists forsook their social revolutionary project in favor of the humanistic, culture-oriented New Left model; and (4) Islamists embraced a cultural version of Islamism, one that retained very little of their original political project. In all cases, intellectuals came to terms with an increasingly repressive political reality by either bringing their ideologies in line with the rulers' objectives or moving from political to cultural opposition.

Now, a few conceptual notes are in order. Intellectuals have been defined in various ways. According to Said, the intellectual is "an individual endowed with a faculty for representing, embodying, articulating a message, a view, an attitude, philosophy, opinion to, as well as for, a public" (Said 1994, 11). Seymour Lipset defined intellectuals as those who "create, distribute, and apply culture" (Lipset quoted in Eyerman 1994, 4). Edward Shils described them as those who "use existing cultural values to elicit, guide, and form expressive dispositions within society" (Shils 1972, 5). Others analyzed types of intellectual, such as the classical intellectual (Benda [1927] 2007), the organic intellectual (Gramsci 1971), and the academic (Jacoby 2000). In this chapter, I am more concerned with the role intellectuals play rather than with how they are defined. To paraphrase Antonio Gramsci, all men are intellectuals, but only a few perform the role of intellectuals (Gramsci 1971, 9). I am only concerned with those few. Those who, as Karl Marx prescribed, aspire to change the world not just interpret it (Marx quoted in Tucker 1978, 145)—'committed' intellectuals who operate within concrete historical situations and engage with real political forces, not those Jean-Paul Sartre dismissed as abstract moral literati (Sartre 1947, 33).

My approach toward intellectuals and their role builds on Said, Gramsci, and Michael Mann. Said stated, "Every intellectual whose métier is articulating and representing specific views, ideas, ideologies, logically aspires to making them work in a society. The intellectual who claims to write only for him or herself, or for the sake of pure learning, or abstract science is not to be, and must not be, believed" (Said 1994, 110). But besides his insistence that intellectuals should challenge rather than justify power, Said was not clear on how exactly they could muster the power to perform that role in authoritarian settings. As the first Marxist to revise the conventional Marxian view of the super-structural nature of ideas, Gramsci argued that if intellectuals act organically—that is, among other things, as 'organizers'—they could become active agents in power struggles. Mann elaborated on this notion of 'organization.' For Mann, actors struggling over the control and direction of society have recourse to four sources of social power (ideological, economic, military, and political). While economic, military, and political powers naturally lend themselves to organization, ideas tend to remain free-floating. That is why Mann stressed that ideas can only have a political impact if they become organized (Mann 1993, 7). In light of the above, I limit my analysis to intellectuals who aspire to intervene in the political field in an organized manner,[1] and among those I focus on academics because of their special training and knowledge,[2] for no matter how much Russel Jacoby abhorred that reality, he himself admitted that in the contemporary world, "to be an intellectual entailed being a professor" (Jacoby 2000, 16).

To summarize, I examine in this chapter how politically affiliated Arab scholars responded intellectually to political repression, and how this very response has helped sustain repression. In other words, the two dialectically related questions that frame my study are those that have typically guided the sociology of intellectuals: how sociopolitical conditions shape intellectuals, and how intellectuals, in turn, influence these conditions (Kurzman and Owens 2002). I begin by reviewing the relationship between intellectuals and regimes in the nationalist and authoritarian neoliberal phases, and then trace the developments that took place in the nationalist, liberal, leftist, and Islamist schools of thought. I conclude with a general discussion of the major trends that characterize the Arab intellectual scene today.

Shaping and Reshaping Political Reality: From Arab Nationalism to Authoritarianism

Contemporary Arab thought has developed in response to two sweeping sociopolitical transformations. The first was the rise of postcolonial nationalist regimes and the building of the military/security-dominated Arab state, and the second was the disintegration of the nationalist project and subsequent rise of the authoritarian neoliberal regimes that prevail today.

For a little over a century (roughly from the 1830s to the 1950s), the Arab intellectual scene was consumed by the struggle between liberals, who wanted to reproduce western modernity under different historical-cultural conditions, and their Islamist rivals, who wanted to preserve Islam's central role in public life. On the margins of this liberal–Islamist divide, leftists were pursuing—without much success—the path of revolutionary change, and nationalists were proposing Arab unity as a substitute for the collapsing Islamic caliphate. By the 1960s, military officers and militaristic tribes and organizations had secured power in almost all Arab countries. Some regimes espoused progressive left-leaning nationalism (such as Egypt, Syria, Iraq, Libya, Algeria, Palestine, and the Sudan), while others combined nationalism with sociopolitical conservatism (as in Tunisia, Morocco, Saudi Arabia, and rest of the Arab Gulf). Still others were torn between the two strands of nationalism (such as Lebanon, Jordan, and Yemen).

In any case, the political sway of nationalism shifted the locus of intellectual struggle away from the liberal–Islamist debate; new lines of division were drawn in response to the new political realities. Despite the political antagonism between progressive and conservative Arab rulers, what Malcolm Kerr refers to as the "Arab Cold War" (Kerr 1966), nationalist intellectuals were welcomed on both sides; their work helped unite the masses with leaders and justified the rulers' policies. The division between nationalist regimes also had no effect on how they treated liberals. Whichever version of nationalism they favored, the new Arab rulers associated liberal intellectuals with western imperialism, something nationalists were bent on resisting. Liberals did not receive institutional support and their ideas became politically irrelevant.

The great divide between progressive and conservative Arab regimes manifested itself in their approach toward leftist and Islamist intellectuals. While progressive nationalists employed developmental and redistributional economic policies to undermine traditional elites and win the support of their overwhelmingly poor populations, conservative monarchs drew on Islam to support their royal privileges. Hence, under progressive nationalism, Islamists were identified as agents of conservatism and thus Islam-based politics was banned, Islamist organizations were dismantled, and Islamist intellectuals were violently repressed through extrajudicial detentions, banishment, and executions. Leftists, in contrast, developed an intricate relationship with progressive regimes. Despite the state-capitalist model adopted by these regimes, most leftists declared—in a remarkable sleight of hand—that statist nationalism was a first step toward socialism and, accordingly, collaborated with the rulers. The opposite occurred under conservative regimes, where leftists were excluded while Islamists were hailed as apologists for conservatism.

The nationalist tide receded gradually from the 1970s onward. The 1967 defeat led to the reconciliation of progressive and conservative regimes, initially with the intention of forming a unified front against Israel. The period following the 1973 War was followed by the ascendancy of a single dominant political order (Ajami 1981, 8–10)—what Said describes as "petty nationalist regimes" (Said 2006, 94). Arab nationalism was gradually "subverted, inverted, perverted into nothing so much as . . . . Right Wing brutality without ideological coherence or mass political grounding" (Said 1995, 225). With the collapse of the nationalist model, Arab intellectuals scrambled once more for a foothold in the new political order.

What are the main features of this postnationalist order? Here we can identify at least three related characteristics: authoritarianism, neoliberalism, and anti-intellectualism. First, though local conditions vary, Arab states became remarkably similar in terms of their authoritarian mode of governance (Schlumberger 2007, 7)—all ruled by a "cartel of authoritarian regimes practiced in the arts of oppression" ("Waking from Its Sleep" 2009, 3). The main principle of domination became personified in the monarch or president, whose chief preoccupation was to consolidate his power and secure the interests of his supporters: military/security officers, senior bureaucrats, ruling party officials, and family members (Hourani 1991, 448–50).

Contrary to popular myth, Arab states "experienced more not less authoritarianism since 1967" (Abu-Rabi' 2004, 22). Whereas nationalist regimes had focused on increasing what Mann described as the infrastructural power of the state—that is, the capacity of the state to control its territories and implement its policies—the new rulers turned their attention to the state's despotic power: the power of state elites over the rest of society (Mann 1993, 59). In a way, authoritarianism evolved naturally from the nationalist regimes' mode of governance. After achieving independence, Arab nationalists felt vulnerable because of the threat of foreign intervention and domestic pressure. They developed entrenched military/ security apparatuses to guard over their state-building projects. In time, they came to see political competition as instability, public debates as inefficiency, and every form of dissent as treason. Such regimes, according to Kees Koonings and Dirk Kruijt, are bound to degenerate into "repressive, closed and corrupt autocracies" (Koonings and Kruijt 2002, 1–2).

Under authoritarianism, the concept of national security was redefined as protecting the existing political order against domestic challengers (Koonings and Kruijt 2002, 20–23). Governance went hand-in-hand with a seemingly endless "low-intensity counterinsurgency campaign" against political opposition; a campaign carried out by a pervasive intelligence-cum-security apparatus that created a climate of fear and constant surveillance (Koonings and Kruijt 2002, 27). The authoritarian state relied primarily on highly developed coercive organs. Rulers drew on surpluses appropriated by the state to finance a large military/security apparatus, as well as a large sector of thugs and informers. State activity became gradually oriented toward political security above all else (Thomas 1984, 89–92).

In the Arab world, the apparatuses of repression developed far beyond those available to nationalist leaders: "If they wished, and if the instruments of repression did not break in their hands, they could crush any movements of revolt, at whatever cost . . . . [Through] a machinery of government larger and more complex than those in the past," the new regimes tightened their grip over society as never before (Hourani 1991, 448–50). One indicator is that the new Arab rulers spent more on the military/security establishment than on any other state institution, creating an "idle and too large military class," whose main occupation was repressing the population (Said 2003, 150–51).[3]

But why did these regimes rely so heavily on repression to maintain their power? The answer is that postcolonial authoritarianism is not only a political–military phenomenon, it is also a "new sociopolitical category" grounded in a specific structural context. This form of authoritarianism emerges in underdeveloped countries where the capitalist class's influence over the state is quite fluid. On the one hand, the ascendant national bourgeoisie understands its dependent role within the international structure of capitalism and props up authoritarianism to help facilitate this role (Thomas 1984, 105–108). On the other hand, authoritarian rulers build "fortress states" with no real mass following, and thus fall back on the support of capitalist centers, which thrive on access to peripheral resources and markets (Beck 2003, 266). Thomas summarized the relationship between capitalist power centers and authoritarian regimes in the periphery as follows:

> The authoritarian state is not purely a national or local phenomenon
> . . . . [Given] a peripheral capitalist society's . . . dependence on the
> international bourgeoisie for investment funds, markets, technol-
> ogy, finance, goods, etc., links between the local and international
> structures of authoritarianism are fundamental to the development
> of authoritarianism in the periphery . . . . This is plainly revealed in
> the role imperialism plays in arming these regimes, in providing them
> with sophisticated methods of internal surveillance, and in training
> personnel to work in the coercive structures of the state. The contin-
> uous upgrading of the military and counter-insurgency apparatuses is
> too well known to need repeating . . . . [In short,] the local authoritar-
> ian state is not only supported by the international structures of dom-
> ination but *cannot exist without them* (Thomas 1984, 93–94; emphasis
> in original).

That is why the second characteristic of the new political order in the Arab word is the dependence of Arab rulers on the support of domestic monopoly capitalists and the representatives of global capitalism. By making themselves useful to domestic and foreign investors, authoritarian regimes secured a huge influx of money and technology, and used it to increase their capacity to control (Abu-Rabi' 2004, 22). Western investors, in particular, were allowed guarantees and privileges to secure the political–military patronage of their governments (Hourani 1991, 422–23). Albert Hourani noted how Arab rulers, starting from the mid-1970s, favored those who controlled the private sector and established strong links with influential transnational corporations. In return, economic elites backed authoritarian regimes because they were able to maintain order, allow the flow of capital, and permit the import of consumer goods (Hourani 1991, 448–50).

A new capitalist elite "associated not with intelligent power, but with conspicuous, even laughable consumption . . . undirected and unmotivated except by short-range profit . . . concerned only with earning more, storing away more, avoiding even the common civil responsibilities of taxes" became the social bulwark of Arab regimes (Said 1995, 233). This new ruling class was composed of reemergent preindependence economic elites, corrupt politicians, state bureaucrats, and businessmen who benefited from state patronage (Abu-Rabiʻ 2004, 76). These groups worked together to maintain the existing political order in order to continue to enrich themselves and facilitate their business operations (Abu-Rabiʻ 2004, 19).

Third, under these conditions, the new rulers welcomed the pragmatism of the neoliberal school of thought (Abu-Rabiʻ 2004, 14). Unlike the nationalist leaders who used state-controlled opinion-making institutions to make their worldview hegemonic in the Gramscian sense, the new regimes promoted a climate of anti-intellectualism (Kurzman and Owlin 2002, 73), or what Bourdieu described as intellectual depoliticization (Bourdieu 2008, 375).[4] The value of ideas was depreciated; intellectual products were "commodified . . . packaged and up for sale" (Said 2003, 97–99). Rulers replaced ideology with the market-based logic of neoliberalism: the promise that economic liberalization and globalization are forces of redemption that can solve the problems of humanity (Beck 2003, 262–63). In that sense, the symbiotic link between authoritarianism and neoliberalism appears natural. As Mann contended, because authoritarian regimes are not pressed to win elections, they are perfectly suited for policies that produce "short-term economic misery for the sake of some dubious neo-liberal vision of the long term" (Mann 2003, 70).

In contrast with neoliberal intellectuals, nationalists were considered archaic and nonthreatening to the new order, while leftists and Islamists were placed at the receiving end of state repression. Nonliberal intellectuals now faced a harsher situation than before. On the one hand, under authoritarian neoliberalism, intellectuals not only suffered from political repression but also became subject to the commercial standards of the market. On the other hand, the regimes they were opposing were far more stable than anything that had ever existed before in the Arab world. Borrowing from Ibn Khaldun, Hourani attributes this stability to (1) the cohesiveness of the ruling group, (2) its ability to link its interests with those of the most powerful economic elements in society, and (3) its success in presenting its agenda in terms of a universal ideology (Hourani 1991, 448–50), that is, neoliberalism.

This stability was reflected in a recent survey of the potential for democratization in ten Arab states (Morocco, Kuwait, Yemen, Egypt, Saudi Arabia, Lebanon, Jordan, Syria, Palestine, and Algeria), which concluded that no Arab regime felt challenged enough to change (Ottaway and Choucair-Vizoso 2008, 261). With the repressive capabilities at their disposal, Arab rulers were steering "a risk-free course," undisturbed by social and political discontent. The few reforms enacted by ruling elites were not intended to allow the sharing of political power, but rather to consolidate their power by developing more "efficiently governed and economically successful versions of existing states" (Ottaway and Choucair-Vizoso 2008, 262), what Heydemann described as "upgrading authoritarianism" (Heydemann 2007).

In the following sections, I examine the response of Arab intellectuals to the rise of the authoritarian neoliberal state: how liberals adopted the now prominent neoliberal creed, and how nationalists, leftists, and Islamists fell back on the culture-oriented doctrines of New Arabism, New Leftism, and New Islamism, respectively.

From Classical Liberalism to Neoliberalism

Arab liberalism was born out of intellectual contact with Europe, starting from the 1830s onward. Classical Arab liberals, such as Constantine Zurayk (Syria), Butrus al-Bustani (Lebanon), and Ahmed Lutfi al-Sayyid (Egypt), were disconcerted by the continuing influence of Islam on Arab politics and society. Convinced that western progress went hand-in-hand with secularism, they claimed that political and legal freedoms could not be attained unless religion was relegated to the private sphere (Barakat 1993, 245–46). The de facto—though not necessarily ideological—secularism of nationalist regimes robbed liberals of their chief cause.

There are also social grounds for the waning influence of liberalism during the nationalist epoch. The political and economic modernization at the heart of the nationalist state-building project undermined preindependence economic elites, mostly landlords and tribal chiefs. These elites, together with a handful of industrialists, represented the social bases for liberal thought in the Arab world. What was missing was a substantial middle class that could have sustained liberalism through the rigorous state-building process that lasted until the late 1970s.

Compared to western societies, the social conditions conducive to the promotion of liberal thought were absent in the Arab world. According to Talukder Maniruzzaman, the bourgeoisie–state relationship in the Arab world developed in a direction opposite to that in the west: "The Western bourgeois revolution grew as the result of a 'revolution from below'—an explosion of creative forces released by tension-ridden society. The bourgeoisies in the [Arab] World has been the artificial creation of the revolution from above." Thus, the Arab bourgeoisie developed through "state patronization rather than initiative and entrepreneurship" (Maniruzzaman 1987, 167–68). That is why Abu-Rabi' described classical Arab liberalism as "a poor version of European liberalism, a cheap imitation copy" that lacked the social context that made liberalism viable in the West. Abu-Rabi' offered two explanations for this: first, colonial powers prevented the emergence of an independent Arab bourgeoisie, and second, Arab feudalism and tribalism proved resilient to a complete capitalist takeover (Abu-Rabi' 2004, 74). The two reasons are related: colonial rulers supported Arab landlords and chieftains because they were the "only social strata" willing to ally with European powers. At the same time, Europeans considered indigenous industrialists as potential market competitors and advocates for independence, and thus undermined their position (Sternberg 1950, 42–43).

Only in the postnationalist phase did Arab liberals reemerge, this time reinvigorated by a new creed (neoliberalism) and new social supporters (state rulers and foreign investors). In the face of authoritarian Arab regimes, many liberal intellectuals decided to postpone the struggle for political freedom, focusing instead on what unites them with the regimes: achieving economic liberalization. In other words, neoliberal intellectuals considered it politically expedient to succumb to the rulers' prioritization of liberal economic development over democracy and civil liberties. This choice was, of course, in line with the social origins of this liberal stratum. Because Arab capitalists developed under authoritarian patronage, they were naturally oriented toward making easy profits through political connections rather than entrepreneurship. It was only natural for such a class, and its intellectual representatives, to pay a subservient role to the state rulers.

Shukri al-Nabulsi (Jordan), who drafted the first Arab "neoliberal manifesto," mentioned two other important differences between Arab neoliberals and their classical liberal predecessors: first, market rationality replaced the reason of the Enlightenment and early European modernity, and, second, global free-market capitalism became the path to progress and prosperity instead of the old national industrial model (al-Nabulsi 2005, 21–25).

Now what are the premises of neoliberalism as an ideology and how did it manifest itself in the postnationalist Arab world? Neoliberalism works in close proximity with the market and derives its logic from market forces. Claiming that capitalist freedom—namely, the right to accumulate, invest, and consume—is the harbinger of all other kinds of rights and freedoms—neoliberals focus their efforts on liberating capitalists from state regulation. Other rights and freedoms: the political, legal, social, and even economic rights and freedoms, understood widely as the right to employment, pensions, and social security and the freedom from need—come second. In fact, they are somehow supposed to follow automatically from capitalist freedoms. Neoliberalism draws its strength from its appeal to efficiency and market rationality. Here, the market model "colonizes the ethical world," claiming to represent universal rationality by ethically sanctioning and freeing human nature once and for all (Tripp 2006, 5). According to Bourdieu, neoliberals erect into moral norms the law of the market, which is, more accurately, the law of the strongest. Arming itself with media power, mathematics, and "falsifications based on the manipulation of statistics and crude trickery," neoliberalism, in Bourdieu's description,

ratifies the spontaneous philosophy of the heads of big multinationals and the agents of high finance, which is echoed throughout the world by politicians and high officials . . . and above all by the world of major journalists, almost all of whom are equally ignorant of the underlying mathematical theory, and this becomes a kind of universal belief, a new ecumenical gospel . . . made up of a series of terms that are poorly defined, such as 'globalization', 'flexibility', 'deregulation' . . . [that] contribute to giving the outward appearance of a message of freedom and liberation to a conservative ideology that sees itself opposed to all ideologies, . . . [a] philosophy [that] has no other purpose than the ever increasing creation of wealth—and, more secretly, its concentration in the hands of a small privileged minority. (Bourdieu 2008, 288–90)

More important, for our purposes, is how this market-based creed affects intellectual production. First, neoliberalism undermines intellectual independence by imposing the standards of commerce and market value on all forms of intellectual production, "establishing profit as the sole principle of valuation in matters of education, culture, art and literature" (Bourdieu 2008, 290–91). Second, neoliberals promote the doctrines of depoliticization, objectivity, and neutrality, claiming that defending economic efficiency is the greatest service one can render his or her society. This notion is of course accompanied by a list of practical necessities, such as privatization, deregulation, and integration into the global capitalist market (Bourdieu 2008, 374–75). This policy of depoliticizing intellectuals "shamelessly draw[s] on the lexicon of liberty, liberalism, liberalization . . . to confer a fatal grip of economic determinism" and obtain the submission of citizens to the "liberated" economic forces (Bourdieu 2008, 379). In short, neoliberalism not only promises an "ideology of false hope" but also reconstructs the intellectual and cultural world in its own image (Abu-Rabi' 2004, 2).

Said conveyed the same impression in his portrayal of the alliance between authoritarian Arab regimes and neoliberal intellectuals—what he designated the New Arab Right. Said described Arab neoliberals and the classes they represent as "visionless and incoherent," with no real philosophy, only firm control over poorly distributed economic power (Said 1995, 224). This class is characterized by its total dependency on the western market philosophy, and although "they pride themselves on their enlightened liberality and technical know-how, they are totally cut-off, ideologically and economically and socially, from the rapidly increasing masses whose accelerating poverty" has become scandalous. Most important, neoliberals and their capitalist associates have become the "mainstays and even mirror images of the regimes and armies they support" (Said 1995, 227–28). Like the new Arab regimes, neoliberals are, in Said's view, insensitive to social needs, uninterested in the results of the policies they advocate, and unversed in either Arab tradition or the western philosophy "they so desperately emulate." Because members of this authoritarian neoliberal alliance are only interested in self-preservation and "having a good time," Said judged them harshly: "No ruling class in history is as unintelligent as this one" (Said 1995, 227–29).

The authoritarian–neoliberal dynamic was very similar to the one that developed between leftists and progressive nationalists, on the one hand, and Islamists and conservative nationalists, on the other, during the 1950s and 1960s. Then, intellectuals, fearing repression, saw wisdom in keeping politics at arm's length and skewing their ideology in a way that emphasized their commonalties with the rulers and downplayed any differences. In the case of neoliberals from the 1980s onward, the points of commonality were mostly economic.

Postnationalist Arab regimes were willing to restructure their economies through privatizing the public sector, deregulating financial institutions, opening up their markets to foreign trade and investments, removing social subsidies, reducing custom taxes, and so on. In justifying their deference of serious political reform, Arab rulers referred to the neoliberal prophecy that economic liberalization, with its almost miraculously transformative effects, is the first step toward political freedom. Neoliberals, for their part, had no major quarrels with this arrangement. It is true that some of them criticized the slow pace of political liberalization, but the intellectual model they propagated—secular, capitalist, and liberal—overlapped considerably with the existing one. In other words, their critique of Arab regimes was quantitative rather than qualitative. They called for more of everything: more secularism, more capitalism, and more liberalism.

Arab neoliberals, such as Khaled Shawkat (Tunisia), stated clearly that their priority at this point was the adoption of the free economy model as a first step toward other freedoms (Shawkat 2005, 100). Hazem Saghieh (Lebanon) justified the prioritization of capitalism over democracy by the fact that majority-rule in the Arab world today is bound to bring undesirable elements to power. Saghieh feared that because of the progressive nationalist and religious tides that have swept over Arab society, political authoritarianism would likely be replaced by a collectivist social order—an anathema to liberals (Saghieh 2005, 68–69). Democracy, according to this view, must wait until Arabs are prepared to make the right choices, which is to support unfettered individualism and the market economy. Because of their reluctance to clash with their rulers, Arab neoliberals busied themselves with defending the economic interests of capitalists instead of promoting political and social freedom for all citizens. In short, they propagated "capitalism without democracy" (Abu-Rabi' 2004, 76–77, 7).

This position secured for neoliberals substantial institutional power. Many of them became members of ruling parties, taught at public and private universities, and headed publicly funded research centers. Some even held ministerial posts, including Ali al-Din Hillal and Abd al-Mon'iem Said (Egypt), Marawan al-Mu'asher (Jordan), and Jawad Hashem (Iraq). Those who remained out of politics and public administration benefited from the fact that the political rulers favored their views. Neoliberals, supported by state officials and the business community, enjoyed access to a wide network of intellectual dissemination, including television, newspapers, publishing houses, and so on. Their access to institutions of intellectual production and their financial capacity to benefit from new forms of commodified culture enhanced their power substantially (Abu-Rabi' 2004, 23–24).

The authoritarian regimes, in turn, profited from adopting the neoliberal discourse in two main ways: first, they secured economic support from domestic monopoly capitalists, and, second, they made themselves useful, perhaps even indispensable, to foreign capitalists. The Arab cities of Dubai, Beirut, Cairo, and others embraced foreign investors, and in return Arab rulers demanded the support of global capitalist centers. In fact, negotiating economic partnerships and free trade agreements with the United States (in the case of Egypt, Jordan, and the Gulf countries) and Europe (in the case of Syria, Lebanon, and North African Arab countries) became a major obsession for Arab leaders.

But defending capitalist freedoms was not Arab neoliberals' only preoccupation. They directed much of their energy to discrediting other intellectual camps. To begin with, neoliberals claimed a monopoly over democracy in the Arab world, lending support to the rulers' assertion that nonliberals, especially Islamists, wanted to use democracy instrumentally to reach power and revoke it afterward. Ahmed al-Baghdadi (Kuwait), for example, stated clearly: "Only liberals are democratic," the rest are hypocrites; and only liberal governance is democratic, no other form of democracy exists other than that of liberal Western countries like the United States, Britain, and France (al-Baghdadi 2005, 113).

Neoliberals also continued the liberal–Islamist intellectual struggle that dated back to the late nineteenth century. From the very start, Arab liberals had sought a "qualitative break with religion" (Abu-Rabiʻ 2004, 73). The classical liberal intelligentsia adopted secularism as the "criterion of progress and ʻcatching up' with the West" (Abu-Rabiʻ 2004, 27–28). This was because the classical Arab liberal project developed on the periphery of world capitalism and was entirely focused on cultural and political themes. Now neoliberals expected Islamist intellectuals not only to accept secularism but also to facilitate the "exigencies of the capitalist order" by legitimating the right to private property, highlighting how social inequality is predestined, distinguishing between permissible banking interest rates and prohibited usury, and refuting the un-Islamic concept of national sovereignty, which fuels anti-globalization sentiments (Abu-Rabiʻ 2004, 27–29).

Furthermore, neoliberals denounced the anti-imperialist positions of Arab nationalists, leftists, and Islamists, considering all forms of identity-based ideology to be a threat to globalization. A liberal world is impossible, according to Kanan Makiya (Iraq), without rooting out the "obsessive and deeply unhealthy hold that identity politics has upon Arab intellectuals" (Makiya 1993, 41). Fouad Ajami (Lebanon) claimed that following the 1967 defeat Arabs should have learned once and for all that they must be part of the international community, they must accept a "subdued coming-to-terms with the world" (Ajami 1981, 5). Similarly, Hazem Saghieh expressed his hope that Arabs would transcend the traditional loyalties of family, nationality, and religion, and embrace the individualism of the new global culture instead (Saghieh 2005, 17, 11). Kemal Gabriel (Egypt) defended globalization against identity politics, stating that in a liberal world there is no place for the kind of "fascist identities" propagated by Arab nationalists and Islamists. Gabriel added that these dogmatic Arab intellectuals must realize "that history has ended, [and] that ideology is dead (Gabriel 2005, 79–80).

In fact, what Arabs needed most on the intellectual level, according to neoliberals, was to stop blaming others for their "self-inflicted wounds" and take responsibility for their own misdeeds. Ajami accused Arab intellectuals of inventing a history that has always pointed outward, despite the fact that Arab divisions are real and "not contrived points on a map or a colonial trick of divide-and-conquer." The tendency to attack the West is, in Ajami's view, the main "Arab predicament" (Ajami 1981, 3). Makiya concurred:

The painful thing to observe is the unrelenting stridency of the Arab intelligentsia's attempt to blame every ill on the West or Israel. The language gets more unreal, hysterical, and self-flagellating, the less the Arab world is actually able to achieve politically and culturally in modern times . . . . A very large number of people have invested much of their lives in constructing and defending this 'rejectionist' paradigm, which has now become second nature to a new generation of Arabs. (Makiya 1993, 235–37)

But why do Arab nationalists, leftists, and Islamists adopt this antagonistic worldview? In Ajami's view, the "losers in the world system," those who fail in their "quest for the Occident's power and success . . . and glamorous world," retreat into their shells and fall back on the things that are familiar to them, especially language, history, and religion (Ajami 1981, 251). Identity-based paradigms, in other words, compensate for the fact that Arab skills could not match those of westerners (Ajami 1981, 21). In short, Arab neoliberals believe that all other intellectual doctrines in the Arab world stem from deeply held inferiority complexes vis-à-vis the West.

Finally, the position that summarizes the neoliberal view better than any other is the explanation for the persistence of authoritarianism in the Arab world. After vindicating not only western powers but also ruling regimes, neoliberals place the full blame on nonliberal intellectuals. According to Makiya, the Arab world's failure to achieve democracy is neither the responsibility of the west nor that of Arab regimes; it is the outcome of a degenerate Arab culture. The Arab malaise, in Makiya's words, "lies principally in its intelligentsia, not in its regimes . . . . It arises from the inner logic of the governing ideological paradigm—cultural nationalism—which includes in its totalizing embrace Marxists, nationalists, and Islamists" (Makiya 1993, 322). Arab intellectuals are incapable of bringing about freedom because they are "fossilized, backward-looking and steeped in a romanticism of 'struggle'" (Makiya 1993, 282). It is the intellectuals and not the "unsavory collection of tyrannies, monarchies, and autocracies that wield the guns" that the young Arab generation should hold accountable for Arab authoritarianism (Makiya 1993, 324–35). In Gabriel's formulation, tyranny in Arab societies lies not in the corruption of the rulers but that of the "corrupted corruptors"—the nonliberal intellectuals who delude the masses and turn them against the liberal, secular West (Gabriel 2005, 76).

From Arab Nationalism to New Arabism

Arab nationalism first began to take shape in the writings of Sati' al-Husari (Syria) in the early twentieth century. Al-Husari was influenced by nineteenth-century German cultural nationalism, which inspired the Romantic movement that swept Europe at the time. In European nationalism, as well as in its Arabized version, unifying the 'nation'—defined basically as members of the same cultural community—was a sacred act that promised to return individuals to their true selves (Dawisha 2003, 298–300). From the very beginning, in Leonard Binder's description, Arab nationalism presented a "hodgepodge of vulgarized European philosophies":

> There is the usual reflection of Herder in the view that every nation has a peculiar mission to perform and through that mission each will contribute to international harmony. There is the Hegelian emphasis on history and the national teleology.... There is reflection, of course, of Rousseau's general will.... The Marxist theory of class struggle also appears, and considerable emphasis is placed upon the economic basis of politics. (Binder 1964, 159)

Arab nationalism was, however, different from the European version in one crucial sense: it was largely undertheorized. In fact, the main protagonists of Arab nationalism, Michel 'Aflaq and Salah al-Din Bitar (Syria) and Gamal Abdel Nasser (Egypt) criticized abstract thinking and "intellectual hairsplitting" and rejected the necessity to theorize nationalism. In their view, "nationalism is love . . . an identity as intimate as one's name . . . [it] needs no justification, and hence needs no theory" (Binder 1964, 162–63). What was required instead was the promotion of nationalist consciousness and the liberation of the submerged Arab identity. In other words, Arab nationalism as a premise should be "accepted on faith; the rest follows logically" (Binder 1964, 163–64). As the nation's vanguard, nationalist thinkers were only supposed to mobilize the masses behind the dream of Arab unity, not theorize it roots (Binder 1964, 162–64). Stephen Humphreys emphasized this single point: Arab nationalists were more concerned with persuading Arabs that they all shared the same identity than with formulating sound theoretical bases for a united Arab state (Humphreys 2005, 66–67).

This lack of theory could be explained by the fact that most Arab nationalist intellectuals were activists, propagandists, and state officials, not philosophers. But a more social-historical explanation is that Arab nationalism drew its strength from Arab militaries, not the masses. Arab militaries were greatly influenced by the western colonial powers that helped train them (as in the cases of Iraq, Jordan, Egypt, Syria, and Algeria, among others). Because armies in the West were vanguards of nationalism and state-building, western-trained Arab soldiers became indoctrinated nationalists. As the military came to dominate Arab politics in the mid-twentieth century, Arab nationalism spread from the state downward.[5] In that sense, Arab nationalism was an instance of what Roger Brubaker referred to as a "category of [state] practice," not a natural manifestation of a substantial and enduring collectivity called the Arab nation. It was a set of nation-oriented idioms that became "suddenly and powerfully" institutionalized in state discourse and practice, not an elaborate theory of identity and belonging (Brubaker 1996, 10, 21).

This lack of theory clearly influenced Arab nationalism's economic doctrine, which was either progressive or conservative depending on the rulers' agendas (Binder 1964, 2). Progressive nationalists collaborated with leftists, usually through institutional forms, such as the merging of the Ba'th Party and the Arab Socialist Party to form the Ba'th Socialist Party in Syria in 1954, and the Egyptian Communist Party's metamorphosis into the state-controlled Arab Socialist Union in Egypt a decade later, in addition to the hybrid nationalist–socialist parties that emerged in Palestine following the 1967 defeat, such as the Popular Front for the Liberation of Palestine and the Democratic Front for the Liberation of Palestine. In contrast, conservative nationalists in countries like Saudi Arabia, Morocco, and Jordan adopted right-wing economic policies and favored Islamists over leftists.

Only the nationalist–leftist alliance produced an economic doctrine worthy of the name, though here, too, there was theoretical ambivalence. Progressive nationalist thinkers supported the redistribution of land and wealth, increasing workers' benefits, limiting private ownership and investment, state control over market fluctuations, the nationalization of most of the industrial and financial sectors, the regulation of foreign trade, and the state's provision of public goods and services. Arab nationalists labeled this doctrine 'Arab socialism,' a version of socialism that stood halfway between Marxism and state capitalism. In Arab socialism, the entire society was expected to rally around a state that pursued the interests of all citizens (Hourani 1991, 406). This version of socialism, naturally, did not lead to a dictatorship of the proletariat, but rather to the "dictatorship of the lower middle class [state bureaucrats]" (Binder 1964, 83–84). While army officers and bureaucrats benefited substantially, and landlords and industrialists were badly hurt, it is still not clear how other groups were affected (Binder 1964, 217). Abu-Rabi' is probably right in suggesting that instead of leveling social classes, what Arab socialism ended up producing was a "nationalist petty bourgeois state" ruled by state bureaucrats (Abu-Rabi' 2004, 32).[6]

The same reluctance to theorize characterized Arab nationalists' treatment of Islam. Unlike liberals and leftists, who had well-defined positions toward religion, Arab nationalists adopted a convoluted logic about Islam. Islam was, on the one hand, an important part of Arab identity and heritage, which helped fuel the anti-western rhetoric of Arab nationalists, but it was not allowed to overwhelm Arabism as an ethnic-cultural identity, on the other. In 'Aflaq's writings, for example, he made it clear that although Islam is one of the "characteristics constituting the Arab nation," it must not be allowed to surpass Arab nationalism as a unifying ideology. In his view, "Arab nationalism comprehends Islam" (Binder 1964, 168). Similarly, Nasser's attitude toward Islam reflected his belief that religion should only bolster the ideology of Arab nationalism (Binder 1964, 172). In more radically secular nationalist settings, such as Algeria, Iraq, and Palestine, Arab nationalists excluded Islam from their doctrines, replacing it with the notion of the sacred bond of Arab brotherhood (Abu-Rabi' 2004, 69).

Following the collapse of Arab nationalist regimes and the rise of the authoritarian neoliberal model, the "sun, which has shone so brightly on Arab nationalism [seemed to have] finally set" (Dawisha 2003, 251). Many declared the death of Arab nationalism as a political ideology (Makiya 1993, 327; Abu-Rabi' 2004, 80), and Arab nationalism was supplanted by a number of local and regional creeds that held the interest of each Arab state above all else (Said 1994, 115). It became commonplace for Arab rulers to rally their people behind divisive slogans such as "Egypt First," a practice adopted not only by Egypt but also by Iraq, Jordan, Tunisia, and the Gulf states. It was Arab statism (wataniya) not nationalism (qawmiya) that defined the postnationalist era (Dawisha 2003, 254). With the political ascendancy of the new order, the concept of the inviolable sovereignty of each Arab state had not only become the fundamental premise of interstate Arab politics but it invaded Arab consciousness (Dawisha 2003, 274).

Despite the above, as Said pointed out, something still united the cultures of Arab countries; the feeling of commonality did not entirely disappear (Said 2006, 94). What continued to live on, however, was "Arabism *not* Arab nationalism" (Dawisha 2003, 252). How was Arabism different from Arab nationalism? According to Dawisha, the goal of Arab nationalism was to bring all Arab countries under one political authority. This goal was irretrievably lost. Arab rulers and ruled acknowledged their belonging to a single cultural space, but no serious intellectual called for the creation of a pan-Arab state anymore. Arab nationalist thinkers now called for Arab solidarity, not political unity (Dawisha 2003, 252–53). In that sense, Arab nationalism was transformed into "cultural Arabism," one that merely required politicians to keep sight of Arab cultural bonds when making decisions (Dawisha 2003, 274). Whatever these intellectuals hoped to achieve, it was certainly clear that they were not planning to "challenge or even question the legitimacy and sovereignty of the Arab state" (Dawisha 2003, 281). Shibley Telhami described this new intellectual trend as "New Arabism," which, unlike traditional Arab nationalism, was a bottom-up movement led by "disaffected intellectual elites trying to chart a political course independently from the state" (Telhami 1999, 56–57).

We can observe today how typical voices of Arab nationalism, whether Muhammad Hassanein Heikal's (Egypt) revisiting of history in his weekly program on Al Jazzera, or Jihad al-Khazin's (Palestine) daily column in *al-Hayat*, are mostly nostalgic, mourning a past long gone, rather than advancing a concrete political project. Dawisha concluded that Arab nationalism is "meaningless *without* its ultimate goal of Arab unity." There is nothing ideologically inspiring, in his view, about a region with a multiplicity of states, the vast majority of whose population happens to speak Arabic and share a set of cultural values (Dawisha 2003, 12).

From Socialism to the New Left

The challenge that confronted some of the first Arab socialists, such as Shibli Shumayyil (Lebanon), Henri Curiel (Egypt), and Salama Musa (Egypt), was how to untangle socialism from its foreign and elitist background and bring it to Arab workers. It was not an easy task in light of the feudal and commercial nature of Arab economies, and the scarcity of industrial production. By the time the Arab world began to industrialize, under the modernizing military/security-dominated regimes of the mid-twentieth century, socialists seemed to have lost their chance at triggering a purely socialist revolution. Whether in Egypt, Syria, Lebanon, Iraq, Algeria, or Palestine, nationalism, not socialism, proved to be the overwhelming ideology.

Arab socialists who aspired for more than the piecemeal left-wing socioeconomic reforms that the Arab nationalists were willing to offer were severely repressed. The support institutions that Arab leftists had developed before the nationalists took power were no match for the newly established military/security-dominated states. Their only choice was to collaborate with the rulers "in the hope that Arab nationalism was a stage in the society's transition toward full socialism" (Abu-Rabi' 2004, 83–84). But even the few leftist gains of the nationalist phase quickly eroded under the new authoritarian–neoliberal alliance: the public sector was sold, most social subsidies were lifted, and Arab markets were opened to all manner of venture capitalism. Furthermore, the new Arab regimes were quite intolerant toward socialists who tried to appeal to, let alone organize, domestic workers.

In response, more and more Arab leftists began to adopt the western-inspired New Left model, which was developed by European Marxists in the 1920s and 1930s to compensate for their failure to take political power and halt the expansion of capitalism. Those who inspired the New Left, mainly Antonio Gramsci, György Lukács, the first generation of the Frankfurt School, especially Herbert Marcuse and Theodor Adorno, and the group of scholars that coalesced around the *New Left Review*, were different in many ways, but what united them was the belief that cultural reform is the key to political change. Instead of developing a contemporary version of Marxism, New Leftists presented an incoherent set of proposals, all aimed at undermining bourgeois culture. Moreover, their "universalization of Marxist phraseology" produced a diffused ideology, capable of supporting various social causes: cultural pluralism, feminism, secularism, anti-imperialism, as well as literary and artistic criticism (Kolakowski 1981, 487). Following the worldwide students' and workers' protests of 1968, the New Left advanced a global democratic agenda, thus becoming even more generalized and abstract. New leftists now envisioned themselves as the harbingers of an international utopia of justice and freedom. As Leszek Kolakowski commented, the New Left encompassed a collection of left-leaning intellectuals that did not offer "any intellectual results worth the name" (Kolakowski 1981, 487–91). They were, in Said's words, a conglomeration of intellectuals "who call themselves Marxists" without being involved in any radical political struggle (Said 2006, 107).

For Arab intellectuals, the New Leftist emphasis on emancipation through culture and the postponement of political dissent until the cultural battle was won was conducive to the repressive political environments within which they operated. Also, the New Leftist focus on the global front was a source of relief to those who were weary of the prospects of confronting Arab regimes. As a result, New Leftism became the ideology of choice for most 'New Arab leftists': a host of left-leaning Arab intellectuals who had little in common with each other, and even less in common with orthodox Marxism (Abu-Rabi' 2004, 80). Benedetto Fontana was even harsher, proclaiming that the "politics of the left [today], characterized by identity issues, diversity and multi-culturalism, rather than offering an alternative to the prevailing order, is the purest reflection of that order" (Fontana 2009, 86).

Borrowing from European Marxists was not new to the Arab Left, which has yet to formulate an Arab version of Marxism that springs from the sociohistorical experience of Arab workers (Abu-Rabi' 2004, 80–82). Mahmoud Amin al-'Alim (Egypt) admitted that Arab intellectuals did not produce a coherent Marxist theory for the Arab world. Instead, the Arab Left adopted western Marxism without contributing any meaningful ideological insights, and thus remained "theoretically aloof and confined to a small circle of elite intellectuals" (Abu-Rabi' 2004, 85). Hisham Sharabi (Palestine) reiterated this point:

> The dilemma of the leftist Arab intellectual [is] in a growing political alienation from the West on the one hand, and an increasing intellectual and cultural attraction to it on the other. For while socialism—which, after all, is a European importation to the Middle East—may serve to draw him toward the communist political orbit, at the same time it ties him to European sources of his intellectual creed. This psychological polarity has given rise in recent years to an impassioned movement of political and cultural emancipation. (Sharabi 1967, 197–98)

What made New Leftism particularly attractive, however, was that it allowed Arab leftists settle for the role of cultural critics, and legitimized their almost full-time occupation with cultural themes, such as religious intolerance, feminist and minority rights, literary production, avant-garde art movements, and changes in popular culture. Examples include Galal Amin (Egypt), Abd al-Kebir Khatibi (Morocco), al-Tayyib Tizzini (Syria), and Husayn Marwa (Lebanon). Developments in current Arab leftist thought were thus primarily cultural, sometimes with a global humanistic flavor and sometimes without.

Sharabi, for instance, claimed that the techniques and conventions of child rearing in Arab society explain political authoritarianism. The dominance of the father and other senior male figures is internalized by family members and then reproduced on the state level; the political leader is extended the same treatment as the family patriarch. In Sharabi's view, the "neo-patriarchy" that infests Arab culture not only discourages political opposition, but also has forestalled a much-needed Arab cultural renaissance. Sharabi recommended a gradual change in the Arab family structure, and its associated values, if Arabs were to reverse the dynamics of political subjugation (Barakat 1993, 264). Along similar lines, Sadiq Jalal al-ʿAzm (Syria) blamed traditional Arab culture, especially religion, for the social alienation, economic underdevelopment, and political despotism prevalent in the Arab world. Al-ʿAzm insisted that radical political change will never occur unless Arabs liberate themselves from traditional metaphysical thinking and social bonds, and some of their abhorrent cultural habits (Barakat 1993, 64–65).

Abdallah Laroui (Morocco) offered a more elaborate cultural critique. He first asserted that the "roots of backwardness in the modern Arab world are to be found in the . . . cultural environment, and not so much in the realms of economics or politics." Laroui then explained that the Arab proletariat could not fulfill the revolutionary role prescribed to it by Marx as long as Arab society remained culturally retarded. Laroui attacked the Arab obsession with preserving cultural authenticity and continuity against cultural 'others,' especially western civilization. Arab culture, in his opinion, stopped developing because Arabs could not conceive of their collective self as being anything other than a negation of the West; they could not overcome the bitterness caused by the West's aggression against them over the course of the past two centuries (Abu-Rabiʿ 2004, 346–47). Laroui underlined the need for an Arab cultural rebirth that would promote secular pedagogy and liberate the "poor masses and workers from the hegemony of religion and traditional ideas" (Abu-Rabiʿ 2004, 367). Finally, he offered "universality as a substitute" for a past that has failed to prepare Arabs for the modern age (Abu-Rabiʿ 2004, 347).

Samir Amin (Egypt) shared both of Laroui's concerns: the negative effects of tradition and religion, and the need for a universal culture. With regards to the first issue, Amin accused Islamists and other religiously oriented intellectuals of furthering the goals of imperialism, arguing that their narrow-mindedness reduced culture to a blind affirmation of belonging to a particular religion and fostered divisiveness among world citizens, thus diminishing the prospects of global cooperation (Amin 2007, 84–86). A typical example of a globally oriented Arab leftist, Amin justified focusing on the global instead of the national front by reminding us that "capitalism has built a global system, and therefore it cannot be transcended except on a global scale." Convinced that national struggles are insufficient to challenge a capitalism that has gone global, Amin established a number of international leftist forums, such as the Third World Forum in Dakar in 1980 and the Alternatives International in Cairo in 1997 (Amin 2006, 255–57). His aim was not only to unite national leftist movements in a global struggle against capitalism, but also to lend support to a host of social movements struggling for a humanistic global culture, movements that include human rights activists, feminists, and environmentalists. Amin's intellectual project calls for a joint front against a multitude of social ills: racism, ethnic cleansing, gender-based persecution, cultural chauvinism, global warming, and, finally, economic exploitation (Amin 2006, 255–57). At the opening of the World Social Forum in January 2006, Amin presented what he considered a *Communist Manifesto* for contemporary times. The Bamako Appeal called for an "internationalism of peoples" and the creation of a global "cultural consensus" to counter America's "militarized globalization" (Amin 2008, 108–109).

In effect, contemporary Arab leftist intellectuals directed their effort away from opposing their politically repressive, economically exploitive regimes toward attacking what they perceived as cultural backwardness and social conservatism. Although they kept up their anti-regime rhetoric, most of their theoretical contributions were directed at undermining Islamism and, to a lesser extent, nationalism.

From Islamism to New Islamism

An Islamist political project for modern times emerged in the early twentieth century. In the writings of Rashid Rida, it became apparent that Islamist thinkers had moved beyond trying to absorb, sometimes even sanctify, European modernity, to developing an authentic political alternative derived from Islamic texts and history. The group of political ideologues that coalesced around al-Ikhwan al-Muslimun (The Society of the Muslim Brothers)—Hassan al-Banna and Abd al-Qader 'Awdah (Egypt), Mustafa al-Siba'i and Said Hawa (Syria), Hassan al-Turabi (the Sudan), and others—drove their disciples into the political fray to impose what they believed to be a proper Islamic order. Following the military-backed nationalist takeovers of postcolonial Arab states, Islamists were either repressed by or incorporated into the state. In the postnationalist phase, the repression of Islamist thinkers and activists increased, especially in light of the global war against Islamist militancy, which began in the 1990s and escalated after the 11 September 2001 attacks.

Nonmilitant Islamists responded first by lowering the ceiling of their political demands, but ended up compromising on most of them and turning their attention to cultural themes—a shift described as "post-Islamism" (Roy 1996; Kepel 2002; Bayat 2007), "new Islamism" (Baker 2003), or a "remaking of Muslim politics" (Hefner 2005). This was basically a reinvention of Islamism as a social movement that renounced radical political opposition and embraced the long-term path of cultural reform. What this amounted to was a "privatization of Islamization" as opposed to the previously hoped for "Islamization of the state." In other words, it indicated the relocation of Islamism from the arena of political struggle to the privacy of Muslim homes. According to Assef Bayat, this "metamorphosis" represented a "tremendous shift" in intellectual discourse. Under repression, politicized Islamist intellectuals began, quite haphazardly, to "marry Islam with individual choice and freedom, with democracy and modernity," thus turning the original Islamism of the mid-twentieth century "on its head" (Bayat 2007, 10–11).

Although Islamist parties remain politically active, they seem to have run out of intellectual steam. Islamism has become less of a political ideology than a sociocultural creed. Islamist intellectuals assumed the role of moral entrepreneurs, consoling their followers with the belief that gradual cultural reform is bound to produce political change in the future. Oliver Roy noted how the failure of Islamist movements to achieve political transformation triggered an intellectual drift toward a puritanical, preaching mode that engaged Muslim individuals and ignored the regimes (Roy 1996, 25). After suffering heavily from political confrontations with Arab rulers, Islamist thinkers decided that a "reinvestment in the social sphere" on the level of morals and piety might be more effective (Roy 1996, 77). Roy summarized this new trend as follows: as the Islamist political campaign reached a dead end, the new Islamist intellectuals fell back on the argument that although an "Islamic society exists only through politics, . . . political institutions function only as a result of the virtue of those who run them, a virtue that can become widespread only if society is Islamic beforehand. It is a vicious circle" (Roy 1996, 60).

How did Islamists justify the intellectual shift from the explicitly political to the cultural? In Bayat's view, Islamist thinkers became convinced that through their cultural production and mentorship they could establish new social facts on the ground, "new lifestyles, new modes of thinking, behaving, being, and doing," which could then be acclimatized in a long-term campaign to socialize the state from below—"conditioning the state and its henchmen to societal sensibilities, ideals, and expectations" (Bayat 2007, 204).

Islamist thinkers around the Arab world have defended this new ideological strategy as authentically Islamic. Youssef al-Qaradawi (Egypt), for instance, argued that political power alone does not create a truly Islamic society, which must be based on Islamic cultural values. These values, al-Qaradawi added, need to be nurtured first, before politics. Similarly, Muhammad al-Ghazzali (Egypt) claimed that the main problem with Islamic societies was the colonial deformation of Muslim identity and cultural heritage. The real danger lay in the tendency of Muslims to forsake Islamic values and adopt the "ways of the conquerors." This primarily cultural disease, in al-Ghazzali's view, must be remedied at the cultural level before moving on to politics (Baker 2003, 42, 7–10). Rashid al-Ghannushi (Tunisia) also rejected Islamists' obsession with politics, arguing that the "takeover of the government should not be the biggest achievement possible. A bigger achievement would be if the people would love Islam and its leaders" (Abu-Rabi' 2004, 207–10).

A similar tone rings through the writings and speeches of Salman al-'Awdah (Saudi Arabia), a previously militant and highly politicized Islamist intellectual. Al-'Awdah encouraged Islamists to direct their time and effort to their homes and families, which he described as "full-fledged institutions" that include a "full cross-section of society" and represent its building blocks. Al-'Awdah devoted most of his writings to such themes as cultural dialogue, tolerance, pluralism, and coexistence. In an article entitled "Positive Alternatives," al-'Awdah called upon

Islamists to partake in a "broader social awakening" by appealing to people's religious sensibilities in order to get them engaged in social and cultural reform. In fact, al-'Awdah stated that in order to avoid repression and conflict, Islamists must adopt a new discourse that does not promote any specific political doctrine or alternative, but rather engages rulers and ruled, Muslims and non-Muslims, East and West, with openness, compassion, and constructive solutions (al-'Awdah 2007a, 1).

The new Islamist treatment of the economy is also quite revealing. The original Islamist approach of the mid-twentieth century outlined an economic philosophy that differed radically from that of capitalism: it treated wealth as a divine endowment, not an earned individual privilege; it related income to production, thus prohibiting usury, speculation, and undeserved commissions; it frowned upon affluence and material comfort because of their corrupting effects; it highlighted the social obligations of proprietors; and it granted the political ruler the right to redistribute wealth to remedy social inequalities. For new Islamists, however, even economic reform was linked to a wider cultural transformation. Instead of providing an original economic alternative to the capitalism that has pervaded Arab societies since the 1970s, Islamist intellectuals again stressed the need to change the ethics and values of the individual first.

Islamists focused on substituting the social values associated with capitalism with the self-affirming values of an ideal Islamic community, immune to worldly corruption (Tripp 2006, 194–96). For Islamist intellectuals, the priority was to fortify the individual Muslim spiritually, to transform him or her into the "main bastion of resistance to a world driven mad by the pursuit of profit, [and] the gratification of material desires." Reconnecting individuals with their true moral selves and drawing them closer to the repository of Islamic virtues was, for Islamists, the "principal undertaking" in the economic field (Tripp 2006, 200). The hope was that with the "reassertion of the quality of [Islamic] fellowship, the all-devouring logic of the capitalist system will be stopped in its tracks" (Tripp 2006, 48).

As for economic development, Islamist intellectuals assumed that combining the "neutral" criteria of economic efficiency with Islamic norms and culture was bound to produce an economic alternative that was both "morally superior to market capitalism, and more effective at delivering the material benefits of economic development" (Tripp 2006, 198–99). On this moral-cultural solution to the socioeconomic disparities that besets the Arab world, Tripp commented:

Those who devoted themselves to the theoretical elaboration of an Islamic economy began with an idealized set of principles which would, by definition, safeguard the spiritual and ethical values of the community, protecting its identity as a distinctively Muslim community. It lent to their writings a curiously moralistic air, but also an idealist flavor since they were more concerned to refer their prescriptions to an established body of Islamic jurisprudence . . . than to the actual workings of the global economy . . . . [There was an] a priori assumption that any arrangement which secured the moral economy of an idealized Islamic community must be better in all senses than any alternative, let alone one driven by the acquisitive egotism and commodity-based logic of capitalism. (Tripp 2006, 198–99)

Apart from making Muslims "impervious to the material attractions of a profit-oriented system of economic life," Islamist intellectuals also offered a few piecemeal institutional responses: Islamic investment companies, Islamic banking, Islamic charity organizations, and so on (Tripp 2006, 6–7). These new institutions, which, according to Charles Tripp, combined secular capitalist practices—minus usury—with Islamic cultural idioms were only symbolic responses to the challenge posed by capitalism. Islamic banking, for instance, not only failed to offer an alternative to capitalist banking but also became "a full player within it," offering customers a unique way to contribute to capitalist economy without moral guilt (Tripp 2006, 194–96, 199).

Of course, those who had been propagating an Islamist cultural response to capitalism soon discovered that while their moral dictates might help, cosmetically at least, to reconfigure some capitalist practices, without a comprehensive economic alternative they could do little to "shack the underlying assumptions and drives which underpinned capitalist expansion" (Tripp 2006, 194–96). In short, the new Islamist inclination to subsume everything under cultural reform prevented Islamist thinkers from formulating a viable path to transcending capitalism (Abu-Rabi' 2004, 28).

The same logic that governed the new Islamist response to political authoritarianism and capitalism—basically reducing them to cultural problems—permeated the rest of the new Islamist doctrines. Said observed that Islamists failed to develop an ideological program of any sort, preferring the role of social critics and moral preachers. Said explained that the large mass following that Islamists commanded was based on religious sentiment, not the belief in any specific intellectual alternative (Said 2006, 90–93). Although the Islamic *da'wa* (literally, the 'call' or 'invitation'; in this context, to enter into, or return to, Islam) incorporated some basic political values, it was mostly devoted to cultural themes (Ibrahim 1999, 41).

This practical negation of politics in favor of culture—what Bayat described as "'governmentality' in reverse"—had the advantage of minimizing the possibility of a head-on clash with the ruling regimes (Bayat 2007, 204). By focusing on culture, Islamists projected themselves not as political contenders, but rather as cultural reformers, confronting an elusive enemy that is at times the morally bankrupt West, at other times Arab secular intellectuals, and less often state technocrats who offend Islamic sensibilities. Ultimately, this prioritizing of culture over politics on the part of Islamist intellectuals diverted the energy of Muslims from defying the rulers to rediscovering their religious identity, reexamining their spiritual lives, and channeling all their energies into attaining a higher degree of piety—an escapism of sorts. That is why *The Economist* reported in 2009 that the growing pattern among Arabs with strong Islamist affiliations was to turn away from politics and "devote themselves to personal lives of extreme piety," a new phenomenon that can be labeled apolitical Islamism ("Waking from Its Sleep" 2009, 14).

Conclusion

Arab thought has changed in the past few decades. New ideas have been produced and new discourses articulated and rearticulated across the intellectual spectrum. Yet Arab *political* thought has become markedly scarce and incoherent. While Arab intellectuals continue to scorn their rulers and lash out frequently against one policy or another, their sporadic critiques no longer amount to viable political alternatives. They have lost the ability to galvanize and mobilize, posing instead as history's disgruntled witnesses to all that has gone wrong in the Arab world. That is why Abu-Rabi' lamented that the most salient feature of contemporary Arab thought is its "lack of a system of thought" (Abu-Rabi' 2004, 89).

A closer examination of the changes in the Arab intellectual scene, however, reveals another interesting pattern: the systematic shift from oppositional politics to culture. Under the watchful eyes of the military/security-dominated postcolonial Arab state, intellectuals who failed to secure state patronage turned to culture to avoid persecution. As the state's grip on society tightened, more and more intellectuals evaded state repression by limiting their work to moral and sociocultural themes, claiming that cultural reform is the first step toward long-term political transformation. According to Bahaa Taher, in societies where security officers control all institutions and intellectual production (schools, universities, newspapers, publishing houses, and the rest), Arab intellectuals learned to accept the futility of challenging political authority (Taher 2009, 5).

Under prolonged political repression: (1) liberals abandoned the classical causes of Arab liberalism—protecting sovereignty, promoting political freedoms, and building a strong and independent national economy—and adopted their rulers' neoliberal agendas, defending capitalist freedoms above all; (2) nationalists shifted their efforts from trying to achieve Arab political unity to promoting a common Arab culture; (3) leftists embraced cultural reform, identifying themselves with the European New Left and global humanistic movements, and forsaking their revolutionary role in organizing and radicalizing domestic labor; and (4) Islamists set aside their ambition to establish an Islamic state, focusing instead on cultural and moral reform. So, far from spearheading political transformation, intellectual opposition in the Arab world today has become a cultural activity performed by a closed circle of associates on talk shows and blogs, and in sidewalk cafés. Arab intellectuals have become the archetype of Russel Jacoby's bohemians "thinking too much and doing too little" (Jacoby 2000, 29).

Said attributed this "unparalleled . . . intellectual poverty" in Arab thought to state repression. It is the growing brutality of this "unthinking" ruling class, which is uninterested in anything other than "blundering on from second to second" and is "intolerant of everything except its own fantasies and appetites," that has either coopted Arab intellectuals or coerced them into silence (Said 1995, 230). In Said's view, the most important development in recent Arab history has been the unrivaled potency of the national security ideology, the notion that the security and stability of the political order supersedes everything else (Said 1995, 232–33). Similarly, Ajami described how Arab modernization was reduced in the last few decades to making the regimes' methods of control more effective, their means of surveillance more refined. Ajami was skeptical about the possibility of producing serious political thought in a world ruled by the logic of national security, a logic that rests on "political terror, a primitive cult of personality and an unyielding notion of the state as a virtual possession of the man at the helm" (Ajami 1981, 25–27). In short, the cultural orientation that characterizes contemporary Arab thought is a response to the consolidation of authoritarianism in the Arab world.

The confusion, submission, and powerlessness of contemporary Arab intellectuals are all indicators of the difficulty of ideologically driven political regeneration under repressive regimes—a conclusion that can be generalized beyond the Arab world. The defeat of almost all Arab intellectual projects during the second half of the twentieth century went hand-in-hand with the rapid development of the Arab state's capacity for surveillance and repression. The current state of Arab thought is a reflection of this "sense of defeat and failure," Said concluded (Said 2003, 78). Arab intellectuals have either joined their rulers out of fear or greed, or thrown their lot with low-risk cultural wars, thus becoming politically irrelevant.

Notes

1   Of course, the Arab world has been simmering in the past few decades with towering cultural icons of the caliber of Bahaa Taher (Egypt), Elias Khouri (Lebanon), and Tayeb Salih (the Sudan) in literature; Adonis (Lebanon), Mahmoud Darwish (Palestine), and Nizar Qabani (Syria) in poetry; and Marcel Khalifa (Lebanon), Souad Massi (Algeria), and Naseer Shama (Iraq) in music. In fact, Abu-Rabi' contrasted the Arab intellectual scene, which is "replete with obsolete and meaningless works," with Arab artists, who stood their ground against the repressive political order (Abu-Rabi' 2004, 62). But while I acknowledge the capacity of this category of intellectuals to reflect and impinge on political reality, even inspire political action at some point, I am not enough of a cultural critic to be able to venture into the multilayered, convoluted relationship between art and politics. Even among politically affiliated thinkers I decided to exclude some quasi-intellectual types: first, the hordes of pamphleteers, bloggers, newspaper columnists, and talk show hosts who voice bold yet sporadic criticisms of the status quo, and whose "journalistic intellectualism," as Bourdieu called it, agitates with no clear end in sight (Bourdieu 2007, 61–64); second, activists and political party members who operate, quite intermittently, among various constituencies (workers, students, peasants, syndicate members, and so on) in order to irritate rather than replace the incumbent regimes; third, intellectual outliers (if one can describe them as such), such as Abdallah al-Na'im (the Sudan), Mohammed Shahrur (Syria), and Nasr Hamid Abu Zeid and Nawal al-Sa'dawi (Egypt), whose contentious ideas attract few followers and are therefore politically inconsequential.
2   Universities, according to Said, are the only place where "collective learning and the development of knowledge occur" (quoted in Ghazoul 2007, 27–28). It is the institution from which intellectuals derive their power, and as it rises and falls in

influence, so too do intellectuals (Said 1994, 67). Foucault described universities as political centers of power all intellectuals either pass through or remain associated with (Foucault 2000, 126–27). Bourdieu underlined the role of scholars who devote themselves to the scientific study of the mechanisms of social and political change and produce "scholarship with commitment" to guide political change (Bourdieu 2008, 380–81). In fact, Samir Amin attributed the failure of the Arab intelligentsia to the fact that Arab academics surrendered to narrow-minded professionalism or political opportunism at a time when their scholarly training was needed most (Amin 2006, 263). Along the same line, al-Bitar blamed the "unscientific dispositions" of Arab intellectuals for the current political stagnation, arguing that Arab scholars have abandoned proper scientific thinking, posing instead as moral preachers and political commentators (al-Bitar 2002, 11–12, 51). Said also related the weakness of Arab intellectuals to the decline of universities, which have been re-conceived as extensions of the "national security states," and "remade in the image of the ruling party." In Said's words: "The atmosphere of the university has changed from freedom to accommodation, from brilliance and daring to caution and fear, from advancement of knowledge to self-preservation" (quoted in Ghazoul 2007, 30–35).

3   A retired Egyptian official stated that his country alone employs more than two million people in the security sector ("Waking from Its Sleep" 2009, 9).

4   Scholars who analyze contemporary western societies, from Herbert Marcuse (1991) and his Frankfurt School colleagues to Pierre Bourdieu (2008) and other French poststructuralists, have attributed this anti-intellectualism or depoliticization to the institutions of late capitalism, not repression. One has to be careful, however, before adopting this explanation when analyzing the anti-intellectual climate in the Arab world. In democratic and economically advanced countries, political oppression and social justice can be easily mystified, undercutting the need for new worldviews or comprehensive systems of thought. But with the everyday violations of political freedoms and the widespread poverty that characterize Arab societies, intellectual passivity cannot be disassociated from repression.

5   In fact, at one point, Arab nationalism became virtually identified with the policy of the United Arab Republic, in which 'Aflaq was appointed minister of education, Bitar headed the foreign ministry, and Nasser was (Binder 1964, 204, 214).

6   This version of socialism, however, was quite useful to nationalist rulers: first, it helped them curb the power of traditional economic elites who opposed military rule (Binder 1964, 185–86); second, economic centralization gave the rulers direct control over economic resources and allowed them to prevent the rise of autonomous economic power centers; and finally, socialist rhetoric secured the support of the Eastern Bloc and the Soviet Union (Hourani 1991, 401–402).

5

Women's Empowerment Hammers Patriarchy: How Big Is the Dent?

Ola AbouZeid

Since the early 1970s, the Arab region has witnessed a rising interest in women's issues at both the state and the regional level. At the regional level, the League of Arab States (LAS) established, at the turn of the 1970s, a Women's Committee within its secretariat-general to act as an advisory body on issues related to women's advancement. In 1988, the Arab ministers of social affairs approved the first "Arab Strategic Plan for the Advancement of Women until the Year 2000." This was followed, in 1994, by the "Plan for the Advancement of Arab Women until the Year 2003," which was endorsed in preparation for Arab participation in the Beijing Conference (1995). In 1996, the Arab foreign ministers convening in Jordan adopted a program for Arab regional cooperation that included a separate section on women (AWO 2005, 2–4).

At the state level, the majority of Arab states have joined women's international agreements, declarations, and conventions, the most important being the Convention on the Elimination of all Forms of Discrimination Against Women (CEDAW), the Beijing Platform of Action, which declares gender equality as its main objective, and the Millennium Development Goals (MDGs), which include women's empowerment and gender equality as the third goal (UNIFEM 2004, 24–35).

Interest in women's issues in the Arab world accelerated considerably after the Beijing Conference (1995), when it began to take on a new dimension. The beginning of the twenty-first century is characterized by the institutionalization of the endeavor of advancement of Arab women. At the state level, national mechanisms ranging from gender units in governmental bodies to women's councils to ministries of women's affairs were established in almost all Arab states (Mosaad 2008, 24–25). At the regional level, the first intergovernmental Arab institution, the Arab Women Organization (AWO), was established in 2001 with the ultimate goal of empowering women of the region in seven sectors: education, health, economy, politics, media, legislation, and social policies (AWO General Policies, 5–16).

The same period witnessed the mushrooming of civil society organizations in the Arab region, particularly those focusing on women. The number of these organizations tripled in 2008 compared to 1995 (Arab Network for NGOs and AWO 2005, 15–25; also see Chapter 2 in this book by Amani Kandil). One direct result of the rise of these governmental and non-governmental, national and regional institutions is a significant increase in the number of projects for women's empowerment, designed and implemented in almost all Arab states to initiate positive changes in the status of Arab women in various vital sectors.

This chapter indicates that significant positive change in the status of Arab women occurred in the 2000–2009 period, coinciding with the rising number of governmental and non-governmental women's empowerment projects. However, it also argues that the road to the effective empowerment of Arab women remains a long one.

The objective of this chapter is twofold: first, to provide a descriptive analysis of the current status of Arab women in relation to men in the sectors of education, health, economic and political participation, and legislation, and, second, to examine the obstacles that still block the way to the advancement of Arab women and to indicate the way forward for their greater empowerment.

The Current Status of Arab Women

Years of serious effort, at both the state and the regional level, to empower Arab women and to bridge the gap that separates them from men seems to be bearing fruit. National, regional, and international reports assessing progress toward women's empowerment and gender equality record important achievements in all sectors, the most impressive of which are in the fields of education and health (Abdul Ghani 2007, 6; Leelah 2007, 11; ESCWA 2005, 1, 2, 4–5; UNDP 2006, 215–16).

Education

Improvement in Arab women's access to education has taken place at all levels in the past three decades in all Arab states. If we look at literacy levels, we find that adult women's literacy rates have seen dramatic progress in many Arab countries during the past few decades. In Bahrain and Jordan, these rates increased from below 40 percent in 1970 to 85 percent in 2002. In Oman, the same rates increased from less than 10 percent in 1970 to 65 percent in 2002. Women's literacy rates reached 80 percent, 75 percent, 70 percent, and 70 percent in 2002 from a rate of only 45 percent, 20 percent, 18 percent, and 11 percent in 1970 in Kuwait, Syria, Saudi Arabia, and Libya, respectively. Even in countries like Morocco and Sudan, where female literacy rates in 2002 were comparatively low, hovering around 38 percent and 49 percent, respectively, it is worth mentioning that these rates witnessed an increase from less than 10 percent and 20 percent in 1970, respectively (al-Shamsi and Ali 2008, 10).

Likewise, literacy rates for young Arab women aged 15–24 years followed the same upward trend during the past three decades. Overall, this rate increased from 38 percent in 1970 to 79 percent in 2002. At the national level, young women's literacy rates improved in 2002, to range from 60 percent in Morocco to around 95 percent in Bahrain, Jordan, and Oman (al-Shamsi and Ali 2008, 10–11).

Despite this progress, a gender gap in both youth and adult literacy can still be detected. According to the United Nations, the Arab region has one of the highest rates of female illiteracy in the world (UNDP 2006, 7). This is despite the fact that projects in the field of education make up the biggest share of female empowerment projects in the region and focus, mainly, on the problem of female illiteracy and drop-outs (AbouZeid 2007, 13).

Figures for 2003 indicate that a disparity in literacy rates between young boys and girls still exists in most Arab countries. The only exceptions are Bahrain, Jordan, and Oman, where this gap almost disappears. At the same time, the gap is highly pronounced in Egypt and Morocco (AbouZeid 2007, 10–11). This situation worsens alarmingly in rural areas, where the differences in numbers of girls and boys aged between 8 and 10 not attending school is high (UNIFEM 2004, 45).

According to the Economic and Social Commission for Western Asia (ESCWA), a gender gap also exists with regard to female adult literacy rates. In 2003, the adult literacy rate of Arab women was 51 percent, compared to 73 percent for men. Although women are marginally more literate than men in Jordan, Qatar, and the United Arab Emirates (U.A.E.), a considerably wide gender gap in adult literacy is still being recorded in Yemen, Iraq, Morocco, and Egypt (ESCWA 2004).

If we move to enrollment levels, available data reveals remarkable improvements in the gross and net female enrollment rates in both primary and secondary education. As a result, the gender gap in primary and secondary education is about to disappear in many Arab countries (al-Masri 2008, 26–27). The figures are even better in higher education where the female enrollment rate exceeds that of males in about one-third of Arab countries (al-Masri 2008, 29).

It is worth noting that despite aspects of improvement in female literacy and enrollment levels in the Arab states, experts in the field note that Gender Parity Indices (GPI) for Arab countries show gender disparity and inequality. GPI are the measures of equality in educational attainment between men and women and are calculated as a ratio of women to men. With reference to GPI for 2003, Arab women are significantly less literate than men. Except for Qatar and the U.A.E., the GPI for the female adult literacy rate indicate inequality in favor of men. Similar gender inequality is recorded with regard to youth illiteracy rates in all Arab states, Palestine being the only recorded exception. As for primary education, GPI for 2001–2002 indicate equality in net enrollment in only four out of the twenty-two Arab countries. These are Bahrain, Jordan, Oman, and Palestine. Net enrollment rates in secondary education for the same year show that nine Arab countries—Algeria, Bahrain, Jordan, Kuwait, Oman, Qatar, Palestine, Tunisia, and the U.A.E.—achieved equality. It is only in higher education that the GPI for the same year shows inequality, but in favor of women, in six Arab states: Bahrain, Kuwait, Lebanon, Qatar, Oman, and Saudi Arabia. In another two states, Jordan and Libya, GPI point to equality between males and females in higher education. In all Arab states that are not mentioned here, the GPI indicate that inequality in favor of men still exists at all levels of literacy and enrollment (al-Shamsi and Ali 2008, 8).

Thus, when compared to men, we can say that, in general, women in the Arab region continue to suffer from knowledge poverty. Compounding the problem is the fact that the countries that suffer the most from this (Yemen, Algeria, Sudan, and Egypt) are those with the most limited resources. They do not have adequate resources to face the complicated problems of female education, particularly female illiteracy and female drop-outs. It is noteworthy that international donors, as well as national private sectors, are usually reluctant to fund projects targeting these problems, either because such projects are regarded as unprofitable enterprises or because the problems they deal with are intense and widespread, making it difficult for them to achieve tangible results in a reasonable period of time (AbouZeid 2007, 34, 36). Experts also notice that the contribution of civil society organizations to the enhancement of Arab female education is rather limited. A main reason for this is the limited human and financial resources available for these organizations, a fact that prevents them from standing up for such complicated problems (al-Masri 2008, 17)

The prevailing culture in the region is another explanation why Arab women continue to suffer more than men from knowledge poverty. Family and social attitudes and practices continue to deprive women of the available opportunities to acquire knowledge, particularly in the case of poor families and the inhabitants of remote areas (al-Masri 2008, 17).

Health
Among the complementary health targets that are defined for the Millennium Development Goals (MDGs), the improvement of maternal health was set as a target to be achieved by 2015. Accordingly, the majority of Arab states channeled their efforts into programs of awareness and enhancement of services in the sector of reproductive health. In spite of this, discrepancies remain between Arab states with regard to the level of improvement achieved for women in the health sector in general and reproductive health in particular. Hence, it is expected that not all Arab states will be able to achieve the health targets of the MDGs on time (Haffadh 2008, 5).

However, there has been impressive progress in the female average life expectancy rate in the Arab region. A review of World Health Statistics between 2003 and 2006 reveals that the average life expectancy at birth in Arab countries has improved dramatically. This is attributed mainly to the improvement of the female average life expectancy in comparison to that of males, as Tables 1 and 2 illustrate.

Table 5.1: Life expectancy at birth by gender in selected Arab countries (2003)

Country	General average life expectancy	Female average life expectancy	Male average life expectancy
Egypt	59	60	58
Jordan	61	62	60
Morocco	60	61	59
Somalia	37	38	36
U.A.E.	64	64	64
Yemen	49	51	48

Source: World Health Statistics (2008) as cited in Haffadh (2008, 8).

Table 5.2: Life expectancy at birth by gender in selected Arab countries (2006)

Country	General average life expectancy	Female average life expectancy	Male average life expectancy
Egypt	68	70	66
Jordan	71	74	69
Morocco	72	74	70
Somalia	55	56	54
U.A.E.	78	80	77
Yemen	61	62	59

Source: World Health Statistics (2008) as cited in Haffadh (2008, 8).

Nevertheless, in the field of reproductive health, and despite significant improvements in the general rate of female mortality related to reproductive health, women in the least developed Arab countries still suffer from high rates of risk morbidity and mortality related to pregnancy (UNDP 2006, 7). For instance, while some Arab countries succeeded in lowering the ratio of maternal mortality due to pregnancy and delivery to four per 100,000 live births in 2005, the same ratio rose to as high as 450 and 650 in Sudan and Djibouti, respectively, for the same year (Haffadh 2008, 6, based on World Health Statistics, 2008).

This is the case despite the fact that the highest percentage of projects aimed at women's well-being is implemented in the field of reproductive health (AbouZeid 2007, 14). Attitudes and practices within the family, and in society in general, are the main underlying factors that diminish the positive impact on women's health expected from the implementation of these projects. Experts have found that social discrimination against women, which starts in the family, prevents them from obtaining health services at the appropriate time. They contend that discrimination against women in matters of nutrition and accessibility to healthcare does exist in the Arab region, particularly among the less educated, as a result of prevailing cultural biases against women (UNIFEM 2004, 43; Haffadh 2008, 18).

Economic Participation

Access to labor markets is one important factor in achieving gender equality. Available data indicates that women's share of the total labor force in the Arab world has increased significantly in the past decade. Between the years 1997 and 2007, the rate of female labor force participation increased by an impressive 7.7 percent for countries of the Middle East (al-Shamsi and Ali 2008, 14–15). However, if we look at individual states, we find that the highest rate of female labor force participation among Arab states did not exceed 35 percent and was registered in Morocco, followed by Tunisia (33 percent), Egypt (31 percent), then Lebanon and Sudan (30 percent each). All other states with available data registered a rate of female labor force participation for the same year that was below 30 percent. In the case of Jordan, for instance, the rate of female participation in the labor force did not exceed 26 percent in 2003, even while the female labor force grew in absolute terms by more than 50 percent compared to 1990 (al-Shamsi and Ali 2008, 16). Hence, female participation in the labor force in the Arab world as a whole remained the lowest compared to any other region in the world. In 2007, Arab women's participation rate was only 33 percent for the Middle East and 23.8 percent for North Africa, as compared to 53 percent worldwide and 67 percent for the East Asian countries, for instance (al-Shamsi and Ali 2008, 15). This means that Arab women are, to a large extent, economically dependent on men.

It is also worth mentioning that despite the rise in female labor force participation rates, the Arab region has the highest women's unemployment rate of any region in the world. For the past decade, this rate has been hovering around the 12 percent mark (ILO 2004).

Over the span of one decade, a slight increase in the percentage of female-employment-to-population ratio in the Middle East and North

Africa (MENA) region was recorded (from 20.4 percent in 1993 to 23.5 percent in 2003). In 2007, the female-employment-to-population ratio stood at 28.1 percent for the countries of the Middle East and at 21.9 percent for North Africa, while the equivalent ratios for male employment ranged from 69.1 to 70.3 percent for both regions. The situation is worse for female youth as their employment-to-population ratio did not exceed 19.5 percent for the Middle East region and 14.7 percent for North Africa in the same year (al-Shamsi and Ali 2008, 14–15). Moreover, data for 2007 indicates that on average the unemployment rate is higher for Arab women than it is for men (16 percent and 10 percent, respectively). Young women suffer even more: in 2007, female youth suffered a 32 percent unemployment rate, as compared to 16 percent for adult women (al-Shamsi and Ali 2008, 15).

More alarming still is the fact that the quality of jobs reserved for women is usually inferior to that enjoyed by men (ILO 2004). Experts report the overrepresentation of Arab women in lower-paid jobs and nondecision-making positions. This is true despite the abundance of qualified female human capital, as the figures discussed above, indicating Arab female secondary and higher education enrollment, demonstrate. However, studies show that higher levels of female education do not necessarily translate into the attainment of better jobs or lower female unemployment (al-Shamsi and Ali 2008, 14; al-Masri 2008, 36). Part of the problem derives from cultural stereotypes that portray men over women as being preferable for certain types of employment and as primary bread winners (Korany 2008, 28; al-Shamsi and Ali 2008, 26). The same cultural factors are responsible for the fact that the majority of female university students are encouraged to specialize in the liberal arts, with comparatively fewer women studying the sciences, particularly engineering (al-Masri 2008, 30; al-Shamsi and Ali 2008, 12). The type of education to which women are 'culturally' channeled results in more disparities with regard to employment opportunities and earned income. Experts note that the type of education (liberal arts versus sciences) women receive reduces their opportunities to obtain well-paid jobs (al-Shamsi and Ali 2008, 12).

Political Participation

The trend over the past decade with regard to Arab women's political participation reveals a marked improvement. Despite the fact that women's presence in government at the ministerial level is still very limited in all

Arab states, as it did not exceed 0.1 percent in 2005, with the only exception being Iraq, which recorded 0.2 percent, progress has been dramatic with regard to female participation in legislative bodies. Available data reveals that, with the exception of Egypt and Yemen, a tremendous increase in the seats held by women in lower/single houses was recorded for 2005, as compared to 1990. The most impressive progress took place in Iraq, Tunisia, Morocco, Djibouti, and Sudan, where female participation in lower/single houses in 2005 was 31.6 percent, 22.8 percent, 10.8 percent, 10.8 percent, and 9.7 percent, respectively, rising from 11 percent, 4 percent, 0 percent, 0 percent, and no recorded percentage in 1990 (UNDP 2006). All five countries with the highest record of female participation in the lower/single house endorse some kind of quota system.

Despite the fact that many Arab governments have committed themselves to promoting the participation of women in the political sphere by endorsing mechanisms such as the quota system, which has resulted in significant progress for women in terms of political participation, levels of female political participation in the Arab region in general remain very low, as compared to the rest of the world. According to information provided by national parliaments to the Inter-Parliamentary Union (IPU), by the end of October 2008, the presence of women in upper and lower houses of government in the Arab states constituted 9.1 percent, compared to 14.9 percent in the Pacific, 18.2 percent in Sub-Saharan Africa, and 18.1 percent in Asia. Out of the 188 countries included in this survey, Arab country rankings were in the bottom quintile (IPU 2008b).

Moreover, even when women do make it into parliament or other decision-making posts, cultural stereotypes place them in certain gender-specific roles. Female members of parliament are often assigned roles in committees that deal with female affairs. Likewise, the essential ministries that allocate resources (ministries of finance, foreign policy, and internal or external security) are almost always reserved for men, while female ministers, despite their small numbers, are usually assigned to ministries of women or of social affairs (UNDP 2006, 203; IPU 2008, 62–68).

The relatively low level of female participation in political life is the result of a number of interconnected factors that are common to most countries of the region. One is the nature of the political processes themselves. The region's weak democratic systems restrict rights of association and use violence to maintain control. Within this context, political participation is viewed as high-risk in terms of personal security and safety.

It is expected that women would opt out of political life if they are not provided with a safe and secure environment in which to be politically active and involved (AbouZeid 2001, 33). In addition, political parties in the region are highly centralized and dominated by powerful families and/or elites. This undemocratic structure limits the opportunities open to ordinary citizens, women in particular, for political involvement (AbouZeid 1995, 64–65).

Another explanation for the low levels of female political participation is the patriarchal social structure, which confines women's sphere of influence to the private domain, with men dominating public spheres. This rigid delineation of gender roles is reinforced by conservative religious codes and cultural stereotypes. More often that not, women themselves conspire in the preservation of this division of roles, for they are an integral part of the culture producing it (AbouZeid 2001, 32; 2000, 181–82).

The Legal Sphere
In the legal sphere, impressive changes in favor of women have taken place over the past few years as a result of governments' commitment to altering iniquitous legislation. An assignment undertaken over the last five years by the "Legal Arab Group," one of the AWO task forces, reveals that, on the whole, laws are not biased against women in the Arab region. In many cases the actual problem lies not in the legal text but partly in the fact that women lack an awareness of their legal rights and partly in the application of these texts to real-life situations. This application is left to the judiciary and the police force, two institutions that, in the Arab world, are for the most part male-dominated. Personal status laws, in particular, remain conservative in many Arab states and resistant to development into a national personal status code (UNDP 2006, 19). As a result, Arab women feel insecure in their private sphere; consequently, they tend not to participate too much in the public sphere (AbouZeid 1995, 61, 65; 2000, 187–88).

The analysis above has shown that significant progress has been made in the status of women in the Arab region since 1990, but it also highlights the fact that Arab countries continue to show clear evidence of gender biases. Despite the establishment of national and regional platforms that design and implement projects for women's empowerment, the progress achieved is still below the desired level. A major reason for the low level of women's advancement is the nature of the female empowerment projects themselves. A critical assessment of the performance of these projects is therefore due.

Arab Female Empowerment Projects:
A Critical Assessment

A significant increase in the number of female empowerment projects in the Arab region occurred in the period that followed the first Beijing Conference (1995). The contribution of these projects to the advancement of Arab women is the focus of a pioneering project that has been conducted since 2004 by the AWO. By 2007, this endeavor surveyed a sample of over six thousand projects targeting Arab women in five sectors: education, health, media, economy, and politics. The sample was drawn from thirteen Arab states and analyzed by sixty Arab experts (Abdul Ghani 2007; Kiwan 2007; Leelah 2007; al-Za'aneen 2007; al-Zu'abi 2007). In 2007, the AWO published a regional report titled "Projects of Arab Women Empowerment: Present Status and Future Prospects" (hereafter PAWE) (AbouZeid 2007). The report sought an answer to the question: Did Arab women empowerment projects succeed in advancing Arab women in the period between 1995 and 2005? The PAWE arrived at the conclusion that such projects succeeded in bringing about positive changes in the status of Arab women. It also concluded that the level of the progress achieved was still way below target. Several defects in the planning, implementation, funding, and evaluation of these projects were highlighted. These defects need to be reversed if the women's empowerment projects are to fulfill their goals.

Planning of Women's Empowerment Projects

In general, projects of Arab women's empowerment suffer from serious ailments that relate to the planning process. The goals and objectives of such projects are not clearly defined and the confusion of overall goals with intermediate objectives occurs frequently. Most of the time, the projects fail to target the groups or areas that are in real need of services. The projects' activities are not properly attuned to their objectives and the time allotted for the implementation of a project's activities exceeds the overall timeframe of the project. The entities involved in the supervision and implementation of the projects lack coordination. Those employed to work on the projects lack the appropriate qualifications. Moreover, objective evaluation of the projects is nonexistent, a fact that hinders effective remedy of deficiencies or weaknesses and prohibits projects from benefiting fully from the experience of other projects (AbouZeid 2007, 61).

As mentioned, several essential groups, areas, and issues that should be targeted by the projects of Arab women's empowerment are being neglected. The negative impact of this negligence on the level of accomplished advancement for Arab women must not be underestimated. Both young girls and elderly women are ignored by Arab women's empowerment projects. Disregarding elderly females will soon cost states dearly when they attempt to compensate for decades of deprivation of basic life needs. The failure to target female youth is by no means less costly. Youth constitute one-third of the population of the Arab world and female youth make up half of that percentage. The importance of female youth lies mainly in their potential impact on society, as this age category is the most susceptible to change and development. Failure to invest in this group should be regarded as a failure to invest in the future.

Rural and Bedouin women constitute another sector that is not usually targeted by women's empowerment projects, despite the fact that the countryside and the desert are the dominant geographical environments in most Arab states. More important, they are the most underdeveloped, so they are the most in need of empowerment projects if equitable development is an aim. Remote areas fail to obtain the recognition of women's empowerment project planners. Project implementation is usually concentrated in the capital and the big cities. This fact hinders the realization of balanced and sustainable development.

Female university graduates do not get sufficient attention from women's empowerment project planners. To the contrary, most projects target illiterate women or, at best, those women whose education ended at the pre-university level despite the fact that investment in university graduates, by enhancing their skills and involving them in capacity-building projects, would prove a much easier and more rewarding endeavor.

Men are not targeted by women's empowerment projects despite the necessity of approaching women's issues from a gender perspective. Ensuring that men are involved in the process of female empowerment is a must, otherwise the changing of traditional power relations between men and women could lead to grave tensions that would endanger the achievement of equitable development.

Men of religion and media personalities, who can be influential in modifying and improving the culture that discriminates against women, should be encouraged to participate in the planning of women's empowerment programs, but no serious attempt is being undertaken by project planners to gain their support or alter their discourse to be in favor of women (AbouZeid 2007, 64–65).

Implementation of Women's Empowerment Projects

Because female empowerment is a complex issue in the Arab region, its confrontation requires the efforts of all potential actors. The private sector, civil society, and universities emerge as leading candidates in this regard. However, studies show that not one of these actors contributes, as expected, to the empowerment of Arab women.

The private-sector contribution to the process of women's empowerment is one of the lowest compared to the other entities involved, notwithstanding the incentives and guarantees received by the private sector, in almost all Arab states to encourage it to invest in the categories and geographical areas that are in serious need of empowerment initiatives. The private sector in the Arab region is still reluctant to bear its fair share of social responsibility when it comes to the issue of women's empowerment (AbouZeid 2007, 65).

Arab civil society suffers, in general, from a centralized, elitist structure and is characterized by an absence of democratic values and practices. Because the culture of volunteerism is unpopular in the Arab world, civil society organizations experience shortages of volunteers, who ought to make up the core of their workforce. They also suffer from the undertraining and underqualification of the available labor force. Moreover, it has been noted that the majority of Arab non-governmental organizations adopt a "basic need" strategy in their work with women, rather than a comprehensive empowerment strategy. These shortcomings limit severely the ability of civil society to act successfully as an influential partner in the process of the implementation of women's empowerment projects (AbouZeid 2007, 65; Arab Network for NGOs and AWO 2005, 52–55).

Universities are plagued with the problems that usually afflict scientific research in the Arab region. Stagnant research methods and limited resources prevent universities from being active and influential centres of expertise that provide solid research, develop gender-sensitive indicators, and provide appropriate training and awareness services.

Arab regional organizations, meanwhile, do not take the role expected from them seriously, either in implementing or in funding women's empowerment projects. The PAWE reports that they rank at the bottom of the list of agencies that implement and fund regional Arab women's projects (AbouZeid 2007, 65–66).

Funding of Arab Women's Empowerment Projects
With the exception of a few wealthy Arab countries, most Arab states need to secure some form of international funding for their women's empowerment projects (AbouZeid 2007, 66). This is particularly true in light of the reluctance of the indigenous private sector to get involved, the limited resources available to local civil society institutions, and the refraining of Arab regional organizations from contributing to this endeavor.

But grave problems come in the wake of international funding of women's empowerment projects. In most cases, international funding agencies choose to finance short- or, at best, medium-term projects that confine activities to simply training and awareness raising. They avoid financing long-term ventures that address widespread and deeply rooted problems, despite the fact that such projects are the ones needed to ensure the realization of women's empowerment. International funding agencies also favor particular countries in the region, which they shower with funds, a fact that hampers regionally balanced development. These factors call for an objective evaluation of the return value of international expenditure on women's projects in the Arab region.

The partnerships flourishing between international funding agencies and indigenous civil society organizations is another issue to be considered here. It has become common practice for international funding agencies to stipulate that the projects they fund must be implemented by civil society organizations. It is true that these organizations can easily reach out to the targeted groups and gain their confidence. However, they suffer some very serious structural problems. Hence, the channeling of international funds toward them and placing them as *the* main actor in the process of the implementation of women's projects places a huge responsibility on their shoulders at a time when they are not adequately equipped to successfully carry it. Undoubtedly, this situation has a negative impact on the achievement of the goal of women's empowerment in the region (AbouZeid 2007, 66).

The negative impact of this partnership on the process of female empowerment in particular and on development in general is further aggravated by the fact that international funding agencies, when offering funds to civil society organizations, also stipulate the key issues that they should address. Most of the projects that international funding agencies choose to fund are short term and address a narrow issue for which limited activities are tailored. On the whole, such projects fail to contribute effectively to women's empowerment. Moreover, the imposition by international funding agencies of their own agendas prevents local civil society organizations from addressing priority women's issues that constitute national goals, a situation that impedes their effective engagement as partners for development. Moreover, the fact that civil society organizations implement the projects dictated by international funding agencies crushes bridges of trust between these organizations and domestic government entities, thus depriving Arab women of the benefits of any partnerships between these national parties.

More serious still is the fact that civil society organizations compete with each other to win international funds, a situation that usually leads to interorganizational conflict. This undermines any opportunity at successful consensus-building and explains why civil society organizations tend to work individually rather than collectively and fail to agree upon a national agenda of work toward women's empowerment.

The problems pointed to above, which occur as a result of international funding for women's projects, necessitate an earnest attempt to widen the circle of Arab financing sources in order to guarantee a constant flow of funds for women's empowerment projects as well as freedom in the formulation of an agenda of women's issues. These issues should be defined in line with an overall Arab strategic plan that aims at comprehensive, sustainable, and equitable development (AbouZeid 2007, 67).

Evaluation of Women's Empowerment Projects

Agencies in charge of female empowerment projects in the Arab region suffer serious shortcomings when it comes to the process of evaluation. One such shortcoming relates to the documentation of women's projects and must be highlighted here. The absence of appropriate documentation limits the possibilities of scientific evaluation that can set present and future projects on the right track. Determining points of weakness, understanding causes of problems, measuring and assessing the consequences of problems, and arriving at sound recommendations to eliminate problems all require reliable data. Lack of data also has a negative impact on the development of effective strategic planning aimed at combating gender inequality, which requires continuity and an accumulation of experience. This, in turn, can only evolve if precise, accurate, and sex-disaggregated databases of the projects are available. Data is vital not only in order to comprehend gender inequality and measure its impact in a country, but also to assist in allocating resources toward achieving the goal of equality.

As such, accurate documentation and the constant updating of project data are pivotal factors in the ability of empowerment projects to achieve their goals (AbouZeid 2007, 67–68; al-Shamsi and Ali 2008, 26).

The above analysis indicates that projects of Arab women's empowerment suffer serious problems that relate to their planning, financing, implementation, and evaluation and that limit their ability to achieve their stated goal.

Toward More Effective Empowerment for Arab Women

Along the road to the empowerment of Arab women, a considerable advance in their status has been achieved over the past decade. This advance relates, to a great extent, to the establishment of women's institutions at both the state and the regional level and to the vitality of civil society organizations that target women and the implementation of a huge number of women's empowerment projects in various sectors. However, analysis of this research shows that the road ahead is still a long one. I concluded above that more effective women's empowerment calls for a serious revision of the performance of women's projects and the rectification of the shortcomings of the processes of planning, funding, implementing, documenting, and evaluating these projects. However, success in achieving women's empowerment hinges not only on the abovementioned efforts but also on other factors, including:

Achieving Qualitative Change in a Gender-discriminating Culture

Most researchers and experts who study and deal with the issue of Arab women's empowerment point to the prevailing culture of discrimination against women as a major factor slowing down the process.

In order to counter the stereotypes of women that pervade the Arab region, three areas need to be tackled. The first is the religious discourse prevalent in the region, which embraces a distorted perception of women and their role in society that derives from a conservative interpretation of the sources of *sharia*. As long as this conservative religious discourse dominates more progressive discourses, efforts to empower Arab women will be stifled (AbouZeid 2007, 60–68).

In order to remedy this situation, and in light of the fact that men of religion enjoy noticeable influence and status in Arab societies, serious work must commence to identify enlightened men of religion and bring them to the forefront. They should be allowed the appropriate channels to reach out to ordinary people with their views. It is also important to include them in the planning of female empowerment initiatives. This is particularly important in relation to projects that address issues that touch on deeply rooted social beliefs and convictions (such as female genital mutilation, family planning, female political participation, and so on). This is necessary in light of the synthesis of traditions with religion in the Arab region, where deeply rooted social beliefs often claim their legitimacy from religious teachings. Thus, it is very important to support the rise of a moderate religious school of thought that can develop enlightened interpretation of the sources of *sharia* and clearly draw the line between traditional, as opposed to religious, social beliefs pertaining to women.

By no means less important is media discourse, which is the second area in need of remedy. The importance of the media emerges from the pivotal role it plays in formulating the beliefs and convictions of the masses. Its dominant role in shaping societal culture grows in light of the unprecedented development of its tools, methods, and ability to reach everyone anywhere and at any time. If the media can play a pivotal role in formulating culture, it can play as strong and influential a role in reforming and refining it.

Unfortunately, the messages that the media transmits about Arab women do not reflect the true role women play in the social and economic life of their societies. The media fails to detect and to fairly portray female participation in and contribution to public life. Consequently, it contributes to the development of a distorted image of Arab women and to diminishing the acceptability of female empowerment projects and, hence, their ability to deliver positive results.

The development of a full-fledged strategy that concentrates on the media message, as well as on those who implement and transmit this message to the public, is crucial. The ultimate aim must be to reinforce positively and influence the media sector to convey balanced messages about Arab women and to portray a positive image of them. It is hoped that through this shift in outlook and orientation, the media would initiate positive social awareness of women's issues and roles that would defeat the perceptions and traditions that marginalize women and lend Arab societies to discriminate against them and violate their rights (AbouZeid 2007, 69).

The legal framework is a third key action area. It is a known fact that the constitutions and laws of any state are a reflection of the culture that dominates its society. The legal structure itself contributes to the formulation, reformation, and refining of this culture, if it is allowed sufficient time to settle and plant its roots firmly in the fabric of the society. The cultural environment within which a legal system operates can act as an insurmountable obstacle that hinders legal development toward the realization of justice and equity for women. This happens when the environment fosters discriminating religious discourse reinforced by a patriarchal social structure. In such a situation, political engagement seems inevitable. The importance of governments committing to legal reform and altering iniquitous legislation that reflects rigidly prescribed gender roles cannot be overemphasized. Parallel to this must go action that serves to raise awareness and alter the convictions of those involved in the legislative process. Persistence in this direction will ultimately lead to filling the gap between the law and its inappropriate interpretation and execution (AbouZeid 2007, 70).

Developing a Comprehensive Strategic Vision

When undertaking planning for the advancement of Arab women, it is crucial to percieve and hence deal with women's problems as a single issue, rather than as a number of separate and disparate problems. It is vital that this approach prevail among key policy-makers, for its absence would have alarming consequences.

Overlapping policies would be endorsed by various authorities and entities involved in women's empowerment initiatives, leading to a conflict of efforts and interests as well as the possible duplication of similar projects time and again—a situation that acts as a drain on both energy and resources. There is also the great risk that a majority of projects will be minor, haphazard, and dissociated if they are not interwoven into a well-defined strategic plan for women's advancement that is integrated in the overall development plan of a given country. Another negative outcome is the rise of sporadic, as opposed to committed, interest in a specific women's issue—a situation that results in the rise of projects tailored for certain events and occasions. Moreover, the absence of such a comprehensive grasp of the issue of women's empowerment would prohibit the integration of women's projects implemented in a certain sector as well as across different yet related sectors, thereby restricting their ability to produce the cumulative effect that leads to women's empowerment. Last but not least, lack of cooperation and coordination between the different entities, governmental and non-governmental, involved in the design, funding, and implementation of female empowerment initiatives will also continue (AbouZeid 2007, 61–62).

Promoting Coordination Between Entities Involved in Arab Women's Empowerment

Joint Arab work is a great opportunity to fortify regional human and institutional capacities from which female empowerment endeavors can benefit at both the state and the regional level. But joint work requires coordination, a prerequisite deeply lacking in a culture that does not enshrine the value of teamwork. Where coordination is weak, efforts to empower women will be stripped of much of their ability to produce any real change in the status of women (AbouZeid 2007, 62).

The existence of a body that promotes, advocates, and monitors coordination between women's empowerment initiatives, at both the state and the regional level, is crucial. At the state level, it is important that projects in different sectors coordinate, particularly those targeting the same groups or areas, or addressing the same issues. Different national women's platforms involved in the implementation of these projects must collaborate effectively to prevent duplication and to encourage mutual support through the systemized exchange of experiences. Stronger linkages and capacities for coordination between the funding agencies of these projects must be created to ensure that funds will not be released time and again to the same bodies to the exclusion of other, more efficient ones. Achieving better coordination between funding agencies can also combat destructive competition for funds between implementing entities. Bridging the gap between the academics and the policy-makers is another important target of coordination.

At the regional level, it is essential to promote intercountry coordination with respect to the efforts exerted to empower women both within a certain sector and between diverse sectors. Better coordination in this respect can help bring down the start-up costs of women's empowerment projects and accelerate the process of women's advancement. The creation of permanent regional coordinating bodies can facilitate the bringing together of experts in the region, with the ultimate aim of arriving at a better vision of women's empowerment projects (AbouZeid 2007, 63).

Conclusion

This analysis shows that significant advances have been achieved in the Arab world since the end of the 1990s in the education, health, political and economic participation, and legal status of women, notwithstanding the fact that different levels of progress have been attained by different Arab states. At the same time, this research also sheds light on the fact that Arab countries, in general, continue to show clear evidence of gender gap. This is reflected in the overall high rate of female illiteracy and female unemployment, as well as female underrepresentation in decision-making positions.

Gender biases that negatively affect the advancement of women are not limited to one sector or another; rather, they are pervasive. The Global Gender Gap Report issued by the World Economic Forum in 2007 used qualitative and quantitative indicators to measure this gap in countries around the world in four vital areas, all examined in this chapter, namely, education, health, the economy, and politics. According to the report, the Arab world's overall ranking was in the bottom quintile (World Economic Forum 2007, 3–4, 7–12).

Several factors account for this, the most important one being the prevalence of a culture that favors men and discriminates against women and rigidly prescribes gender roles that deprive women of their right to contribute to the development process through their active involvement in the public sphere. Another is the inability of projects of women's empowerment to contribute effectively to the realization of gender equality and women's advancement because of serious drawbacks they experience in the stages of planning, funding, implementation, documentation, and evaluation.

The eradication of gender disparities and the realization of women's empowerment call for reform of the prevailing culture and correction of the performance of women's empowerment projects. This requires the collective effort of the whole society, government, the private sector, civil society, higher education institutions, media, and enlightened thinkers and men of religion. With the development of a comprehensive vision of the requirements of the process of women's empowerment, and with the rise of reasonable coordination between the various entities that work for women's advancement, the goal will ultimately be achieved.

6

Continuity and Change in Islamist Political Thought and Behavior: The Transformations of Armed Islamist Movements in Egypt and Algeria

Omar Ashour

Armed Islamists and the Phenomenon of Deradicalization

In July 1997, the "historical leadership"[1] of al-Jama'a al-Islamiya (Islamic Group; hereafter, IG)—the largest armed Islamist movement in Egypt during the 1980s and 1990s—declared a unilateral ceasefire. Known as the Initiative for Ceasing Violence (ICV), the declaration ran against the group's traditionally militant literature, the previous vows of its leaders to continue armed struggle until the Mubarak regime had been toppled, and the increasingly violent tactics used by IG affiliates since the late 1970s. In 2002, the leadership of the IG not only dismantled its armed wings but also renounced its radical literature. Members of the *shura* (consultative) council of the IG issued several books explaining its new nonviolent ideology. This seemed to indicate a deradicalization process that had taken place not only on the behavioral (strategic/tactical) level but on the ideological level as well. By 2008, the IG's deradicalization looked to have been consolidated: no armed operations since 1999, no significant splits within the movement, and around twenty-five volumes authored by IG leaders to support their new ideology with both theological and rational arguments. Two of the volumes were critiques of al-Qaeda's behavior (Zuhdi and Ibrahim 2002a; 2003) and a third was a critique of the "clash of civilizations" hypothesis, arguing instead for cultural dialogue (Ibrahim and Zuhdi 2005, 225–47). The drafting of these volumes by the same movement that co-assassinated President Anwar Sadat was a significant development. This process of deradicalization removed more than 15,000 IG militants from the Salafi–Jihadi camp currently led by al-Qaeda.

In 2007, al-Jihad Organization, the second-largest armed organization in Egypt, with strong ties to al-Qaeda, also initiated a deradicalization process. The process is being led by the former amir (commander) of al-Jihad (1987–93) and al-Qaeda's ideologue, Dr. Sayyid Imam al-Sharif (alias 'Abd al-Qadir ibn 'Abd al-'Aziz, as well as Dr. Fadl). To recant his old views, al-Sharif authored two books entitled *Wathiqat tarshid al-jihad fi Misr wa-l-'alam* (A Document for Guiding Jihad in Egypt and the World, 2007) and *al-Ta'riya* (The Uncovering, 2008). In addition, al-Sharif and other al-Jihad commanders toured Egyptian prisons between February and April 2007 to meet with their followers and discuss the abandonment and delegitimization of violence. That process has been only partially successful, however, as at least three factions within al-Jihad still refuse to uphold it. These factions also refuse to leave the organization and one of them is in solid alliance with al-Qaeda. The process is thus ongoing at the present time.[2]

In Algeria, similar deradicalizing transformations occurred in 1997. Like the IG, the self-declared armed wing of the Islamic Salvation Front (FIS),[3] known as the Islamic Salvation Army (AIS), declared a unilateral ceasefire. The ceasefire led to disarmament and demilitarization processes that aimed for the reintegration of AIS members as well as other armed Islamist factions into Algerian society. The demilitarization process included militias from the notorious Armed Islamic Group (GIA) and the Salafi Group for Preaching and Combat (GSPC).[4] These groups and factions issued several communiqués to explain and legitimize their decisions to dismantle their armed wings. Unlike the Egyptian groups, however, the Algerian groups did not produce any ideological literature to reconstruct a new ideology.

The phenomenon of deradicalization has not been confined to Egypt and Algeria, nor has it been confined to the Middle East. In the 2000s, it took place in several other countries, albeit on a relatively smaller scale. Instances of deradicalization have occurred within Libyan, Saudi, Yemeni, Jordanian, Tajik, Singaporean, Malaysian, and Indonesian armed Islamist groups, factions, and individuals. Additionally, deradicalization processes and programs have influenced several British and other European Islamist leaders (Ashour 2009, 14–18).

Despite the fact that the aforementioned armed Islamist movements have shown remarkable behavioral and ideological transformations in favor of nonviolence and even though these movements' deradicalization processes have removed tens of thousands of militants from the ranks of al-Qaeda supporters and acted as disincentives for would-be militants, very few studies have addressed the reasons behind the renouncing (behavioral deradicalization), and delegitimization (ideological deradicalization) of violence. That the phenomenon of deradicalization remains largely understudied is even more surprising when one considers the huge volume of literature on Islamism produced after the September 11 attacks.

This chapter attempts to explain ideological and behavioral transformations toward nonviolence within Islamist movements that have long glorified armed struggle and upheld continuity. Their decisions to abandon violence can been seen as examples of sudden, 'big bang' types of change, but the ideological and organizational transformations were more of the steady and cumulative type. Also, milestone events and critical junctures, most notably September 11, had a major impact on state policies and governments' inclinations to support these transformations, especially in the Egyptian case.

The main focus of this chapter is on the processes of deradicalization in Egypt and Algeria. Transformations where the "foreign variable" (a foreign military presence or occupation) exists are dealt with elsewhere in this book. Where such a variable exists, the process of legitimating political violence and the organizational dynamics of change (as in the cases of Hezbollah and Hamas, for example) can be quite different from cases where a foreign military presence does not exist, as in Egypt and Algeria.

Processes of Change within Islamist Movements

Radicalization, deradicalization, and moderation are processes of relative change within Islamist movements, which can occur on the ideological and/or behavioral levels, evenly or unevenly across issues considered central to the Islamist cause. The three processes hinge on the changes in the stated positions and views of Islamist leaders and groups on violence and democracy.

Radicalization is a process of relative change in which a group undergoes ideological and/or behavioral transformations that lead to the rejection of democratic principles (including the peaceful alternation of power and the legitimacy of ideological and political pluralism) and possibly to the utilization of violence, or to an increase in the levels of violence used,[5] to achieve political goals.

Deradicalization is another process of relative change within Islamist movements, one in which a radical group reverses its ideology and delegitimizes the use of violent methods to achieve political goals, while also moving toward an acceptance of gradual social, political, and economic changes within a pluralist context. A group undergoing a deradicalization process does not have to abide ideologically by democratic principles, whether electoral or liberal, and does not have to participate in an electoral process.[6] Deradicalization primarily consists of changing the attitudes of armed Islamist movements toward violence, rather than toward democracy. Many deradicalized groups still uphold misogynist, xenophobic, and anti-democratic views.

Deradicalization can occur on the behavioral level only. On that level, deradicalization means abandoning the use of violence to achieve political goals without a concurrent process of ideological delegitimization of violence. Deradicalization can occur on one of the two levels. It can also occur on both levels concurrently. There is also a third level of deradicalization. Following the declaration of ideological and/or behavioral deradicalization by the leadership of an armed group, there is usually the challenge of organizational deradicalization: the dismantling of the armed units of the organization, which includes discharging/demobilizing members without internal splits, mutiny, or internal violence.

Finally, 'moderation' is a process of relative change within Islamist movements that mainly affects the attitudes of these movements toward democracy. Moderation can take place on two levels. On the ideological level, the key transformation is the acceptance of democratic principles, most importantly the legitimacy of pluralism and the peaceful alternation of power. On the behavioral level, the key transformation is participation in electoral politics (if the organization is so permitted). Different levels of moderation can occur within both nonviolent radical and moderate[7] Islamist movements, unevenly, and across different issues.

The Common Cause of Islamist Transformations

The proposed argument for explaining Islamist transformations is that a combination of charismatic leadership, state repression, interactions with the 'other'[8] and within the group, and selective inducements from the state and other actors is the common cause of deradicalization. There is a pattern of interaction between these variables. State repression and inter-action with the 'other' affect the ideas and behavior of the leadership of a radical organization and probably lead them to initiate three endogenous processes: strategic calculations, political learning, and *weltanschauung*(s) revision(s). The first process is based on rational-choice calculations and cost–benefit analyses. The second process is a product of socialization and interaction with the 'other,' through which the leadership updates its beliefs and reassesses its behavior according to the behavior of its inter-action partner(s). The third process is mostly based on perceptional and psychological factors. It is a process in which the leadership of an armed Islamist movement modifies its worldviews "as a result of severe crises, frustration and dramatic changes in the environment" (Bermeo 1992, 273–74). Following these processes, the leadership initiates a deradicaliza-tion process that is bolstered by selective inducements from the state as well as by internal interactions (lectures and discussions, and meetings between the leadership, mid-ranking commanders, and the grassroots in an effort to convince them of the merits of deradicalization). Also, deradi-calized groups often interact with violent Islamist groups and, in some cases, the former influence the latter.

Leadership: The Enduring Role of Neopatrimonialism

Since change in general and change toward demilitarization in particular is often conflated with "betraying the struggle" in many militant Islamist movements, only a leader/leadership that is perceived by the majority of followers as credible, pious, theologically knowledgeable,[9] and, preferably, possessing a history of 'struggle'[10] could cast legitimacy on the deradicaliza-tion processes. In other words, a leader can be said to be charismatic when his followers see him as extraordinary as a result of the aforementioned fac-tors and are therefore dependent on him for guidance and inspiration. As a result of this, the leader exerts control or a high level of influence over the followers' behavior, thereby eliminating or limiting splits and internal con-flict. Without a leadership that has these characteristics, armed Islamist movements tend to fragment under state repression. In most cases, that fragmentation leads to splintering and further radicalization in the form of anti-civilian violence and extreme anti-system ideologies perpetrated and upheld by loosely structured organizations. Also, fragmentation may engender internal violence within the group.

Egypt: Leadership and the Comprehensive Deradicalization of the Islamic Group

In Egypt, one of the main reasons behind the relative success of the deradicalization process of the IG was the leadership's charisma and resulting influence over its followers. Before the 1997 ceasefire declaration, there had been at least fourteen attempts to put a partial stop to the violence between the IG and the Egyptian regime.[11] The most notable of these attempts are:

1. **1988–94:** Several attempts are made by al-Azhar[12] scholars to convince the IG leaders and members that violence against the state and society is not sanctioned by Islam.
2. **1993:** The so-called "committee for mediation"[13] attempts to reconcile the regime and the IG. The mediation fails, mainly because it is publicized as "negotiations with terrorists," and therefore embarrasses the regime.[14]
3. **1993:** General Abdul Ra'uf Salih, head of the Prisons Department in the Interior Ministry, suggests that the IG cease violence against tourists. 'Abbud al-Zummur, who is on the IG shura council, calls in exchange for the regime to comply with the IG's demands, including releasing political prisoners. The process fails as a result (al-'Awwa 2006, 226).
4. **March 1996:** Khalid Ibrahim al-Qusi, the former IG commander in the southern city of Aswan, calls for the cessation of violent activities during a military tribunal. The attempt is unsuccessful because of a lack of support from the IG leadership.

Two factors were common to all of these attempts. First, before 1997, no consensus existed among the IG's historical leadership over completely ceasing violence. A related, second factor is that all such attempts lacked ideological justification. Since *fiqh al-'unf* literature (Islamic jurisprudence justifying violence) had been produced by the leadership, recanting it and providing a new literature that ideologically de-legitimized violence and then convincing IG members and sympathizers to uphold that new ideology were tasks that would be most likely to succeed if undertaken by those same historical leaders. In the eyes of their followers, the historical leadership was the only possible source that could bestow "Islamic legitimacy" on an ideological delegitimization of violence. Other sources were not credible enough and were usually dismissed as regime sympathizers, agents who had been coopted (such as some al-Azhar scholars) into delegitimization or were weakened as a result of repression, as in the case of Khalid Ibrahim.

From the IG members' perspective, the historical leadership is credible enough and beyond cooptation and weakening. This perception was made clear on several occasions. In June 2002, during a conference held in Wadi al-Natrun detention center, where more than one thousand IG members were imprisoned, the followers showed signs of great respect for their leaders. This included the kissing of hands and beards of leaders,[15] as well as hanging signs and pickets on the walls of the conference site featuring phrases such as, "Welcome Our Sheikhs, Delight of Our Eyes!" (Ahmad 2002a, 1, 12). In the question-and-answer session, almost all members started their questions with an expression of praise or welcome, or a verse from a poem.[16] In another conference, in August of the same year, in the Istiqbal detention center, where around two thousand IG members were held, followers addressed their leaders only with the opening *mawlana* (our master/lord), in spite of the fact that most of them could argue that the years they had spent in detention or in hiding, as well as being tortured, could be partially attributed to their leadership's policies, rhetoric, and incompetence. Thus, rather than hold their leaders accountable for disastrous decisions, the members rallied around them.

Despite these clear signs of support, convincing their followers that they had been wrong for the last two decades was not an easy task for the movement's leadership. To limit potential dissent, the historical leadership had first to make a unanimous decision to stop the violence and then to convince other segments within the IG to put an end to violence and uphold the new ideology. These consisted mainly of the leadership abroad, imprisoned mid-ranking commanders and grass-roots members, and commanders of small units and grassroots members in hiding. The largest group consisted of detainees, who numbered at more than 15,000 according to official sources.[17]

Hamdi Abdul Rahman, one of the movement's historical leaders and a *shura* council member, explained in an interview that the conferences held in detention centers to convince grassroots members of the wisdom of the Initiative for Ceasing Violence (ICV) were just the final stages of a long process that had begun in 1997 (Ahmad 2002b). The historical leaders had been communicating and debating with their followers in detention centers across Egypt between July 1997 and December 2002. The reactions in 1997 varied inside the prisons, mainly due to miscommunication and lack of direct contact with the leadership. However, there were no reported splits as a result of the unilateral ceasefire declaration of 1997. In 2002, during the conferences, critical questions that reflected the concerns of IG members were raised. These included questions about the reasons behind the delay of the ceasefire initiative, the fate of deceased IG members, and the returns/compensations that the IG would get from the Egyptian state.[18]

Algeria: Leadership and the Pragmatic Deradicalization of the Islamic Salvation Army

Algeria presents us with two cases of deradicalization, one of which was successful and one which was a failure. The successful case is that of the Islamic Salvation Army (AIS), whose process of deradicalization took place between 1997 and 2000. The leadership of that organization was able not only to dismantle the AIS but also to influence smaller armed organizations and factions to join the deradicalization process. By contrast, the Armed Islamic Group (GIA) experienced mixed results. Whereas some of its affiliated militias joined the AIS-led process, the bulk of the group failed to deradicalize. Instead, part of the GIA was completely destroyed by 2005. Another part broke away as early as 1998 and renamed itself in 1999 the Salafi Group for Preaching and Combat (GSPC). By 2008, a part of the GSPC was still negotiating laying down its arms and abandoning violence (behavioral deradicalization), but the largest faction underwent even further radicalization by internationalizing its cause and allying with the al-Qaeda network. That splinter of the GSPC called itself "al-Qaeda in the Islamic Countries of al-Maghreb" (QICM). The AIS and the GIA both began their armed action in the crisis environment that plagued Algeria after the January 1992 coup by the Algerian military, in which parliamentary elections that would have brought the FIS to power were cancelled by force.

The first AIS cells were established in western Algeria in 1993. In 1994, the AIS was mainly operating in the west and east of Algeria under the joint leadership of Ahmad Ben Aicha and Madani Mezraq, respectively. Both figures were mid-ranking leaders in the FIS in 1991. Ben Aicha was an elected member of parliament in al-Chelf district, who had turned to armed action after the cancellation of the elections, his subsequent arrest, and then two attempts on his life after he was released (Ben Aicha 2000). Mezraq was a former activist in the al-Nahda Movement.[19] He had no leading role in the FIS except after the Batna Conference in 1990, during which he was appointed the FIS representative in the Jijel province and a member of the FIS national committee for monitoring elections.

When the coup occurred in 1992, the FIS had no leading figures to organize armed action and no militias operating in its name.[20] In 1994, Muhammad Said and Abd al-Razzaq Rajjam, both former provisional leaders of the FIS, joined the GIA instead of organizing or leading the AIS cells. Others, like Said Makhloufi, a former military intelligence officer, a veteran of Afghanistan, and a former member of the Consultative Council of the FIS, had also joined the GIA.[21] In Ben Aicha's words, the armed men of the FIS became "orphans" after these leading figures joined another organization (Ben Aicha 1996).[22] However, Mezraq and Ben Aicha emerged as the new field commanders who upheld the FIS's "original line."[23] Their leadership was challenged on several occasions, for example, during the negotiations of 1997 and in the aftermath of the unilateral ceasefire declaration, when around thirty AIS detained affiliates, suspected sympathizers, and relatives of members were summarily executed in the area of Umm al-Thalathin,[24] which is close to some of the hills controlled at the time by the AIS guerrillas. This action took place just before a meeting between General Muhammad Lamari and Mezraq. The latter interpreted it as an attempt by other factions in the military establishment to "drive his followers crazy" before the talks. "They wanted to tell us that the authorities have no intention to reach a resolution . . . and possibly drive one of our men to kill their delegate [General Lamari]," Mezraq recalled. Despite the incident, there was no violent retaliation on the part of the AIS, and Mezraq was able to control his militiamen. However, Mezraq argued that the commanders of other armed organizations in Algeria were following the emotional and radical views of their soldiers: "Weak commanders in other organizations were leading their soldiers via the concept of 'whatever the listeners want' because these commanders loved leadership and fame . . . that was a disaster for the [armed Islamist] movement."[25] Following that second challenge, the talks developed into a negotiation process that finally led to the dismantlement of the AIS and several other smaller organizations in January 2000.

Another challenge came after January 2000, when the political leaders of the FIS, Mezraq and Belhaj, expressed their support for behavioral deradicalization, but their opposition to the terms of the agreement between the AIS and the regime. The two leaders refused the dismantlement of the AIS and other pro-FIS militias (Ben Hajar 2000). Mezraq sent a letter to Ali Ben Hajar, the amir of the Islamic League for Jihad and Preaching (LIDD) and a formerly elected FIS member of parliament in al-Medea (Ben Hajar 2000).[26] In it, he asked Ben Hajar to keep his arms and men, refused to reveal the details of the Lamari–Mezraq agreement, and called for a resolution along the lines of what he had proposed in 1994 and 1995 during the talks with the regime.[27] When asked directly if he thought that Mezraq approved of the dismantlement of the LIDD, Ben Hajar answered, "I do not know . . . but Sheikh Abbasi is a wise politician, he knows that we did not put down arms except under duress,[28] and that we did not abandon our duty" (Ben Hajar 2000). Ali Belhaj and Abd al-Qadir Hachani,[29] the provisional leaders of the FIS who led the party to the electoral victory of 1991, had similar views. They both approved of an end to the violence, however, they wanted better terms in the agreement with the regime, especially with regards to rehabilitating the FIS and allowing its members to be politically active.

Despite that stance from the FIS's political leaders, the dismantlement of the AIS and the deradicalization of other groups and factions were successful. The AIS militiamen were following the orders of their direct commanders, who were in turn following the orders of the AIS's national amir, Mezraq. Mezraq was also able to convince the amirs of other armed organizations to deradicalize. In addition to the crucial role played by the leadership, the other three variables of state repression, social interaction, and selective inducement contributed to the success of these groups' deradicalization process.

State Repression

State repression is defined here as "a behaviour that is applied by governments in an effort to bring about political quiescence and facilitate the continuity of the regime through some form of restriction or violation of political and civil rights (Davenport 2006, 6). This behavior incorporates a broad range of actions, including "negative sanctions, such as restrictions on free speech, violations of life integrity rights, such as torture and political imprisonment" (Carey 2002), as well as state-sponsored terror in the form of assassinations, civilian slaughters, and mass murder. In short, state repression comprises all confrontational activities, both violent and non-violent, that are directed from the ruling regime toward the population in general and the political opposition in particular.

Whereas the variables of the roles played by the leadership, social interaction, and selective inducements were evident in the deradicalization process described above, the role of state repression was not as clear. Was repression a cause of radicalization, an obstacle to deradicalization, or a cause of deradicalization? The empirical evidence suggests all three. I focus here on repression as a cause of deradicalization, as it is the most relevant to the topic of this chapter.[30]

Egypt: The Politics of Torture[31]

In several interviews, historical leaders of the IG have referred to state repression as a reason for revising their behavior and ideology. Repression forced the IG leadership to reassess the costs and benefits of violently confronting the Egyptian regime. They found that the costs of confrontation outweighed the benefits and, therefore, came to the conclusion that *jihad* was Islamically forbidden in this case (Abdul Rahman et al. 2002, 66). "*Jihad* is not an end in itself. It is just a means to attain other ends. If you cannot attain these ends through *jihad*, you should change the means," said Nagih Ibrahim to the IG members during the Wadi al-Natrun conference. Ali al-Sharif, another leader, and co-author of *Taslit al-adwa' 'ala ma waqa'a fi-l-jihad min akhta'*, added during the same conference that the members fought for the IG's right to preach Islam,[32] as well as for their detained "brother." What they received as a result was a complete ban on preaching, more detainees, and incredibly repressive conditions.[33] According to the leadership's new perspective, since 'Islam' was hurt by '*jihad*,' the latter should be banned.

In addition, repression seems to have affected the worldviews of some leaders. In an interview, Mamduh A. Yusuf, the commander of the IG's military wing (1988–90), discussed some examples and consequences of repression in detention centers, including rampant tuberculosis, malnutrition, bad ventilation, and bi-monthly beatings of all political prisoners, some of which resulted in deaths. Outside the prisons, the families of detainees were suffering from economic deprivation, social alienation, and systematic discrimination by the state. Yusuf argued that if God had been "on their side" these things would not have happened to the IG members and their families. He therefore concluded that there had to be something "theologically wrong" with the decision to confront the regime.[34]

Algeria: The Politics of Massacres

Algeria was plagued by several types of violence and repression following the cancellation of the elections by a group of incumbent army generals in January 1992. In 2005, Algerian President Abdelaziz Bouteflika estimated the war's toll at 150,000 fatalities between 1992 and 2002 (Bouteflika 2005). In addition, a group of researchers documented 642 massacres that occurred between 1992 and 1998 (Bedjaoui et al. 1999).[35] Most of these massacres took place in districts that voted for FIS candidates in 1991 elections (Bedjaoui, et al. 1999, 25–30). While the GIA took responsibility for some of these massacres, some researchers, opposition figures, and former Algerian intelligence officers and diplomats accuse the regime of being complicit in or even directly responsible for others (Samroui 2003; Souidia 2002; Roberts 2001).

In addition, following the 1992 cancellation of elections, between 30,000 and 40,000 FIS supporters, suspected supporters, and sympathizers were detained, mainly in detention centers in the Algerian desert, known as *al-muhtashadat* (concentrations). In 2006, a government committee appointed by President Bouteflika blamed the security services for 6,146 'disappearances' between 1992 and 1998 (Cosantini 2005; 2006a; 2006b). According to the government, the total number of disappeared persons in this period was more than 10,000 (Oyahia 2007), a number that exceeds the total for any other place in the world except Bosnia in the 1990s.[36] The same committee declared that the security establishment arrested more than 500,000 Algerians during the crisis as "terrorism suspects." Finally, Prime Minister Ahmad Oyahia declared in 2006 that the security forces had killed 17,000 "armed Islamists," out of an estimated 25,000[37] operating between 1992 and 1997 (Costantini 2006b, 19; Oyahia 2007, 1). These figures reflect the general level of state repression in Algeria in the 1990s. This section, however, focuses on a specific type of repression—that directed against the AIS and its affiliates—as well as how that repression affected the AIS decision to deradicalize.

Between 1993 and 1997, the AIS faced a double threat. First, its guerrillas were at war with the official National Popular Army (ANP), pro-regime militias, and the GIA.[38] The AIS dealt with this threat relatively better than with the other one. Contrary to the GIA between 1994 and 1995, the AIS did not pose a significant threat to the ANP during the crisis. However, it was able to hold its own in the face of ANP offensives, and the ANP was unable to destroy it. The second threat to the AIS came partly from the GIA and, allegedly, from factions within the military security establishment. That threat came in the form of massacres of mainly civilians in electoral districts that had voted for the FIS in the 1990 municipal elections and 1991 legislative elections. The massacres became a regular phenomenon in 1997, with a massacre occurring almost every day that year (the total number in 1997 exceeded 300 massacres).

These massacres had a strong impact on the AIS decision to disarm and dismantle. The AIS was the self-declared armed wing of the FIS, but, it could neither protect the families of its members nor FIS supporters, especially in central Algeria. For example, in 1997, the GIA claimed responsibility for the mass killing of thirty-one "convicted apostates" in Ktiten village in al-Medea province.[39] The "convicted apostates" were mostly women and children from the extended family of Ali Ben Hajar, the amir of the LIDD, who was coordinating with the AIS and whose militia assassinated Djmel Zitouni, the GIA amir, in 1996 (Izel et al. 1999, 415). In Bentalha, a small town south of Algiers whose residents overwhelmingly voted for the FIS in 1991, 417 civilians were massacred, allegedly by the GIA, in one night (22–23 September 1997) (Nasrullah 2007, 13).[40] Many of the victims were relatives of AIS members. Awad Bou Abdullah (alias Sheikh Nur al-Din) was the AIS commander of the sixth zone, the nearest area to Bentalha in which the AIS had a militia (Bou Abdullah 2006). Bou Abdullah recalls that after hearing the news of the massacre, he sent an armed detachment to Bentalha to defend relatives and supporters but it was "too late" (Bou Abdullah 2006).[41]

Answering a question in an interview about the causes behind the unilateral ceasefire, Mezraq mentioned that the AIS declared it because the "jihad was just about to be buried by its own sons." By this, he meant that the whole concept of jihad in Algeria was being tarnished by the massacres and by intra-Islamist fighting. There was consequently no point in continuing the fight against the regime, due to waning popular support (Mezraq 2005).

Mustafa Kabir, the AIS commander of the east of Algeria argued that among the main reasons for the declaration of the unilateral ceasefire was the ongoing massacres. "We were used as an umbrella to hide the perpetrators of the massacres . . . and we therefore had to remove this umbrella and dismantle our organization" (Kabir 2002). Kabir was referring to the fact that many Algerians and non-Algerian monitors did not distinguish between the AIS and the GIA. They were all regarded as armed Islamists fighting against the regime, and the massacres hurt the reputation of Islamists in general. By declaring the unilateral ceasefire, the AIS wanted to send a message to Algerians and to the rest of the world that they were not behind the massacres and that they were laying down arms to "expose whoever is behind them."[42]

In addition to the 'regular' forms of repression (imprisonment, torture, extrajudicial executions, media smear campaigns, and others), the massacres had a strong impact on the AIS decision to deradicalize, regardless of who was really behind them. Whether it was the GIA practicing its takfiri ideology, army factions using the massacres as a 'counterinsurgency' tactic,[43] or a mixture of both,[44] the massacres were the main cause behind the AIS decision to declare the unilateral ceasefire.

Social Interactions

Social interaction is a variable with internal and external dimensions. External interaction is a subvariable featuring a sequence of interactions between a movement and any actor/entity who/which does not belong to that movement's ideological camp or is not recognized by the movement.[45] Internal interaction is another dimension of social interaction and takes place on the internal level among the leadership, the mid-ranking commanders, and the grassroots members of the same movement. In the cases under study, social interaction took place mainly in prisons, detention centers, and remote mountainous locations (where Islamist guerrillas were operating).

Egypt: Prison Socialization
Two factors should be highlighted as forms of external interaction in the IG case: interactions with other Islamist movements and interactions with other political prisoners. In their conferences, interviews, and new literature, the IG's historical leaders have mentioned that one of the reasons behind

the ICV declaration in 1997 was their fear of an Algeria-like scenario (Ahmad 2002b, 17; Ahmad 2003, 193; Zuhdi and Ibrahim 2002b, 123; Ibrahim 2005a, 59–60), by which they meant the loss of control over their followers and the fragmentation of the IG during the confrontation period. The Algerian parallel was the loss of control over the armed factions by the FIS leaders.[46]

In addition, there were external interactions with detained secular liberals and human rights activists. Renowned pro-democracy activist and former political prisoner Dr. Saad Eddin Ibrahim has described some of those interactions.[47] He mentioned that the leaders were first interested in knowing why the international community was outraged by his detention but not by the detention of thousands of Islamist suspects.[48] That question started debates between the detained Islamist figures and Professor Ibrahim about Islamism, democracy, and human rights. The ideas expressed in the IG's new literature, as well as the references cited, reflect those debates and show the strong influence of modernist and postmodernist theory, albeit recycled in an Islamist framework.[49] These ideas include upholding ideological and theological uncertainty over determinism (Ibrahim 2005b, 17), cultural and historical dynamism over rigidity (Ibrahim 2005b, 81), cultural dialogue rather than a clash of civilizations (Zuhdi and Ibrahim 2002b, 236; Ibrahim and Zuhdi 2005, 225–49), and the necessity for renewing religious rhetoric (Ibrahim 2005b).[50] Karam Zuhdi, head of the IG's shura council, went as far as citing the controversy regarding the role of religion in U.S. foreign policy, concluding that at least before September 11 there had been no Christian crusade against Islam led by the U.S., as al-Qaeda have assumed (Zuhdi and Ibrahim 2002a, 64).

Finally, I should point out that at no point did IG leaders admit that they had been influenced by secular intellectuals, literature, or ideas. Despite that, they have expressed their gratitude to those secular intellectuals and politicians who supported the ICV, as well as their basic human rights (Hafiz and Majid 2002, 46). They have also condemned those leftist leaders[51] who rejected the ICV and argued in favor of state repression of Islamists. Such a stance is by itself a new development, as secularists were, with no exceptions, usually the objects of the IG's harsh criticism, fiery rhetoric, and even on occasion its bullets.[52]

As for internal interactions, the historical leaders toured all known political detention centers and prisons, from Damanhur in the north to al-Wadi al-Jadid and Asyut in the south, for a period of ten months in 2002. These tours and meetings aimed to illustrate the meaning of the ICV, to explain new ideological perspectives,[53] and then to address the questions, comments, and critiques of the movement's members. The historical leaders would first hold meetings with second-in-line commanders[54] to illustrate the general guidelines of the ICV and the new ideology. Then, a 'general assembly' would be convened, which all the members would attend and where they would meet with the historical leaders. The leaders would begin with a discussion of the four new books, followed by an extended question-and-answer period. Afterward, the leaders would meet with the members in their cells and in prison corridors to discuss transformations taking place directly in small groups (Zuhdi and Ibrahim 2002b, 21–23).

In their book *Nahr al-zikrayat* (2002), eight historical IG leaders described the interactions with their followers during the meetings and conferences as one of the main reasons for the relative success of the ICV (Zuhdi and Ibrahim 2002b, 25). Before the long process of interaction, argumentation, and discussion, there had been little support, if any, for the ICV among middle-ranking leaders and grassroots members. Yusuf mentions that when second-in-line leaders received ICV-based orders, they complied with them but with little conviction: "We would ask the individual members to comply, but between us [second-in-line leaders], we still did not agree."[55]

Aware of the opposition, Karam Zuhdi called for transferring Yusuf and other second-in-line commanders from the Scorpion prison to the Liman hospital, where Zuhdi was being held for treatment. "Hearing the [theological] exegeses directly from the sheikhs was different. . . . We had heard these before from the Salafis and from al-Azhar . . . [but] we did not accept them. . . . We accepted them from the sheikhs because we know their history," Yusuf explained.[56]

Algeria: Interactions and the Deradicalization of the AIS

Nuances of ideology and behavior separated the AIS from the IG and from other jihadist groups. The main difference was its belief that armed jihad is a last-resort, defensive effort to create an Islamic state after all attempts at electoral politics have failed. The AIS also believed that violence would not resolve the Algerian crisis. Therefore, throughout the civil war it attempted to negotiate a settlement, first via the FIS political leaders in 1995 and then via its own leadership in 1997. The political position of the AIS can be considered partly a product of interactions between AIS figures and nonviolent Islamists and secular groups.

The interactions between the AIS and moderate Islamists and non-Islamists (external interaction) were important in influencing its stance on violence. First, the leadership of the AIS was influenced mainly by the ideas and works of the Egyptian Muslim Brothers, a group that had renounced violence against the Egyptian regime in the early 1970s. For example, when asked about the books that influenced his Islamist ideology and behavior, Medani Mezraq mentioned *Majmu' al-rasa'il*, by Hasan al-Banna, *al-Ikhwan al-muslimun: ahdath sana'at al-tarikh*, by Mahmud Abdul Halim,[57] and Abu Hamid al-Ghazali's *'Ulum al-din*.[58]

Second, throughout the Algerian crisis, the leaders of the Egyptian Muslim Brothers called for dialogue. The position of some of these leaders was quite different from that of the mainstream Algerian Muslim Brothers (Movement for the Society of Peace—HAMS or MSP); in general, they tended to be closer to those of the FIS/AIS than to those of the Algerian military establishment. For example, Yusuf al-Qaradawi, a leading Muslim Brothers scholar, argued in one interview that the struggle of the AIS is a legitimate one. However, he urged all armed Islamists to cease violence, to negotiate a settlement, and, at a later stage, to follow the AIS-led deradicalization process (Qaradawi 1998).

In addition to intra-Islamist interaction, the Rome meeting organized by the Catholic Community of St. Edigio was another chance for external interaction with other political forces in Algeria.[59] Although AIS representatives did not attend the meeting, Rabih Kabir, the head of the FIS executive committee abroad and the closest FIS leader to the AIS,[60] was among the signatories of the accords. As opposed to the GIA and the ruling regime, the AIS upheld the results of the talks and called for continuing negotiations based on them.

Given this inclination to negotiate and the perception that armed jihad is a means to an end,[61] the internal interaction process undertaken to convince the AIS militants to deradicalize was less difficult than those of other jihadist groups. Mezraq and Kabir both mentioned that the internal interactions with their followers aimed at convincing them to disarm and demobilize were not easy, but that they were successful in the end.

Indeed, there were no splits within the AIS, and other factions from the GIA and the GSPC, as independent armed organizations, joined the AIS-led deradicalization process.

Selective Inducements

By selective inducements I mean any explicit or implicit sociopolitical/socioeconomic incentives proffered by domestic and/or international political actor(s) to an Islamist movement in return for behavioral, ideological, and/or organizational changes. Examples of selective inducements range from ceasing systematic torture in detention centers to offering a power-sharing deal for participation in the government.

Egypt: Carrots in Bits? The Psychological Impact of Incremental Inducements

Before discussing the selective inducements proffered by the Egyptian regime starting in 2002, I have to mention that there were two developments preceding it, namely 'de-repression' (1998–2001) and coordination (2001–2002).

When the historical leaders declared the ICV in 1997, there was no coordination with the state (Zuhdi and Ibrahim 2002b, 135). Caught unawares by this unexpected development, the regime initially gave out several negative signals, among which were apathy, rejection, hesitation, and suspicion. By 1998, the state had started interacting with the Islamic Group and this was the beginning of the 'de-repression' period. The violence targeting IG members inside most prisons began to stop. Prison meals improved in both quality and quantity.[62] By 1999–2000, prison visits that had been banned by the State Security Investigations (SSI) since 1992–93 were gradually allowed,[63] and the conditions of the visits gradually improved.[64] By December 2001, the policies of the regime toward the ICV took on a new level: coordination with the IG leadership. That policy change alone merits a detailed analysis given its sophistication, but I cannot elaborate on it here because of space limitations. Suffice it to say that before September 11 the Egyptian regime had been far less supportive of the ICV and the IG transformations. IG leaders were allowed to tour prisons, the state media gave extensive coverage of the transformations, and the regime went as far as funding and disseminating the IG's new publications. The message that the regime wanted to send to the United States and the West was that it had been successful in "taming the beasts" and in coopting a former ally of al-Qaeda, thereby removing fifteen to twenty thousand potential supporters from its camp. The implication, therefore, was that it should receive credit for this despite its inglorious human rights record and repressive policies. While coordinating with the IG leaders, the regime was brutally cracking down on democratic opposition in general and on Islamist opposition groups with no ties to al-Qaeda, such as the Muslim Brothers. The vicious cycle of repressive autocrats breeding violent theocrats did not seem to end at this point.

The stages of 'de-repression' and coordination between the regime and the IG were followed by the selective inducements stage, in 2002 and early 2003, when the regime began releasing IG members and leaders, initially in groups of hundreds and then in thousands (Salah 2006). Karam Zuhdi was released in September 2003, followed by other historical leaders in the same month (Salah 2003). In April 2006, an anonymous security official told *al-Hayat* newspaper that there were only two thousand IG detainees left in Egyptian prisons, and that the number had come down from fifteen thousand, all detained under emergency laws (Salah 2006). By April 2007, only IG members who were sentenced by military tribunals, state security or civilian courts were still left in prison. Their number is in the hundreds.[65] Furthermore, the state helped the IG to publish more books, particularly ones that explain the group's perspectives more comprehensively, criticize al-Qaeda, and call for dialogue with the state and with society. Hosni Mubarak's regime also allowed the IG to launch and administer its new website.[66] Finally, the IG leadership announced that the members of its military wing would be discharged and paid pensions. Zuhdi declared that Nagih Ibrahim would be in charge of paying them, although he failed to mention the source of funding (Ahmad 2002a, 16). Since the overwhelming majority of IG members were imprisoned for long periods, all funding options have to include assistance from, and/or cooperation with, the state. Therefore, the state will either provide direct funding or permit IG activists to raise the funds.

Algeria: A Return to 'Normal' Politics?
To support the deradicalization process, the Algerian regime under President Bouteflika had to address four major issues, namely, political prisoners, the 'disappearances' of individuals perceived to be aligned with

Islamists, social reintegration, and the political rights of the deradicalized groups and individuals. Despite the 2006 activation of the Charter of Peace and National Reconciliation, the legal framework that covers these issues, most of the problems underlying them remain unresolved because of their complex and sensitive nature. Nevertheless, the inducements provided by Bouteflika's government with regards to these four issues were enough to bolster the deradicalization process and make it attractive to thousands of militants.

In relation to political prisoners, the main demand of the AIS was the release of all its detainees, FIS leaders, and other affiliates and supporters. The government complied with these demands, releasing high-profile prisoners like Ali Belhaj and Abd al-Haqq Layada, the founder of the GIA, in 2006. Tens of thousands of other political prisoners had been released between 1999 and 2005.

Reintegration was another inducement that the Bouteflika regime had to provide. It was mainly centered on socioeconomic issues and safety concerns. The two socioeconomic issues were reemployment/employment and compensation for families that had been victimized by the regime during the Algerian civil war. Although some of the AIS leaders became successful business entrepreneurs, others were still denied jobs as a result of their history. Many former militants were denied a passport and were continuously harassed by the military and security agencies. These conditions forced Bouteflika to apologize and "ask for forgiveness" from former guerrillas in a gathering at al-Chelf Stadium attended by thousands of former AIS members and other former militants (al-Chelf is one of the towns in western Algeria in which the AIS had a strong presence under Ahmad Ben Aicha).[67]

As to matters of safety, the state provided personal arms, mainly to the commanders of the AIS, to protect themselves against the GIA and its splinter groups, pro-regime militias, and other potential threats. This did not prevent various reprisals such as the assassination of Ali Murad, a member of the AIS joint leadership staff, by one of the pro-regime militias in Souk Ahras province in 2006, not to mention the more recent attempt on the life of Mustafa Kertali,[68] the former AIS amir of central Algeria, in which he lost a leg.[69]

Another sensitive topic is that of political rights. On several occasions, the commanders of the AIS have mentioned that they would not accept being "second class citizens," by which they refer to the *de facto* ban on their political rights.[70] Mezraq is, for the second time, in the process of applying for a permit to launch a political party, although he expects the Algerian authorities to deny his request. The AIS leaders assert that the agreement with the regime upheld their political rights. However, Bouteflika has mentioned on several occasions that he could not find "anything written" with regards to that (Bouteflika 2005; Muqaddim 2005). Given the regime's stance, Ali Ben Hajar, former amir of the LIDD, went so far as to refuse to call on the GSPC and the QICM militants to put down their arms. He argued in one interview that the regime did not honor its promises and that he believed the reconciliation process to be "symbolic but not real" (Ben Hajar 2000).

Conclusion

This chapter analyzed the deradicalization processes of once-armed Islamists in Egypt and Algeria. The Islamic Group and the AIS have shown a remarkable ability to change on the behavioral, ideological, and/ or organizational levels. Behaviorally and organizationally, both groups shunned the path of political violence. Ideologically, the IG delegitimized it. Although the IG's current political stance falls far short of embracing electoral or liberal democracy, it does not represent the end of its transformations. Several sympathizers and former members of the IG participated in the 2005 Egyptian parliamentary elections (al-Zayat 2005). In a 2006 interview, Karam Zuhdi explained that the current IG position on democracy could change, subject to the IG's interests,[71] implying that pragmatism and opportunity structures have final say in the behavior of the IG. As for the AIS, the leadership has accepted electoral processes since its foundation and is currently attempting to form a political party. The hurdles in this case are not ideological but structural.

This chapter also explored four causal variables behind the initiation and the relative success of deradicalization processes: state repression, social interaction, selective inducements, and leadership. A comparison of these variables could be the subject of future research, as could an investigation of the effects of those causal variables on other countries, as the proposed framework is not limited to Egypt and Algeria.

In conclusion, external social interaction aiming to influence Islamist leaders, coupled with selective inducements, could be key factors in deradicalizing militant groups. Elimination of the 'spiritual'[72] leadership of a militant movement, which could be perceived as a media/psychological victory for a government, could also make a comprehensive deradicalization process less likely to succeed. Such leaders are necessary to legitimize deradicalization and initiate a genuine dialogue with their followers (internal social interaction). Finally, moral considerations aside, while durable, intense, and reactive state repression was correlated positively with deradicalization in both cases, the consequences of that type of repression were not limited to deradicalization; they included the initial radicalization of the IG and the AIS, as well as the fragmentation and further radicalization of other militant groups.[73] The four variables, however, provide the necessary bases for understanding the deradicalization of armed Islamist movements. The larger framework in which these variables operate is that of change, whether the sudden, 'big bang' type of change or the more steady, cumulative type.

Notes

1 The term 'historical leaders' was coined by the Egyptian media and it refers to the IG leadership of the 1970s. Almost all of them were sentenced in the so-called al-Jihad trials of 1981, following the assassination of President Anwar Sadat. Most of the historical leaders were still serving their sentences or administratively detained by the regime in 1997. They currently represent the majority in the shura council of the IG. The leaders who were still alive in 2008 were Karam Zuhdi, Nagih Ibrahim, 'Asim Abdul Majid, 'Essam Dirbalah, Hamdi Abdul Rahman, Usama Hafiz, Ali al-Sharif, Fouad al-Dawalibi.

2 By early 2008, most al-Jihad factions had joined the deradicalization process. The main exceptions were the faction led by Ayman al-Zawahri, which joined al-Qaeda, and two small factions in Egyptian prisons whose refusal was based on their rejection of the ideological component of the process (see, for example, Jahin 2007).

3 In general, I shall use the acronym by which an Islamist group is best known, regardless of which language it is based on. Particularly in the cases of Algerian, Moroccan, and Tunisian groups, the acronyms are based on their French initials. Otherwise, acronyms are largely based on the English initials.

4 Now the GSPC is known as "al-Qaeda in the Islamic Countries of al-Maghreb" (QICM).

5 Examples of increasing the level of violence would be expanding the selection of targets to include civilians, the use of indiscriminate violence, and, in terms of technique, suicide bombings. After 1994, the methods utilized by the Algerian GIA exemplify increasing the level of violence.

6 The main example is the Egyptian Islamic Group, which, based on its understanding of Islam, still rejects democracy. However, its newly developed ideology delegitimizes violence and views the 'other' not necessarily as an enemy.

7 An example of a higher level of moderation is accepting liberal, substantive democracy as opposed to electoral, formal democracy.

8 The 'other' is defined here as any social actor or entity who/which is not Islamist or who/which is not recognized by the movement(s) under study as 'Islamist.'

9 Theological training and credentials and a history of issuing *fatwa*s (religious rulings) usually help in legitimizing leaders to followers.

10 Usually armed action against 'secular' national regimes or against foreign military presence or invasion.

11 By 'partially,' I mean that those attempts were not intended to stop the violence completely like the 1997 Initiative for Ceasing Violence (ICV). More specifically, those attempts either aimed to stop a specific operation or to stop 'excesses' in the use of violence, which led to killing or hurting bystanders or neutral civilians. Those attempts aimed as well to cease regime-sponsored violence against the IG and its affiliates.

12 al-Azhar is a world-renowned Islamic institution, mosque, and university. It is considered by many Sunni Muslims to be the most prestigious school of Islamic learning, despite the fact that it was established by the Shi'i Fatimid dynasty in the tenth century.

13 The committee was led by the late Sheikh Muhammad M. al-Sha'rawi, a popular cleric from al-Azhar. The committee members were mainly from the Muslim Brothers and other independent moderate Islamists. State-owned and leftist media outlets criticized the attempt and called on the regime to stop negotiating with Islamist terrorists.

14 This led to the sacking of General Abdul Halim Abu Musa, the interior minister who was behind the process.

15 A traditional way to show great respect

16 Another traditional way to show respect to the leaders

17 The IG leaders put the number at more than 20,000. For estimates see: Ahmad 2002b; Zuhdi and Ibrahim 2002b, 237.

18 See Ahmad 2002b; Zuhdi and Ibrahim 2002b, 116–29. Also, at some points, the discussion stalled. In an interview I conducted with one of the attendees of the *Istiqbal* conference in August 2002, he mentioned that the members were so critical of the ideological reform that Essam Dirbala, one of the leaders and a Shura Council member, said, "Okay, brothers, should we cancel the initiative?" There was a moment of silence, until one of the IG members from Asyut broke it by saying, "Carry on, *mawlana*, we are listening."

19 This was created by Abdullah Djaballah and was mainly based in eastern Algeria (and is therefore sometimes known as the 'eastern group').

20 There was an initial assumption that all armed Islamist organizations in 1992 were fighting for the FIS and its leaders. That assumption was incorrect, especially after the GIA's official establishment in September 1992. Also, in 1991, when tensions were rising between the FIS and the Algerian regime, one of the FIS leaders suggested to Abbasi Madani that the FIS should form an armed wing as a precaution. Madani refused the suggestion. See Ben Aicha 2000.

21 He co-established an autonomous armed organization, Movement for the Islamic State (MEI), in 1992. This organization joined the GIA in May 1994.

22 Said and Rajjam probably joined for pragmatic reasons rather than ideological affinity. Those reasons included the actual strength of the GIA, its control of 'liberated zones' in central Algeria and the large number of Afghanistan-veterans and Algerian army personnel who joined the GIA and therefore contributed with their experience to its military might.

23 By the "original lines of the FIS," AIS activists usually mean the acceptance of electoral democracy, to distinguish themselves from the GIA and Salafi-Jihadi groups who reject all forms of democracy. They also mean loyalty to the leadership of the FIS (Madani and Belhaj).

24 Known as the Umm al-Thalathin Massacre, it occurred in July 1997.

25 That problem confronted not only armed Islamist group leaders but also the FIS leaders from the very beginning. As a result of the populist rhetoric of the FIS leaders, outbidding by followers was a common phenomenon. For example, there was a widespread chant used by FIS supporters in 1991, before the elections, which was heard again in 1997 after the ceasefire declaration: "Ya Ali, ya Abbas al-Jabha rahu Hamas" (O Ali [Belhaj], O Abbas [Medani], the Front has become like Hamas). Hamas (currently Hams or MSP) is the Algerian Muslim Brothers party, which has been in an alliance with the military regime since 1992. It is perceived by FIS supporters as being too compromising and as betraying Islamist ideals (Muqaddim 1999, 6; Shahin 1997, 160). That chant was a condemnation of the FIS leadership's 'lenient' positions.

26 The LIDD is a 300- to 500-men-strong Islamist militia operating mainly in al-Medea, in central Algeria. Its affiliates were able to ambush and kill the GIA amir, Djmel Zitouni, in July 1996.

27 These included the freedom for him and other FIS leaders to consult with the military commanders of the AIS and other groups. In addition, Madani insisted that any agreement with the regime should have neutral witnesses (Ben Hajar 2000).

28 He meant by this the fact that the AIS had struck a deal with the regime and was already dismantling its armed units. The LIDD was a part of those units at this point in time, and Ben Hajar was following Mezraq's orders.

29 He was assassinated on 22 November 1999, allegedly by a GIA member named Fouad Boulemia. His death mainly served military generals who did not want a political role for the FIS. Hachani was coordinating with several political leader from the left (Louisa Hannoue, WP) and the Right (Abd al-Hamid Mehri, FLN), demanding more political freedoms in the country, as well as the rehabilitation of the FIS. His alleged assassin was convicted in a controversial one-day trial, sentenced to death, and then released in 2006. Boulemia mentioned during the trial that he was tortured by the military and threatened by General Toufik (the alias of Mohamed Mediene, head of the *Département du renseignement et de la sécurité*) to write a confession saying that he had killed Hachani by mere "coincidence."

30 For more on the role of repression see Ashour 2009.

31 The argument in this section is based on empirical observations and inductive analysis. At the core of it, there is an obviously problematic moral element that is not addressed here. However, the argument should not be understood as recommending or supporting state repression or any violations of human rights.

32 Which means, in this case, the IG's understanding of Islam.

33 For example, former detainees who were held in Scorpion Prison mention that they were held in solitary cells from 1993 until 1997. In addition to bimonthly beatings and torture, they were not allowed to leave these cells for four years. When they were finally allowed to interact with the outside world in 1997, the last news they had heard about the world was from 1993 (former IG detainee, interview by author, October 2002, Cairo, Egypt).

34 See interview with Yusuf in: al-'Awwa 2006, 145.
35 A massacre is defined as a violent event in which more than five civilians are murdered; see Abdul 'Ati 2002; Urwa 2001.
36 In addition to the humanitarian tragedy, Algeria's economy was devastated with the loss of billions of dollars in revenue (an estimated $30 billion between 1992 and 1998), a dramatic increase in security expenditures by the regime, ballooning external debt ($30.7 billion in 1997), and rampant unemployment.
37 According to Faruq Costantini, the head of the regime's Consultative Commission for Human Rights in Algeria, this number does not include the supporters of armed Islamists inside cities and towns (Costantini 2006b, 19).
38 The war with the GIA started with skirmishes in 1995 and intensified in 1996 and 1997.
39 GIA 1997, communiqué no. 13.
40 Bentalha is a small town south of Algiers that voted for the FIS in the 1991 elections. Many inhabitants were initially in favor of the FIS/AIS Islamists and some had joined them.
41 It was unclear what he meant by "too late." However, during the massacre the army was blocking all entrances and exits to Bentalha and reportedly shot dead a policeman who attempted to interfere. Security forces were stationed on the edge of Bentalha and were aware of what was going on but did not interfere. The neighborhood of al-Djilali, which was specifically targeted by the attack, was repeatedly illuminated by huge spotlights recently installed in a nearby field by the police. Also, a military helicopter hovered over the scene throughout much of the six hours in which the massacre took place. Given these conditions, it was almost impossible for an AIS detachment to reach Bentalha (see the details in Nasrullah 2007 and Roberts 2001).
42 AIS Communiqué 1997, 1.
43 In his book La Sale Guerre (translated from French to Arabic: see Souidia 2002) and in several interviews, Lieutenant Habib Souidia mentions that he drove some Algerian Special Forces officers and soldiers to the homes of Algerian civilians who had voted for the FIS. The group that he drove massacred the voters. Souidia mentions that he is ready to stand trial for these and similar actions. If these accounts are correct, it shows that some units in the army were directly involved in the massacres and not just lacking the will to interfere or providing indirect support for the GIA as in the case of Bentalha. For comparative cases of targeting civilians as a counter-insurgency tool, see: Izel et al. 1999.
44 Like an infiltration of the GIA's units or even leadership structure, as Colonel Mohamed Samraoui and others argue. Given the simplistic mobilization methods and the lack of recruitment screening, as well as the basis for 'promotion' within the GIA, the infiltration scenario is not unlikely.
45 In other words, external social interaction takes place between an Islamist movement and what it perceives as the 'other.'
46 The relationship between the IG and the Algerian FIS is no secret. Several IG leaders had ties with FIS figures in the late 1980s and early 1990s. Muhammad al-Islambuli and his mother have visited Algiers and participated in one of the FIS rallies in 1990, in which they were greeted as heroes by FIS supporters. Tal'at Fu'ad Qasim (alias Abu Talal al-Qasimi), a former IG spokesperson, issued several statements supporting the FIS in the 1990s. In his sermons recorded on

audiotapes, Qasim prayed for the release of Madani and Belhaj (Tal'at Fu'ad, Friday sermon, cassette, 1994). In 1997, the IG historical leaders issued a statement congratulating Abbasi Madani, the FIS leader, for his release from prison (see Zuhdi and Ibrahim 2002b, 136).

47 Ibrahim 2004; Saad Ibrahim, interview by Omar Ashour, 21 March 2007, Montreal, Quebec, Canada.

48 Ibrahim 2004; Saad Ibrahim, interview by Omar Ashour, 21 March 2007, Montreal, Quebec, Canada.

49 Although the new literature merits analysis and discussion, I will not attempt to do that here because of space limitations.

50 It is worth mentioning that in the IG's old literature, most of these arguments were refuted as a form of heresy and/or conspiracy (see, for example, Ibrahim et al. 1984; Ibrahim 1990).

51 The new development here is that the condemnation was directed against *some* leftists. Usually, the IG would attack the whole ideological camp.

52 One example is Dr. Farag Foda, a leading secular intellectual who was assassinated by IG activists in June 1992.

53 The general features of the new ideology are based on the first four books that were mentioned before.

54 These are the leaders who ran the IG outside the prisons throughout the 1980s and led the confrontation with the regime in the early 1990s.

55 See interview with Yusuf in: al-'Awwa 2006, 202.

56 See interview with Yusuf in: al-'Awwa 2006, 206.

57 One of the leaders of the Muslim Brothers in Egypt. His three-volume book is one of the most detailed accounts of the history of the Muslim Brotherhood in Egypt.

58 The latter book is a classic of four volumes that deals mainly with theology, jurisprudence, spirituality, and Islamic philosophy. It is one of the classics that the Muslim Brothers teach and emphasize in their curricula.

59 The Rome Accords (also known as the St. Egidio Platform) were considered to be a political victory for the FIS and the Algerian pro-democracy opposition. In January 1995, the accords were signed by several major opposition figures and parties in Algeria, including Islamists (FIS, al-Nahda Party, Contemporary Muslim Algeria), nationalists (National Liberation Front—Abdelhamid Mehri), socialists (Socialist Forces Front—Hocine Ait Ahmad), Trotskyites (Workers' Party—Lousia Hanoune), nationalist democrats (Movement for Democracy in Algeria—Ahmad Ben Bella), human right activists (Algerian Human Rights League—Ali Yahia), and even the anti-Islamist Rally for Culture and Democracy (Hocine Esslimani). The accords were brokered by the St. Egidio Catholic Community and provided the basis for a peaceful resolution of the crisis via the establishment of common principles that all the cosignatories accepted and vowed to respect.

60 His brother, Mustafa Kabir, was the AIS amir of the east starting in 1995.

61 Not an end per se. The latter was an ideological preference for the GIA.

62 See interview with Yusuf in: al-'Awwa 2006, 144.

63 The exact time period depends on which prison is in question.

64 For example, Samir al-'Arky, one of the IG members who was detained in al-Fayoum Prison explains that after January 2000, when the ban on visits was revoked, there were usually two fences between the detainee and his visitors. Given the large number of detainees and visitors in the same location at the same time, hearing and

interaction were very difficult. By late October 2001, the detainees were allowed to sit with their families with no fences between them. Samir al-ʿArky mentions that when this happened, many detainees went down on their knees and prostrated to perform *sujud*, an Islamic ritual for thanking God (see Samir al-ʿArky, "Rihlat al-Fayyum . . . zikrayat wa shujun." Interview by Islamic Group. [Online]), http://egyig.com/Public/chapters/mobadra/6/38809650.shtml (accessed 1 January 2007).

65   See interview with Nagih Ibrahim, "Ibrahim yakshif al-sitar ʿan ahdath akhbar al-mubadara," by Usama Abdul Azim, http://egyig.com/Public/chapters/interview/6/83640472.html (accessed 20 July 2007).

66   Although the history and the old literature of the IG are not available on it.

67   After apologizing, Bouteflika said that the AIS militants had honored their word (with regards to abandoning violence), whereas the state did not honor its commitment to them.

68   This was the second attempt on Kertali's life. The first was organized by a pro-regime militia in the town of Larbaa. It ended with a gun fight in which one of the assailants was injured and Kertali survived unharmed.

69   al-Qaeda later "apologized" for the attack, mentioning that one of its members decided to act on his own, without the leadership's consent.

70   For example, former AIS members were not allowed to run in the Algerian parliamentary elections of May 2007.

71   Interview with Karam Zuhdi. 2006. *Liqa' khas,* Al Jazeera, 23 August.

72   As opposed to the organizational leaders of a group.

73   Most notable are the Algerian cases of the Armed Islamic Group (GIA) and the Salafist Group for Preaching and Combat (GSPC) (which has now become al-Qaeda in the Islamic Countries of al-Maghreb).

7

Nonstate Actors: A Comparative Analysis of Change and Development within Hamas and Hezbollah

Julie C. Herrick

Introduction

In accordance with the broad theme of a changing Middle East, this chapter will explore the emergence of alternative forms of governance, namely the rise of nonstate actors (NSAs) as political entities increasingly wielding legitimacy and influence at domestic, regional, and international levels. More specifically, this chapter will compare and contrast the development of Hamas and Hezbollah, two of the largest and most high-profile NSAs currently operating in the Middle East.

Hamas and Hezbollah are often perceived and categorized as being alike, as a result of similarities in their organizational structure, ideology, and activities. Hamas and Hezbollah exhibit comparable characteristics, as they both represent sociopolitical agendas while adhering to ideological paradigms of political Islamism. They are similarly known for their utilization of violence against Israel in an effort to further their political goals. Hamas and Hezbollah are highly entrenched in their respective territories (the Occupied Palestinian Territories (OPT) and Lebanon), yielding considerable legitimacy and authority among their respective populations. They are also demonstrating an increasing connectivity and resonance within the dynamic and changing region of the Middle East.

As addressed by Bahgat Korany in the Introduction, attitudes and perceptions of the Middle East generally conform to an "intellectual laziness" or assumption of the unchanging and often static nature of regional actors, state and nonstate alike. This point can be refined to encapsulate mainstream perceptions concerning the singular 'terrorist nature' of organizations such as Hamas and Hezbollah. Attitudes and analyses concerning Hamas and Hezbollah are typically conducted within the realm of international security, in the context of the containment of 'terrorism,' a complex and often self-serving term used by politicians and pundits to serve specific political and foreign policy agendas. Contrary to this established vein of analysis, a more productive research endeavor is concerned with why NSAs have emerged as an alternative form of governance in the region of the Middle East. Considering the dynamic and volatile territories in which these actors emerged, a worthwhile research question concerns the degree to which Hamas and Hezbollah have developed as a result of strategic pragmatism and/or dynamic adaptation. These research questions are essential to understanding the nature and future political trajectory of NSAs.

In accordance with the theme and focus of this book, this chapter seeks to address why, how, and in what manner Hamas and Hezbollah have changed and developed since their inception. 'Developed' in this context is not intended to denote a qualitative value judgment, for Hamas and Hezbollah's controversial aspects, including the use of violence and terrorism, are extremely well-documented.[1] Rather, this chapter will serve as an assessment of observed change within the institutional structures and activities of these NSAs. Such an analysis will facilitate an increased understanding of the development of Hamas and Hezbollah in order to better predict future patterns of interaction among states and NSAs in the changing Middle East.

This chapter offers a comparative longitudinal analysis of change and development within Hamas's and Hezbollah's institutional structures and activities to demonstrate several points. First, the formation and development of the two organizations are a consequence of the spillover or 'multiplier' effects stemming from two 'big bangs': the creation of the State of Israel in 1948 and the collective failure of the Arab states in the June 1967 War (see Korany in this volume, Chapter 1). Hamas and Hezbollah have developed by capitalizing on the qualitative disconnect created by the culmination of these two milestone events. This disconnect, combined with the failure of the authoritarian Arab states to fulfill promises of regional growth and development, resulted in the creation of opportunity structures for alternative forms of governance.[2] Second, development within the institutional structures and activities of Hamas and Hezbollah is the result of dynamic adaptation and strategic pragmatism. The organizations developed to capitalize upon emergent opportunity structures resulting from formative conditions of domestic and regional instability in their respective territories of the OPT and Lebanon. As a result of this continuing instability in their territories, Hamas and Hezbollah employed a multifaceted developmental approach, engaging in a broad range of activities in the social, political, and military realms. Longitudinally speaking, the result is the complete entrenchment of these organizations within their respective territories. As a consequence, Hamas and Hezbollah have placed themselves on par with the state or central authority, which largely accounts for their increasing political development and participation in democratic mechanisms and processes.

Common Milestones

The theme and conceptual lens of this book emphasizes the impact of 'big bangs,' from war or revolution to milestone events, as catalysts for change. Change and development can occur in the aftermath of such events as a result of multiplier effects that trigger further change and transformation on alternate levels or in parallel realms, as the cumulative impact of such big bangs settles in (see Korany in this volume, Chapter 1). The growth and development of Hamas and Hezbollah can largely be attributed to the big bangs of the creation of Israel and the collective failure of the Arab states during the June 1967 Six Day War. The repercussions from these events factor highly into the domestic and regional instability that characterized the formative context of Hamas and Hezbollah. Contemporarily, these events continue to shape the direction and manner of development and change within the organizations.

The Creation and Policies of the State of Israel

The creation of Israel in 1948 and the concomitant *nakba* forcefully ousted approximately 800,000 native Palestinians from approximately 78 percent of the land of historical Palestine. Presently, Palestinian refugees and their descendants number approximately seven million people and constitute the world's oldest and largest refugee population (PLO Negotiation Affairs Department and UNCCP 1961, 43). The multiplier consequences of this event have overwhelmingly dominated regional politics in the Middle East ever since. The Arab–Israeli and/or Israeli–Palestinian conflict is the longest, most violent, and historically entrenched conflict on earth, spurring numerous Arab–Israeli wars (1948, 1956, 1967, 1973, 1982, 2006, 2008), as well as three Israeli invasions of Lebanon (1978, 1982, 2006) (Warschawski and Achcar 2006, 7).

Israel's creation is relevant to this analysis for several reasons. First, the events of 1948 shaped the territorial parameters of the Middle East. The contrivance of territorial borders continues to weigh heavily upon the politics of the region and factors highly in the rapid growth and development of Hamas and Hezbollah. With regard to Hamas, Israeli–Palestinian territorial grievances are paramount to the recurrent conflict involving Israel and Hamas. Controversy over Jerusalem and the Palestinian right of return has recurrently derailed peace efforts. In relation to Hezbollah, the Israel–Lebanon border and the Israeli security buffer zone have proven the sources of repeated conflict. The second point of relevance concerning 1948 and the creation of Israel is that it effectively created the 'Palestinian Problem,' an issue with the ability to transcend borders and invoke ideological, religious, and nationalist sympathies and sentiments in the Middle East. This does not mean that Arab nationalism is resurfacing or that any Arab state is going to rescue the Palestinians from their predicament, for historical experience points to the contrary. However, it must be noted that the 'Palestinian problem' does inspire a tangible regional sense of solidarity with the Palestinians in light of past grievances and present Israeli policies of superretaliation in response to actions taken or acts of violence by Hamas in the OPT. The cumulative impact of this dynamic can potentially account for the regional symbolism and sentiment evoked by Hamas, and to a lesser extent by Hezbollah, as well as the support for these organizations among state actors such as Iran and Syria.

The Impact of 1967

The impact of the Six Day War on the collective confidence of the Arab states warrants mention as a crucial trigger, one that continues to shape the contemporary nature and dynamics of the Middle East, as well as the development of Hamas and Hezbollah. The events of June 1967 are attributed to a culmination of factors, including twenty years of lingering regional resentment stemming from the events of 1948. In that month, Egypt, Jordan, and Syria began amassing troops and soliciting arms and support from other Arab states, including Iraq and Saudi Arabia. Israeli forces struck preemptively, displaying superior tactical capability and, six days later, capturing territorial control of the Sinai Peninsula, the Gaza Strip, the West Bank, East Jerusalem, and the Golan Heights.

The events of June 1967 forever altered the balance of power in the Middle East. The collective failure of the Arab states to defeat Israel at the height of the Arab nationalist project resulted in widespread regional change, the effects of which still linger to this day. In the wake of this failure, the Arab states reoriented themselves, undergoing a sociopolitical convulsion associated with defeat in war (see Chapter 1, in this volume). The dynamics of the region began to change, and states such as Egypt and Jordan became more moderate. Engaging in dialogue and cooperative peace efforts with Israel and its western allies, states such as Egypt effectively maneuvered for diplomatic status and more influence within the region.

This bears relevance on the development of Hamas and Hezbollah and consists of several interrelated points. It took the Arab states twenty years to acclimate to a region-wide shift in the balance of power stemming from Israel's creation. The inability of the Arab states collectively to reconcile Palestinian grievances, combined with the loss of their own sovereign territory in 1967, had a profound psychological impact, which has been reflected in the policies of the Arab states toward Israel ever since.

Since 1967, several Arab states have pursued policies of nonengagement with Israel, leaving the Palestinian population to "fight their own fight" (Kramer 2008). This dynamic, when viewed parallel to the continued cycles of violence and socioeconomic deprivation within the OPT, has created a normative disconnect between the moderate Arab states and their populations over the Palestinian issue. This disconnect is fueled by widely felt religious and ideological sympathies for the 'Palestinian problem' within moderate Arab states and regionally. Widespread criticism of Egypt's role in the recent Gaza border dispute is evidence of this point (Erlanger 2009). This is not to suggest the imminent resurgence of Arab nationalism, by now a rather subdued sentiment. Since 1967, however, Palestinians in the OPT have existed in a state of limbo, economically, socially, and politically. As a result, longitudinally, an increasingly palpable regional sense of support for the 'victimized' Palestinians grew, which organizations such as Hamas and Hezbollah (obviously, more so with Hamas) effectively tapped into.

The abovementioned triggers provide context and perspective in an effort to explain the spillover or 'multiplier' effects associated with 'big bangs,' such as war. A firm understanding of these events and the interrelated changes they cause, on many levels, produces valuable insight into the formative historical context that contributed to the growth and continued development of Hamas and Hezbollah. The following sections employ historical narrative in an effort to analyze longitudinal development and change in the social, political, and military structures of the two organizations.

Hamas

Hamas operates in the Occupied Palestinian Territories (OPT) of the Gaza Strip and the West Bank. It advocates a nationalist Palestinian agenda yet adheres to a Sunni Islamic ideological frame of reference. The movement emerged from the more radicalized segments of the Palestinian and Egyptian Muslim Brotherhood and continues to have strong ties, ideologically and materially, to the organization today. Hamas is increasingly regarded by the Palestinian people as being a model for resistance against Israel. In addition to its symbolic influence, Hamas is gradually gaining recognition and legitimacy among Palestinians for its wide array of sociopolitical activities, which have rendered the organization wholly entrenched among the poorest segments of Palestinians in the OPT.

As a result of the cyclical violence and instability in the OPT, Palestinians there face a perpetual state of humanitarian crisis. The Hamas *da'wa* attempts to reduce socioeconomic degradation by providing a variety of charitable and social welfare services. The efforts and activities of Hamas's *da'wa* are vital to understanding the process of entrenchment that has served to broaden and increase the movement's legitimacy and influence.

Social Services

The *da'wa* is a network of social services crucial to the development of Hamas. Building upon the civic fundamentals of the Muslim Brotherhood, Hamas helped develop and currently administers a variety of social services in the OPT, including medical, housing, and food assistance. The *da'wa* is essentially a "functional substitute for the social welfare apparatus of the state" and includes educational, medical, and housing services (Levitt 2006, 17).

In an effort to contextualize Hamas's *da'wa*, it is important to highlight the socioeconomic conditions in the OPT. The United Nations Relief and Works Agency for Palestine Refugees (UNRWA) released a 2008 study of the prevailing economic conditions in the OPT. The report estimates that households living below the official poverty line comprise approximately 52 percent of the population in Gaza and approximately 20 percent of the population in the West Bank (UNRWA 2008, 51; Al Jazeera 2008). The UN Office for the Coordination of Humanitarian Affairs documents unemployment in Gaza at 49 percent in 2008, up from 32 percent in 2007 ("UN: Gaza Unemployment," 2008). Considering that these estimates were made prior to the devastation wrought by the December 2008 Israel–Hamas conflict, it is fair to assume that the economic situation of the OPT is much worse now, and bordering on a humanitarian crisis.

In light of the above, it is unsurprising that the provision of material resources has greatly contributed to the increasing influence of Hamas. Azzam Tamimi discusses the importance of the *da'wa* in generating increased legitimacy for Hamas among Palestinians in the OPT, stating that "the Palestinian Islamists may be viewed as pioneers in the way they transformed their intellectual and ideological discourse into practical programs providing services to the public through voluntary institutions" (Tamimi 2007, 37). The voluntary institutions and non-governmental organizations that administer and fund the Hamas *da'wa* include the Islamic Society, the Holy Land Foundation for Relief and Development, and al-Aqsa Education Fund. Other notable organizations that contribute to the *da'wa*'s funding and maintenance include the Islamic Association for Palestine (IAP), the American Middle Eastern League for Palestine (AMEL), the al-Islam Charitable Society, the American Muslim Society Kuwait Joint Relief Committee, the Saudi High Commission, and the Qatar Charitable Society (Levitt 2006, 144).

Through its social welfare and infrastructural activities, Hamas is effectively "filling a governmental void which in some respects resembles the western notion of civil society" (Mishal and Sela 2000, 7). The successes of the *da'wa* are indicative of the degree of organizational effectiveness Hamas has attained in the OPT. Through its network of social services, the organization has developed in such a way as to capitalize on emerging opportunity structures and vacancies created by the failure of central political authorities to attain infrastructural development in the area. Considering the widespread economic degradation and scarcity of resources in the OPT, it is unsurprising that the Hamas *da'wa* fosters a great deal of loyalty among the poorest sections of Palestinians. One highly strategic aspect of Hamas's developmental course concerns the organization's demonstrable ability to translate the influence and legitimacy gained from its *da'wa* activities into political power and influence.

Political

Hamas's political philosophy developed in a steady, incremental manner. What began as an overt rejection of existing political mechanisms and democratic forms of governance developed into a highly organized socio-political movement based on grassroots mobilization. Hamas emerged in late 1987 as a political alternative to the governance of the Palestine Liberation Organization (PLO) under the leadership of Yasser Arafat and the Fatah movement. Hamas issued its first formal political declaration in 1988, the Hamas Charter. The charter serves as an ideological and political manifesto, affirming Hamas's Islamic identity and its dedication to violent resistance against Israel. The charter emphatically denounces the secularism of the PLO as well as its dialogue with Israel. Strategically, the Hamas Charter coincided with a shift in PLO policy spurred by Yasser Arafat's desire for increased diplomatic dialogue and negotiation at the regional and international levels. Hamas capitalized on the dynamic, characterizing the shift in PLO policy as indicative of the increasingly accommodationist policies of the PLO toward Israel. While condemning the shift in PLO policy, Hamas also stepped up its attacks on Israeli targets, resulting in more imprisonment of Hamas fighters and leaders. By maneuvering to position and portray themselves as a political alternative to the PLO and its backbone, the Fatah movement, Hamas benefited when the inevitable failure of the PLO's diplomatic efforts came to pass (Kristiansen 1999, 23–25).

Arafat's diplomatic efforts culminated in the 1993 Oslo Accords, which created the Palestinian Authority (PA), the primary political body in the OPT. Domestically and regionally, Arafat's cooperative efforts with both western and Israeli leaders were perceived as 'selling out' the Palestinian cause in an effort to consolidate Fatah's power and leadership within the OPT. Hamas employed "cautious rejection combined with calculated acceptance" in formulating its political strategy in the post-Oslo political environment created within the OPT (Mishal and Sela 2000, 109). Its leaders perceived Oslo as equatable to an "Islamic state negotiating with infidels"; however, they also realized that political realities within the OPT were overtaking the organizations' ideological considerations. As a result, a shift or development in Hamas's political philosophy occurred, and it "subdued its criticism of Oslo" (Mishal and Sela 2000, 109). Cautious pragmatism contributed to the shift, as Hamas's leaders sought to avoid civil war with their newly victorious Fatah rivals. Civil war would ultimately prove beneficial to Israel, thus Hamas refrained from calling for Arafat's removal and significantly dampened their inflammatory anti-Oslo rhetoric. Shortly after the Oslo Accords, Hamas circulated a Declaration of Principles (DOP), an internal document aimed at determining a consensus on the direction and manner of change in Hamas' political philosophy in light of changing domestic political realities in the OPT.

The immediate post-Oslo period was a politically developmental period for Hamas. Faced with the new political realities of the PA and its Fatah majority, Hamas pragmatically changed its political strategy and pursued a middle ground. In an effort to retain support from its militant Islamist constituency, Hamas would not abandon violent resistance tactics or methods of terror, nor embrace secularism. However, in order to appeal to a larger, more moderate Palestinian constituency, Hamas would need to cut down on its religious rhetoric and embrace its nationalist principles.

During this period, Hamas walked a narrow path to accomplish its goal, concentrating its efforts outside the realm of politics. Its 'cradle to grave' *da'wa* activities continued to address the daily needs of Palestinians, resulting in a small degree of material provision and infrastructural stability (Levitt 2004). In terms of militant resistance and terrorist activities, Hamas walked a fine line by developing a policy of "controlled, calibrated violence" in response to pressure exterted by Israel in 1995 on the Fatah-led PA, which cracked down on Hamas to stop its rocket launches into Israeli border towns (Gruber 2007, 6). Hamas agreed to refrain from attacking Israeli targets in areas controlled by the PA, but Israeli controlled territories were a different matter. By continuing rocket launches into these areas, Hamas could retain its commitment to violent resistance as an outlet against Israeli aggression and resistance, yet also maintain the appearance of mild cooperation with the PA. The dual strategy would appease the radical Islamist segments of Hamas that were committed to violent resistance, while simultaneously not alienating more moderate Palestinians, necessary for further political development (Gruber 2007, 6–7).

Hamas continued to develop politically by participating in the 1996 elections of the Palestinian Legislative Council (PLC), the parliamentary body of the PA. The elections were largely characterized by a lack of competition and the general disarray that prevailed in the aftermath of the Oslo Accords. Khaled Meshaal, Hamas's political leader, stated, "We did not participate in the 1996 elections because they emanated from Oslo, a political program that we reject and oppose. . . . As for our stance toward any future elections that will be decided at that time" (Tamimi 2007, 208). As this statement indicates, Hamas showed a willingness to join future elections in order to test its political viability and strength.

The organization continued to gain political support as a result of its *da'wa* efforts. At the same time, it highlighted and capitalized upon the apparent corruption of its Fatah competitors. Leaders within Fatah were perceived as living relatively opulent lives and as involved in numerous forms of moral and financial corruption, including arresting and torturing dissenting Islamists groups and individuals. In stark contrast, Hamas engaged in a variety of civil and societal activities aimed at improving the lives of ordinary Palestinians, and Hamas leaders were perceived as frugal, pious men living ethical lives in accordance with Islamic principles. This dynamic, combined with the failures of Oslo to effect tangible changes in the everyday lives of Palestinians, contributed to the eventual replacement of Fatah as the symbol of Palestinian resistance by Hamas.

In the wake of the Second Intifada, an additional change occurred within Hamas's political philosophy. The failure of Oslo was evident at this point, with little tangible progress in the OPT or the broader Middle East peace processes. Hamas emerged to capitalize on widespread frustration among Palestinians. Its leaders drafted the so-called Change and Reform List in anticipation of the Palestinian elections in 2006. The Change and Reform List consisted of suggested reforms to the PA written in "secular and bureaucratic" language (Hroub 2008, 14). In the document, Hamas leaders offered suggestions for legislative and judicial reform, reduced corruption, and educational and media policy reforms. The list revealed the extent to which the organization had instituted political development efforts and revealed a "politically mature Hamas that has developed concrete suggestions and reforms . . . in various spheres of society" (Schulz 2007, 11).

In January 2006, Hamas emerged victorious in the Palestinian Legislative Council (PLC) elections. It won 74 out of 132 seats, highlighting its degree of political development and efforts to increase its participation in the PA's democratic institutions. Hamas's win can be attributed to several dynamic factors, including the failure of Oslo to effect change in the daily lives of Palestinians, corruption within the Fatah Party, and the death of Yasser Arafat, as well as widespread frustration among Palestinians over economic and sociopolitical stagnation in the OPT. Domestic political dynamics shifted away from Fatah, partly as a result of its dialogue and cooperative efforts with Israel during Oslo and partly as a consequence of economic stagnation and the complete failure of the Middle East peace process. Hamas capitalized on the resulting dynamics to emerge politically as a changed and developed, highly organized grassroots-based political party and movement. Despite its formative declarations condemning formal democratic processes as an implementation of western values, Hamas pragmatically developed politically to participate in the democratic processes of the PA.

In the wake of Hamas's election victory, the Middle East Quartet (the United States, Russia, the European Union, and the United Nations) imposed three conditions on the Hamas government: recognition of Israel's right to exist, acceptance of all previous agreements between the PLO and Israel, and complete cessation of terrorist activities. The newly elected Hamas government refused to comply with these conditions, and international funding to the PA ceased in April 2006. The total loss of international financial support translated to a two-thirds loss of funding for the Hamas-led government.

Hamas was confronted with a politically developmental dilemma at this juncture: to lose financial support or to engage in ideological compromise, which would mean effectively placing itself on on the same shaky political footing as the party it had just defeated. Critics argued that the embargo on international monetary aid wholly contradicted western principles advocating democratic governance. Hamas was elected democratically and international funding in support of democratic development disappeared amid claims that its victory was tantamount to a hijacking of democracy.

It is unsurprising that in the wake of Hamas's victory, Fatah was reluctant to give up the power and influence it had attained over thirteen years of rule. Large-scale violence ensued between the two parties. Clashes between Fatah militia members and Hamas's paramilitary Executive Force took place in January and February, as well as in May and June, of 2007. In 2007, Saudi Arabia attempted to broker a peace agreement between Hamas and Fatah in order to curb the drastically escalating violence in the West Bank and Gaza, as well as to put an end to the international aid embargo. The outcome was a National Unity Government (NUG) encompassing both Hamas and Fatah. Despite the international agreement, tensions with Fatah continued as conditions in the OPT deteriorated. At the end of 2007, amid increasingly violent clashes, the OPT split in two. The Hamas government took control of the territory of the Gaza Strip, and the West Bank came under the administration of Palestinian President Mahmoud Abbas.

The period of 1988 to 2006, culminating in Hamas's electoral success is demonstrative of an incremental process of development in Hamas's political philosophy. Hamas has pursued a policy of dynamic adaptation and strategic pragmatism in light of the emergent opportunity structures created by domestic conditions of violence and instability. The organization is a complex case to categorize in terms of formal international status. It is a nonstate political party operating in the OPT, specifically in Gaza, yet under the administration and occupation of Israel. As such, despite Hamas's political development, its future in the OPT will be determined largely by Israeli foreign policy and the future of the broader Middle East peace process.

The 2006 legislative elections thrust Hamas into the political limelight at the regional and international levels in part, ironically, as a consequence of the Bush Doctrine's active emphasis on democracy in the Middle East. Overwhelmingly, however, Hamas is best known as a terrorist organization. The following section examines the military or terrorist aspects of Hamas.

Violence and Terrorism

Hamas is primarily known as a terrorist organization, one that utilizes alternative forms of violent guerrilla warfare, including suicide martyrs, kidnappings, and structural and/or car bombings. It is known for its use of suicide martyrs in civilian-populated areas, as well as against Israeli military targets. Hamas perceives its violent methods as an in-kind response to the violence used by Israel (Alexander 2002, 12; Levitt 2006, 8) and has repeatedly described its utilization of violence and terrorism as a conscious and strategic choice in response to the overwhelming superiority of Israel's military forces and tactical capabilities, as well as Israel's policy of super-retaliation in response to violence generated in Gaza.

The military branch of Hamas, the Izz al-Din al-Qassam Brigades (IZZ), is a long-standing resistance wing that predates Hamas itself. The organization's namesake and founder, Izz al-Din al-Qassam, began mobilizing forces from as early as the 1930s in response to the immigration of early Jewish settlers to Palestine. Al-Qassam focused on creating separate, distinct cells within the resistance movement in order to delegate responsibility and achieve a loose autonomous structure that would allow for adaptability and deftness. His cells were divided according to responsibility: arms procurement, intelligence gathering, recruitment, training, and so on. Al-Qassam is a highly influential and enduring figure in the formation of Hamas's military structure and activities, and his organizational efforts are evident in the development and current nature of the armed military wing (Chehab 2007, 54–65).

A hotly debated aspect of Hamas's military activities concerns the separation of the IZZ from the 'legitimate' or sociopolitical activities of Hamas. One of the most vocal authorities on the topic is Matthew Levitt. Levitt argues that the Hamas *da'wa* is primarily a façade or mechanism aimed at channeling funds in support of terrorist activities (Levitt 2007). In a variety of publications, Levitt suggests that the "myth of disparate wings" promoted by Hamas has been most effective in deflecting attention away from its terrorist activities toward its more legitimate sociopolitical activities (Levitt 2007, 2). He argues that the prevalence of this perception has allowed the organization to openly conduct fundraising in the form of numerous charities and NGOs based around the Middle East and Europe (Levitt 2007).

Hamas has benefited immeasurably from spillover legitimacy derived from its wide variety of activities. Its multifaceted development approach translates legitimacy across the broad spectrum of its activities, social to political, military to political, social to military, and so on. Logically, it is safe to assume that Hamas allocates funds at its own discretion. However, the nature and allocation of funds from Hamas supporters, particularly state supporters such as Iran, is known only to the upper echelons of the organization, although the breadth of Hamas's activities would indicate that funds are dispersed to all three of its spheres of activity: political, social, and 'military,' meaning its terrorist acitivies (Levitt 2007, 2). It is important to note that Hamas demonstrated its ability to translate support and legitimacy from one realm to another. The pragmatism behind such a multifaceted developmental strategy must also be acknowledged. Via the "myth of disparate wings," Hamas can continue military or terrorist activities that ensure continued loyalty from its more radical fundamentalist Islamist supporters, while simultaneously engaging in legitimate activities (social and political) that are typically reserved for the state.

A key element in Hamas's continued resonance in the OPT, particularly the Gaza Strip, has been its use of underground tunnels. The tunnels are vital to maintaining Hamas's social, political, and 'military' activities, yet are often cited as being primarily a mechanism for facilitating the transportation of arms and fighters in support of IZZ activities. The tunnel networks used by Hamas run in criss-cross fashion beneath the Egyptian border and throughout Gaza, via a stretch of territory increasingly known as the "Philadelphia corridor" (Sengupta 2009). The development of the underground tunnel network is testimony to the deft and adaptable nature of the IZZ, undoubtedly a result of formative and recurrent conditions of violence and instability characterized by material shortages. Hamas's tunnels are used to transport everything from "rockets to cattle" and provide the "economic life blood" of the OPT in light of border restrictions, supply embargos, and economic sanctions (Sengupta 2009). Numerous sources indicate that the tunnels are used to transport segments of Hamas's estimated force of twenty thousand fighters to training outposts in Iran and Lebanon. Hamas has developed a logistical mechanism that temporarily bypasses Israeli security borders and checkpoints, allowing the organization to receive supplies and arms despite conditions of warfare, violence, and instability (Sengupta 2009). The tunnel network allows the provision of material resources necessary for the maintenance of the Hamas *da'wa*, and simultaneously facilitates the continuance of the violent activities of the IZZ.

The efficacy of the Hamas tunnels was a primary contributing factor to the continuation of Israel–Hamas violence in 2008–2009. Israel engaged in another round of violent conflict with Hamas in the OPT that resulted in widespread infrastructural damage and massive civilian casualities. The conflict began in December 2008, with Israel employing air and ground forces. Israel justified the attack by arguing that Hamas's rocket launching and arms smuggling were detrimental to Israeli security. The IDF used its most aggressive tactics, leaving high numbers of Palestinian casualties.

A large portion of the international community called for an end to the attacks, which culminated in the cessation of hostilities on 18 January 2009, followed by unilateral ceasefires and the eventual withdrawal of Israeli forces from Gaza on 23 January 2009.

As the longitudinal analysis in this chapter has shown, the development of Hamas is largely the result of dynamic adaptation and strategic pragmatism in light of emergent opportunity structures. The inception and longitudinal development of Hamas were determined by the actions and policies of Israel and the Arab sympathies that followed. By building upon the civic fundamentals of the Muslim Brotherhood, Hamas has developed in light of cyclical violence to maintain a network of social services in an effort to build a small degree of infrastructure.

By nature of the territory and people it represents, Hamas is increasingly gaining recognition as a symbol of Palestinian nationalism. As a result of the Israel–Hamas war of 2008, regional and international attitudes toward Hamas are changing. Israeli polices of super-retaliation in response to Hamas violence, and the ensuing disproportionate number of casualties, have produced an increased awareness of Hamas as a political entity. Gradually, regional and international perceptions of the organization are shifting among states and international institutions, partly also as a result of the humanitarian crisis in the Gaza Strip, which is multiplying calls for dialogue with Hamas.

This chapter has thus far analyzed the transformation and development of Hamas in the social, political, and military realms. Hamas has displayed a high degree of organizational learning in developing and changing in a multifaceted manner to effect change in its territories while simultaneously entrenching itself in numerous realms of Palestinian life. In an effort to provide an effective comparison to Hamas, the social, political, and military aspects of Hezbollah are examined in the following section.

Hezbollah

Hezbollah emerged in Lebanon in 1987 out of the radicalized segments of Lebanon's Amal movement, in response to Israel's 1982 invasion of southern Lebanon. Members of Amal who broke off and formed Hezbollah, particularly the charismatic Hussein al-Musawi, felt that the Israeli incursions into Lebanese territory necessitated more radicalized resistance efforts. In a country rife with sectarian conflict, against the backdrop of Israel's "buffer zone" and the shifting alliances of the Lebanese Civil War, Hezbollah emerged in an effort to represent marginalized Shi'i Muslims suffering from the consequences of broad demographic shifts and uneven development in southern Lebanon.

Today, Hezbollah operates in Lebanon within the framework of the Lebanese government. It wields considerable influence, participating aggressively in the formal structures and institutions of the state as a political party, as well as outside the state's structures, domestically and regionally, as a nonstate actor with its own, independent military capability. The following sections highlight change and development within the organizational structure and activities of Hezbollah, using historical narrative to explore the longitudinal development of the organization in Lebanon.

Social Development

Hezbollah maintains a network of social welfare services in Lebanon. Jihad al-Bina is an umbrella organization encompassing numerous sub-committees and organizations engaged in a variety of activities aimed at infrastructural development in areas of southern Lebanon. Initially, Jihad al-Bina sought to facilitate reconstruction amid the devastation of the sixteen-year Lebanese Civil War. Often referred to as the Relief Committee or Reconstruction Campaign (RC), Jihad al-Bina administers and funds a variety of social welfare and charitable activities, displaying a high degree of institutional development, to the extent that in the Dahiyeh district, a primarily Shi'i suburb of southern Lebanon, the infrastructural and social welfare capabilities of Hezbollah often rival those of the Lebanese state (Hamzeh 2004, 71–79).

Jihad al-Bina encompasses numerous organizations devoted to improving medical services. For example, al-Rasul al-A'dham Hospital/Mosque Complex provides medical services in Dahiyeh. Jihad al-Bina also administers and funds primary, secondary, and vocational schools and participating in financial sectors, administering micro-loans aimed at increasing agricultural development in regions devastated by the civil war (Harik 2004, 83–87).

The Martyrs Foundation, or al-Shahid, is a controversial component of Hezbollah's social service network. Al-Shahid cares for the families of suicide martyrs. Educational, medical, and living expenses for those left behind are taken care of by al-Shahid. This aspect of Hezbollah's social network is often cited as evidence of the ominous intent, terrorist nature, and general illegitimacy of Hezbollah's social welfare activities, as the services performed for the families of suicide martyrs create a cyclical dynamic, perpetuating the creation of future suicide martyrs via the children and loved ones of past suicide martyrs (Mounayer 2001).

Controversial elements aside, the legitimate social welfare and charitable activities of Jihad al-Bina broaden Hezbollah's influence by improving infrastructural development among Shi'i Muslims in southern Lebanon. Through these activities Hezbollah capitalizes upon opportunity structures created by the failings of the state. Hezbollah developed its social welfare networks in an effort to demonstrate its developmental and governing capabilities by assuming roles and activities typically reserved as for the state.

This development and maintenance of Hezbollah's activities in the societal realm has resulted in a spillover effect, a translated legitimacy in the realm of politics. Historically and today, Hezbollah is a distinct actor in the Lebanese political scene, one that occupies a larger and more influential role than that of a traditional political party or social movement.

Political Philosophy

Hezbollah's political philosophy is the result of gradual change. At its inception, Hezbollah denounced the decrepit character of the Lebanese confessional system, but gradually it has engaged in a process of change and development that serves as an indication of the entrenched nature, resonance, and future political trajectory of the organization.

Hezbollah's political manifesto, an "Open Letter to the Downtrodden of Lebanon and the World," released in 1985, highlights Hezbollah's early perceptions of the Lebanese political system. The document argues that "the existing political system and its sectarian privileges are the cause of Lebanon's problems" and should be changed "from the roots" (Shanahan 2005, 115). Influenced by the ideological teachings of the charismatic Imam Musa al-Sadr, Hezbollah sought initially to establish an Islamic theocracy in Lebanon modeled on Khomeini's Iranian revolution. Gradually, leaders within Hezbollah realized that this was impossible considering Lebanon's heterogeneous demographic makeup. At this early stage, Hezbollah began the process of dynamic adaptation, recognizing that change and development were politically necessary in order for it to maintain relevance in Lebanon.

In 1989, the domestic political environment in the country shifted with the establishment of the Ta'if Accord, which reestablished a Lebanese parliament in the wake of the chaos and instability of the Lebanese Civil War. Hezbollah initially rejected Ta'if because, under the Lebanese confessional system, it apportioned an equal number of parliamentary seats to Christian and Muslim sects yet barred its Shiʻi constituency from the offices of president and prime minister. However, when Syria invaded east Beirut and ousted interim Prime Minister Michel Aoun in October 1990, "effectively eliminating the last remnants of opposition to Syrian authority," Hezbollah realized the necessity of changing its political position and strategy in order to contend with shifting domestic realities in Lebanon (Gambill 2003).

In the wake of the Ta'if Accord, Hezbollah went through a phase of political development. Its leaders were divided over the future political trajectory of the organization. Considering prior denunciations from Hezbollah leaders of the "decrepit nature" of the Lebanese political system, the organization's leaders argued that formal political participation would contradict Hezbollah's ethos of resistance. Eventually the pragmatism of the late Sheikh Muhammad Hassan Fadlallah, a charismatic cleric within Hezbollah's leadership, prevailed. Fadlallah argued that Lebanon's domestic political environment was changing rapidly amid competing alliances and interests. If Hezbollah desired to maintain relevance within the Lebanese political landscape, its political philosophy needed to develop in order to compete within the existing structure of Lebanese parliament. This would necessitate an ontological shift of focus from violent resistance to "alliance-making, constituent representation and all other activism common to political parties in a parliamentary system" (Shanahan 2005, 118).

Hezbollah's participation in the 1992 parliamentary elections in Lebanon represented a strategic shift within the organization. Parallel to its increased political participation and development, Hezbollah displayed a reluctance to engage in guerrilla tactics—particularly kidnappings—that had successfully attracted attention in the past (Mannes 2008, 40). The organization continued its course of political development by participating in the 1996 Lebanese parliamentary elections. A shift occurred in the standard by which Hezbollah's political candidates were selected in an effort to obtain "new faces to represent the party's desire to cultivate a broader more moderate support base in Lebanon" (Ali 2009). Its leaders selected political candidates who were among the ranks of the educated or business classes, contrary to the prior selection of military or religious leaders as candidates. The change in election candidates is demonstrative of Hezbollah's attempt to change external perceptions of its nature and activities.

In the interim, between the 1996 and 2000 parliamentary elections, Hezbollah released a statement outlining its ideological paradigm and political philosophies. Its "Views and Concepts," released in June 1997, set a cautious yet diplomatic tone. The document outlined Hezbollah's political positions and put forth suggestions for reform. The language and tone of the document reflected Hezbollah's attempts to portray itself as a more mature and pragmatic organization capable of operating in the broader regional and international environment (Alagha 2006, 225).

In an effort to contend with changing domestic conditions, Hezbollah further developed its political strategy in the wake of Israel's 2000 withdrawal, justifying a decline in military activities with the 2000 "victory," and focusing primarily on sociopolitical goals. In 2000, an Amal–Hezbollah alliance, the Resistance and Development Bloc, won twenty-three seats in southern Lebanon and more than a quarter of all seats in parliament (Norton 2007a, 7–8).

The context and outcome of the 2005 Lebanese parliamentary elections served as an indication of the wider role Hezbollah envisioned for itself in Lebanon. These elections were the first elections in thirty years that were independent and free from Syrian or Israeli influence (El-Hokayem 2007, 35). Hezbollah and its allies again won all twenty-three seats in southern Lebanon, gaining two ministerial seats in the new government led by Prime Minister Fouad Siniora (Norton 2007b, 483).

Since 2005, Hezbollah has developed into a major power player on the Lebanese political scene and solidified its distinct role in Lebanese politics. The events of July–August 2006 (addressed in the next section) attest to this influence, regionally as well as internationally. Hezbollah has continued its multifaceted course of political development, steadily increasing its influence by way of participation within the processes and institutions of the Lebanese government.

In 2009, the domestic political character of Lebanon shifted once again. Hezbollah actively participated in the Lebanese parliamentary elections as part of the March 8th Alliance. Its leaders continued to cultivate an appearance of moderation and development, evident from Hezbollah's selection of electoral candidates, including: Nawwaf Mussawi, Hussein Mussawi, and

Dr. Ali Fayyad (Assi 2009). The 2009 candidates, all educated business professionals in addition to long-term Hezbollah supporters, is demonstrative of Hezbollah's desire to cultivate an appearance of moderation and viability as a long-term political actor in Lebanon.

The 2009 election culminated with the March 14th Alliance winning seventy-one seats in the Lebanese parliament.[3] Ironically, the March 14th Alliance won a parliamentary majority yet lost the popular vote (Muhanna 2009). The June 2009 parliamentary elections engendered relief from pro-western supporters of the March 14th Alliance, who feared that Hezbollah's victory might destabilize Lebanon's domestic political scene, as well as mobilize Hezbollah's allies, Iran and Syria, potentially causing regional destabilization. In the wake of its electoral loss, Hezbollah's primary political objective in Lebanon was the retention of its third veto power. Hezbollah attained the veto power via the Doha Agreement, an accord that arose largely as a response to Hezbollah's attacks and riots in Beirut during the summer of 2008. Since taking power, Saad Hariri has opposed Hezbollah's retention of the veto power, claiming it was a temporary provision under the terms of the Doha Agreement. Hezbollah desires a continuance of veto power in order to avoid any restrictions on its independent retention of arms.

Much domestic and regional attention concerns Hezbollah's retention of independent arms capability, an issue that will largely determine its future in Lebanon. A variety of regional and international entities have called for the disarmament of Hezbollah. The Israeli prime minister, Benjamin Netanyahu, recently expressed caution over Hezbollah's role in Lebanon, stating that Hezbollah's disarmament was crucial to Lebanon's future and vowing a harsher Israeli response to Hezbollah attacks. Netanyahu cautioned that the Lebanese government would be held accountable for any violence stemming from Hezbollah. Hezbollah's future development and political trajectory will largely be determined by the degree to which Lebanese forces press the issue of disarmament, which remains to be seen. Hezbollah's perspective is clear from its aggressive stockpiling of arms and fighters; as such it has not displayed any willingness to voluntarily disarm (Ali 2009).

The previous sections have analyzed the usually overlooked social and political aspects of Hezbollah's activities. Hezbollah's political philosophy is the result of incremental change and development. The organization emerged amid the shifting alliances and general chaos of the Lebanese

Civil War. In response to shifting Israeli security policies and in consideration of the widespread devastation of the war, Hezbollah developed in a multifaceted manner, while emphasizing infrastructural and sociopolitical development. Hezbollah's longitudinal development of a political philosophy malleable enough to capitalize on emergent opportunity structures in Lebanon's political and social landscape serves as evidence of this point.

Hezbollah also actively and aggressively engages in violent resistance against Israel. Since its inception, it has used violence as a means of political negotiation and a mechanism with which to address past grievances. The following section will examine Hezbollah's use of violence, terrorism and military activities.

Violence and Terrorism

Hezbollah has historically displayed a willingness to use violence to achieve its goals. It is primarily known as a 'terrorist group' as a result of its use of violence aimed at maximizing Israeli casualties, civilian or military. Hezbollah utilizes suicide bombers, hijacking, and kidnappings. A notable example is the bombing of the Beirut Marine barracks in 1983.

Hezbollah has developed 'military' structures and strategies that effectively maneuver around the overwhelming strength and firepower of the IDF. It has accumulated a weapons stock that consists of an estimated ten to thirteen thousand small- to mid-range Katyusha rockets. These small and highly portable weapons can fire from virtually any building or ground position (Cordesman and Sullivan 2007). This allows Hezbollah fighters to move deftly along the Lebanese border, firing on land into Israeli border towns or on targets at sea, including Israeli defense carriers. These tactics are often cited as elements of Hezbollah's effectiveness in July 2006 amid intense retaliatory strikes from Israel.

Hezbollah has developed an organizational structure that complements its weapons stock, emphasizing small, mobile fighting units. Its military and security apparatus consists of two organs: the Islamic Resistance and Party Security. The Islamic Resistance is comprised of the Enforcement and Recruitment and the Combat sections. The Enforcement and Recruitment section provides recruited fighters with an ideological indoctrination that reinforces party beliefs *(wilayat al-faqih)*. The Combat section consists of four organs that collectively provide training, medical support, and weaponry. These units are self-contained and semiautonomous. Organizationally and administratively speaking, the military units of Hezbollah communicate through "sector command" that is under the supervision of "region command" (Hamzeh 2004, 113–17). Andrew McGregor has explored the tactical advantage of Hezbollah's adaptive and loose organizational structure, noting, "The top-down command structure that inhibited initiative in junior ranks has been reversed. Hezbollah operates with a decentralized command structure that allows for rapid response to any situation by encouraging initiative and avoiding the need to consult with leaders in Beirut" (McGregor 2006, 3).

Hezbollah's military units have the ability to act independently should opportunity or circumstance arise. Hezbollah's tactics have developed to emphasize the movement of small groups of fighters and to increase deftness and deniability in the case of potential capture, as individual units are not apprised of the details of other units (Hamzeh 2004, 113–17).

The efficacy of Hezbollah's military approach was tested in July 2006, when Israel launched retaliatory attacks against Hezbollah in response to an assault that killed five out of seven IDF soldiers who were patrolling the Lebanon–Israel border and led to the capture of the remaining two soldiers. Five more IDF soldiers were killed in a failed Israeli rescue attempt. Israel responded, beginning thirty-four days of fighting, including air and ground incursions into southern Lebanon. Israel held the Lebanese government firmly responsible and accused Hezbollah of continuing hostilities, launching rockets into Israeli border territories, and displacing large segments of the Israeli population. The Lebanese government emphatically condemned the actions of Hezbollah and denounced the Israeli retaliation. The international community called for a ceasefire and the UN Security Council approved Resolution 1701 in an effort to end the hostilities. The resolution included provisions for Israeli withdrawal as well as for Hezbollah's disarmament (Warschawski and Achcar 2006, 61–62).

Considering its proportionally fewer tactical capabilities compared to Israel, Hezbollah's performance in its thirty-four days of conflict with Israel was surprising. Hezbollah's fighters amounted to several thousand against Israel, a major military power. Corey Oakley describes the situation well:

> Israel, the fifth most-powerful military on earth, was fought to a standstill by several thousand well-armed, well-organized fighters. . . . The very fact that Hezbollah survived with its fighting forces intact was a huge victory. Israel's position in the region, the fear it inspires in the

Arab world, is predicated on the presumption that in the final analysis it is futile to take Israel on militarily. (Oakley 2007)

By 2006, Hezbollah had developed military organizational structures and tactics that capitalized on Israeli weaknesses in an effort to contend with Israel's relative tactical advantages. By holding its own against Israel in the so-called July War, Hezbollah demonstrated its "capacity to shake the Lebanese political landscape" (El-Hokayem 2007, 35) and solidified its status as a special and distinct actor in Lebanon.

On the regional and international levels, Hezbollah has proven itself an effective military fighting force. This fact has broad implications for international security arrangements and the wider international environment, which has traditionally focused on state-on-state conflict. The Israel-versus-Hezbollah-in-Lebanon dynamic points to a shift in international security paradigms: a NSA undertaking a major military offensive against a regional power without the sanction of the domestic state within which it resides. Such a conceptual and categorical shift has far-reaching implications for traditional international relations conceptions of power and authority.

This chapter has offered an assessment of the change and development in Hamas and Hezbollah by examining the social, political, and military aspects of these two organizations. It is evident from the longitudinal analysis that change and development instituted by these organizations are the result of dynamic adaptation and strategic pragmatism in accordance with emerging opportunity structures for sociopolitical activity following the violent establishment of the state of Israel in 1948 and the 1967 Arab military defeat.

The rising influence of Hamas can be interpreted as evidence of a spillover or 'multiplier' effect of these events. Hamas capitalized on the declining credibility of the PLO and its Fatah backbone. It emerged to fill the opportunity structure for social and political activity, employing a multifaceted developmental strategy in order to maximize presence, influence, and entrenchment. Hezbollah emerged in a similar context amid the violence and instability of the Lebanese Civil War. In terms of future change and development within these organizations, Hezbollah has become increasingly integrated into the Lebanese political scene. In the case of Hamas, its future course of development is hard to predict, given the cycles of conflict and widespread socioeconomic deprivation within the OPT. The issue of statehood is the primary difference separating these two NSAs and addressed in the following section, which compares the longitudinal development of Hamas and Hezbollah.

A Comparison

Hamas and Hezbollah have undergone a gradual process of change as evinced by the longitudinal development within their social, political, and military structures and activities. In an effort to make a comparative assessment of the degree of change and development within the two organizations, several similarities need to be addressed, as well one distinct difference.

Hamas and Hezbollah have both benefited from the maintenance of social networks and their provision of social welfare and charitable services. The manner of this development is demonstrative of the high degree of connectivity they enjoy in their respective territories. Amid the violence and instability that is largely characteristic of the OPT (cyclically) and Lebanon (particularly during the Lebanese Civil War), Hamas and Hezbollah are increasingly developing to moderate and shift the focus away from their long-term ideological goals in order to pursue small-scale and medium-term sociopolitical objectives and build a degree of infrastructure in their territories. They tend to combine the material provision of resources with the religious principles and ideological elements that they espouse. The result is a highly cogent and effective mix of tangible provision of material necessities and religious, spiritual, ideological guidance. Hamas and Hezbollah appeal to their followers ideologically, by nature of their religious ideology and violent resistance, as well as materially, by nature of their social welfare networks. The Hamas *da'wa* and Hezbollah's Jihad al-Bina have contributed to their efficacy, entrenchment, and resonance, and the impact of this dual dynamic of 'charity and rockets' cannot be underestimated in understanding the efficacy and legitimacy of the organizations, as well as their longitudinal development and future trajectory.

Hamas and Hezbollah employ political philosophies that are the result of gradual incremental development juxtaposed against the violence, instability, and chaos that is largely characteristic of their territories. Domestic conditions of violence and instability created opportunity structures for political activity. Hamas and Hezbollah initially rejected the mechanisms or established institutions of the state or central political authority, but moderated their stance over time for the sake of political or diplomatic advantage or in the face of shifting domestic, and often regional, conditions of violence and instability. Steadily and in an incremental manner, Hamas and Hezbollah have developed politically in an effort to maintain influence and increased participation in the established political institutions, mechanisms, and processes that surround them.

Both organizations display a stark contrast between ideologically oriented Islamist rhetoric and pragmatic political behavior. Hamas and Hezbollah have both displayed a tendency to moderate the more militantly Islamist aspects of their discourse when doing so could prove politically beneficial. Augustus Richard Norton, an expert on Hezbollah, echoes this point: "Politics are dynamic and contingent, . . . political constraints and opportunities are the desiderata of political behavior and ideology takes a back seat" (Norton 2007a, 39). Both Hamas and Hezbollah have continually demonstrated an ability to amend and moderate previous positions or statements in order to gain increased access to domestic political institutions and wield greater power, influence, and legitimacy within domestic activities.

The development and transformation of Hamas and Hezbollah, as evinced by broadened and increased participation in democratic methods and political processes, has prompted debate as to the validity and applicability of foundational charters to the contemporary character of the two organizations. This point is notable considering that the foundational documents of these organizations are often cited as evidence of their singularly terrorist nature for their inflammatory language, their fanatical religious content, and their abolitionist policies toward Israel. Some argue that Islamist organizations such as Hamas and Hezbollah have, developmentally and longitudinally, made considerable strides away from their foundational charters.

This analysis has demonstrated that the use of violence is simultaneously the hallmark, savior, and doom for Hamas and Hezbollah. Their commitment to violent resistance against Israel has produced conflicting and cyclical results. In one respect, the high-profile violence utilized by the groups has increased domestic, regional, and international awareness of their motivations and goals. Hamas's and Hezbollah's commitment to violent resistance against Israel, as well as their refusal to engage in the platitudes of the Middle East peace process, has awarded them a large measure of credibility, contrary to the perceived acquiescence of the so-called moderate Arab states. In another respect, Hamas's and Hezbollah's commitment to violent resistance has resulted in continued degenerative cycles of violence and instability in their respective territories. Israel is known for its policy of super-retaliation to violence or terrorism generated by either Hamas or Hezbollah (one need not look further than the 2006 Israel–Hezbollah and the 2008 Israel–Hamas conflicts as evidence of this assertion). For every rocket or kidnapping Hamas and Hezbollah carry out, the retaliatory violence and in-kind response from Israel acts as a hindrance to these organizations' ability to gain greater access to mainstream political processes, institutions, and mechanisms at the domestic, regional, and international levels.

Toward Increased Radicalization or Deradicalization?

In comparing change and development within Hamas and Hezbollah, it is necessary to highlight previous observations made in this book about armed Islamist movements. In Chapter 6, Omar Ashour explores the processes of transformation within two armed Islamic movements, the Islamic Group in Egypt and al-Jihad in Algeria. He highlights the mechanisms and dynamics that can potentially facilitate a process of deradicalization within such armed Islamic groups "who have long glorified armed struggle." Ashour observes within his case studies a longitudinal process initiated by radicalization, followed by deradicalization and eventual moderation. He argues that this process of change and transformation is framed by the dynamic interaction of several variables including, charismatic leadership, state repression, organizational/selective inducement, and interaction with the 'other,' or non-Islamist entities. The combination of these variables can potentially lead to deradicalization and the eventual adoption of nonviolent tactics. It leads to change and development within Islamist groups, embodied by observed processes of strategic consideration, political learning, and strict cost-benefit analysis. Ashour also highlights the role of perceptional and psychological factors that can lead to change, development, and transformation within armed Islamist groups as a result of "severe crisis and frustration" (see chapter by Ashour in this volume).

Ashour's observations have validity for and bearing upon the present analysis. Longitudinal change and development within Hamas and Hezbollah can effectively be characterized and measured using Ashour's variables. For example, the importance of charismatic leadership as a facilitator and measure of change can be applied to Hamas and Hezbollah, as shown by the significant impact of such formative leaders as Sheikh Ahmed Yassin and Imam Musa al-Sadr, followed by more contemporary leaders such as Hassan Nasrallah and Khaled Meshaal, in shaping the manner of development of the structures and activities of the two organizations.

State repression as a mechanism for deradicalization, change, and development can also be applied to the cases of Hamas and Hezbollah. Israel has repeatedly displayed its repressive foreign policy role in Lebanon, as evinced by the unilateral establishment of the security buffer zone. The Lebanese government, historically and today, has employed caution in negotiating with Hezbollah considering the latter's independent arms capability and its extensive social welfare networks, which foster extensive loyalty among Shi'i Lebanese in the south. Lebanese leaders would undoubtedly like to exert more control over Hezbollah, yet, considering the precarious peace that characterizes the domestic Lebanese political scene, they are unable to do so. The role of state repression is more overt in the case of Hamas. Hamas still operates in the OPT, and more particularly, the Gaza Strip, but Israel still very much determines the territorial borders, security policies, taxation measures, and administration of the OPT.

Ashour focuses particularly on the role of social interaction as a mechanism for change and development. In the cases of Hamas and Hezbollah, social interaction serves as a mechanism for moderation and development, not necessarily as a facilitator of deradicalization or disarmament. The social activities of these organizations in the realm of civil society entrench these organizations in their respective territories. This entrenchment leads to translatable legitimacy and influence in the political realm. By the nature of politics, increased political participation would necessitate moderation of inflammatory ideological and religious elements in order to increase political viability. Whether such moderation leads to deradicalization or disarmament (that is, a willingness to lay down arms) is highly debatable and certainly does not reflect the cases of Hamas and Hezbollah, as both have demonstrated a commitment to violence and terrorism simultaneous to political engagement. In terms of social interaction, it is unlikely that the social wings of these organizations—the Hamas *da'wa* and Hezbollah's Jihad al-Bina—will lead to deradicalization or disarmament. In fact, several of the social and educational activites of these organizations serve to facilitate the continuance of radical Islamist elements, Hezbollah's maintenance of al-Shadid for families of suicide martyrs serving as a case in point (Mounayer 2001).

This chapter's comparative and longitudinal analysis has demonstrated that though manifestly ideologically oriented, both Hamas and Hezbollah have demonstrated an ability to engage in dialogue, prisoner exchanges, and ceasefires whenever absolutely necessary or advantageous. However, moderate elements of progress have recurrently and overwhelmingly been negated by cyclical violence and the refusal of these organizations to give up independent arms and military capabilities.

Hamas and Hezbollah display numerous similarities. Yet it must be noted that the key difference in statehood status fundamentally alters the legitimacy and development of these organizations, as well as their future political trajectory and potential. Hezbollah, to a degree, is considered an example of moderation and development as a consequence of increased political participation. Despite mainstream perceptions of its so-called terrorist nature, academic literature does recognize the longitudinal evolution of Hezbollah. Hezbollah has developed away from its more militant Islamist ideological orientations and goals toward increased integration in the Lebanese state and growing entrenchment of its sociopolitical activity. Comparatively speaking, the obvious distinction in statehood status will forever reflect the political trajectory of Hamas as compared to Hezbollah. This point obviously relates to the status of the OPT as 'occupied,' not to mention Israeli control of borders and supply flows. Considering the present stagnation of the Middle East peace process, it would appear that Hamas's continued development will depend on Israeli foreign policy, which by all accounts favors the leadership of Fatah under Mahmoud Abbas in the OPT.

Conclusion

In line with the broad theme of the changing Middle East, this chapter has examined the rise of two nonstate actors, Hamas and Hezbollah, and the degree of development in their social, political, and military structures and activities. Both movements have undergone a process of change in respect to their organizational structures and activities, in response to emergent opportunity structures created by domestic and regional conditions of violence and instability.

Hamas and Hezbollah are continuing to gain legitimacy and authority within their respective territories, as well as in the Middle East generally. This is a consequence of their multifaceted development, which encompasses a wide range of activities, social, political, and military. By developing activities typically reserved for states, Hamas and Hezbollah have inserted themselves as on par or in competition with traditional state actors, with numerous implications for studies of international relations. The organizations are a clear reflection of the changing Middle East. Both are at a pivotal juncture in their development, trying to reconcile highly formative pasts with future potential. Hamas and Hezbollah have changed to the extent that they are currently navigating uncharted territory in terms of governance, occupying a sphere in which they are neither integrated into nor completely detached from the mechanisms and institutions of traditional state governance. Whether these organizations can make the final transition to solely legitimate political actors in the highly dynamic and transforming Middle East is altogether another question.

Notes

1   Throughout this essay, I refer to Hamas's and Hezbollah's use of violence and terrorism, in addition to their military incursions. I address my thoughts on the term 'terrorism' early on in the chapter, but it is worth noting that all tree terms are intended to denote the general use of force and violence by these NSAs, whether this takes the form of small- to medium-scale suicide bombs, rockets, or tactical ground incursions and organized urban warfare. The scope, variety, and methods in which Hamas and Hezbollah use violence has been debated. As such, several terms are used to describe their use of violence and force. It should also be noted that the distinction in statehood status also complicates the terminology used to describe the use of force and violence by these actors. The OPT is not considered a state and Hezbollah functions within the Lebanese state. As such, I dispense with the distinctions and refer throughout the chapter to Hamas's and Hezbollah's organized use of violence with the terms 'military' or 'terrorist activities.'

2   The term 'opportunity structures' in this context denotes the creation of spaces for new forms of social and political interaction and activity. Opportunity structures frame the dynamic interaction of structure, agency, and timing, and contribute to the formation of collective action, social movements, and organizational learning. Opportunity structures emerge when "fixed or permanent institutional features combine with more short-term, volatile, or conjectural factors to produce an overall particular opportunity structure" (Yavuz 2003, ix–5). See also the collected works of David Meyer, who has written extensively on the subject.

3   The March 14th Alliance is a large political bloc in Lebanon. It is composed of the Future Movement, the Progressive Socialist Party, and the Kata'ib Party. The bloc is named after a 2005 anti-Syrian demonstration in Beirut that came

shortly after the assassination of Prime Minister Rafiq Hariri. Presently, March 14th is primarily in competition with the March 8th Alliance, consisting of Amal, Hezbollah, and the Free Patriotic Movement led by Michel Aoun. For a succinct summary of the 2009 Lebanese parliamentary election, see Amiri 2009.

8

The Challenge of Change and the Necessity of Social Engineering

Bahgat Korany

On the face of it, the Arab region may appear stagnant. After all, political leadership at the top does not change very much. President Bashir of Sudan has been in power for twenty-one years, Tunisia's Zein al-Abdine Ben Ali for twenty-three years, Egypt's Hosni Mubarak for twenty-nine years, and the revolutionary Muammar Qadhafi celebrated his fortieth anniversary in power in Libya in 2009. When Syrian President Hafez al-Asad died after more than thirty years in power, in 2000, his son Bashar succeeded him. To describe this phenomenon of longevity in so many republican regimes, many Arab analysts are using the term *gumlaka,* a combination of *gumhuriya* (republic) and *mamlaka* (kingdom).

But the appearance of continuity at the top of the political pyramid should not hide the incremental, cumulative changes beneath, which the various chapters in this book have delineated. In Chapter 1, I concentrated on developing an alternative conceptual lens and backed it empirically with descriptions of some macro-level 'big bangs' and incremental processes leading to regional restructuring. These changes can also be reflected at the micro, even individual, level. Our personal day-to-day experiences serve to emphasize how persistent, continuous, and vibrant the process of change is. Like many of my colleagues who travel back and forth to the region, I recall that as recently as 1990, to keep track of what was happening, I would be glued from abroad to CNN,

197

the BBC, or short-wave transmitters, such as Radio Monte Carlo, particularly during times of crisis or other big bangs in the region. Now, no matter how geographically distant I am, I consult standard native sources, such as Al Jazeera or Al Arabiya, *al-Nahar* or *al-Ahram* newspapers, and blogs and other Internet sources. Similarly, as Amani Kandil mentions in her chapter, I witnessed in 1983 when Arab human rights activists and academics establishing their first organization could not find an Arab capital to host their meeting and were forced to meet in Cyprus. At present, quantitatively at least, there are 87 such organizations in Egypt and 160 in Morocco.

Although the issue areas they deal with are various and their approaches and bibliographical sources different, all the contributors to this book converge on the identification of change/transformation in the Middle East. Rasha Abdulla, for instance, goes beyond my limited use of 'revolution' in its traditional political sense to identify a revolution of a different genre, in the Arab media sector at large, which acted as both a reflection and a trigger of change. Other chapters, too, not only emphasize change but also point to different degrees and types of change. Ola AbouZeid, for example, points to advances in the status of women in areas such as education, health, and even economic participation, but indicates that far fewer have occurred in political participation and certain aspects of popular culture. Similarly, Julie Herrick looks to the future at the end of her chapter by speculating as to whether deradicalization in Algerian and Egyptian Islamist groups, as analyzd by Omar Ashour, could be replicated in the cases of Hamas or Hezbollah. Amani Kandil, Hazem Kandil and my analyses are equally differentiating and dynamic in tracing the evolution of various civil society groups and their 'generations,' that is, the different clusters of Arab intellectuals/transformations of political thought, or the different patterns of regional order and their pan-Arab or state-centered bases. It is thus undeniable that the region has been going through a process of deep transformation, a process that may at times be blunted or diverted, such as during the short Arab 'Spring of democratization' in 2002–2005, but which will certainly continue (Korany et al. 1998; Ottaway et al. 2009; Salame 1994). In fact, part of the policy-making problem in the Arab world is the discrepancy between overtly imposed political stability and covertly determining change, between an aging leadership and a youthful population, between social transformation and a lack of political transition. We can call this discrepancy 'the volcano underneath.' Even topics that were not directly analyzed in this book demonstrate the discrepancy.

Demographic patterns and their repercussions, for example, attest to creeping change. If medical advances have had any positive impact on the lamentable state of healthcare in the region, it has been in reducing the mortality rate. The birth rate remains high, region-wide. As the 2009 *Arab Human Development Report* puts it:

> For most of the latter half of the 20th century, population growth rates in the Arab countries were among the highest rates in the world. For the period 2005–2010, the population of the Arab region is projected to grow by 2.00 percent per year, and over 2010–2015, the projection is 1.90 percent per year. This is nearly double the world average for those periods—1.20 percent and 1.10 percent respectively (UNDP 2009, 34–35).

As a result, the Arab world's population grew from 172 million in 1980 to 331 million a quarter of a century later, and is expected to reach 385 million by 2015. Without an equivalent development of basic resources and infrastructure, the population–resource gap will widen and the demographic bomb could have catastrophic effects.

The problem of increasing water scarcity could drive the point home. As the majority of Arab countries are in arid or semiarid regions, they count mostly on rivers for their water supplies, but 57 percent of these rivers originate outside the Arab world. As the needs of various riparian countries are increasing, water stress is rising. Intense competition could degenerate into water wars. Even in the absence of such a worst-case scenario, water scarcity is leading to bad urbanization, increasing desertification, and greater dependency on food imports. In 2005, fourteen Arab countries relied on food imports to an extent greater than the world average (UNDP 2009, 13).

It is not only overall population growth that has to be emphasized, but also age distribution. Almost two-thirds of the population of the Arab world is now under thirty years old—the so-called youth bulge. They are part of the dependent group in the age pyramid, in need of schools and good nutrition, and finally, jobs. In fact, data from the International Labor Organization for 2005–2006 shows that the overall unemployment rate for the Arab countries is more than double the world average: 14.4 percent compared to 6.3 percent. The rate among youth is even more worrying, even in some oil-producing countries. Thus the youth unemployment rate is 17 percent in Qatar, 20 percent in Oman, 21 percent in Bahrain, 23 percent in Kuwait, 26 percent in Saudi Arabia, 27 percent in Libya, and as high as 46 percent in Algeria. It is estimated that Arab countries will need about 51 million new jobs by 2020 (Arab Human Development Report 2009, 108–109). Depending on the policies pursued, the growing number of young people could be an asset or a liability, or even a time bomb given their potential recruitability into extremist organizations.

Youth and technology have been at the basis of another major societal change: international communication and technology. Technology, Prometheus's fire unbound, has been the major and continuing trigger of an all-encompassing change that goes beyond interstate relations to the rise and consolidation of civil society. States, despite their authoritarian core and ethos, are losing their grip on their domestic landscape. Profiting from international communication and technology, civil society movements manifest themselves in protest movements, pressure for more democratization, and religiopolitics. These civil society groups and their actions manage to put to the test what seem to be failing states, such as Somalia, Sudan, Lebanon, and Yemen. The impact of this new technology, especially on youth—a dynamic element and the majority of the population—is bound to accelerate the rate of change/transformation.

Although this region is not as Internet-intensive as East Asia or even India, the rate of growth of Internet use between 2000 and 2008 was almost three times that of the world rate: 1176.8 percent versus 290.0 percent (Internet World Statistics 2008). The growth in some countries for 2000–2007 was simply phenomenal: 2,250 percent in Saudi Arabia, 4,900 percent in Syria, and 7,100 percent in Iran. This evolution could result in a revolution in its own way, especially when the sociopolitical impact of bloggers is accounted for.

Arab political bloggers engage in three principal types of activity: activism, bridge-blogging, and public-sphere engagement. These categories are not mutually exclusive, of course, and many individuals move fluidly across boundaries. But distinguishing these modes of action can help to make sense of the different ways in which Arab bloggers could influence politics in the region.

Activists use their blogs for political organization and campaigns to mobilize support for contentious politics. In countries such as Bahrain, Egypt, and Kuwait, blogs have played an important role in historically unprecedented bouts of political activism in recent years. Other Arab blogospheres, such as in Jordan and Saudi Arabia, remain more on the political sidelines, taking note of the exploits of their activist peers (interview with Hossam el-Hamalawy, of the *Masrwai* blog, 27 February 2009). This politically engaged 'activist blogging' stands in sharp contrast with what Ethan Zuckerman has termed 'bridge-bloggers'—Arabs writing in English as interpreters of their communities, less engaged in local politics than in building bridges to western audiences. Given their novelty, such bridge-bloggers receive disproportionate attention from western journalists.

Finally, 'public-sphere' blogs are deeply engaged in arguments about politics, culture, and society. Baheyya, the pseudonymous blog of an Egyptian woman, is a prime example. With biting wit and an intimate knowledge of the contentious politics about which she writes, Baheyya has quickly became a lodestone not only for western readers but for Egyptians as well; no less an authority than Muhammad Hassanein Heikal dubbed Baheyya an excellent source.

Blogging in Tunisia or Syria is an alternative to the national press. This new blog-based public sphere challenges the 'punditocracy' directly, as entrenched elites lose some of their power to dictate the terms of debate and frames of reference. Today's public-sphere bloggers are the tip of an iceberg of politically savvy, engaged, young citizens determined to argue in public about the things that matter to them.

How exactly has all of this played out? In Egypt, for example, Kefaya began as a petition of some three hundred intellectuals in the summer of 2004 and developed an Internet presence with a popular website in the fall of that year. Blogs began to play a key role over the course of 2005, providing coverage at times when the mass media paid little attention. Blogs contributed both to publicity and organization. Bloggers worked with protest organizers to ensure that photographs and narratives of the protests were quickly disseminated online, offering a valuable resource to journalists, international NGOs and Egyptian citizens alike. For all the innovative activism of Kefaya and its associated bloggers, the movement's political impact was assisted by the short-lived opening created by several factors. These included a constitutional referendum, presidential elections with nominally multiple candidates, the presence of some independent candidates in parliamentary elections, the appearance of several new, like-minded independent newspapers, and increased western scrutiny of Egyptian democracy due to the Bush administration's reform rhetoric.

In Bahrain, bloggers and online forums played a direct role in a human rights campaign that infuriated the regime and generated great public controversy. By 2005, some sixty Bahraini bloggers were energetically focusing on local politics in both English and Arabic, many under pseudonyms. They helped to organize and publicize a number of protests over issues such as the arrest of Abdulhadi al-Khawaja of the Bahrain Centre for Human Rights (in December 2004) and constitutional reforms. In response, the Bahraini authorities arrested some of the most active bloggers, such as Ali Abdulemam, and demanded that Internet sites register with the authorities in an attempt to break down the anonymity protecting some of the most outspoken voices. More recently, Bahraini bloggers have been intensely following "Bandargate," a scandal driven by revelations of regime plans to fix the 2006 parliamentary elections. They have also produced a map of the country using Google Earth, revealing vast appropriations for electoral purposes. As a result, the Bahraini government briefly banned all instances of online activism against the royal family.

Kuwaiti bloggers took advantage of several windows of opportunity over the course of 2006. After gaining an audience with their coverage of the succession crisis following the death of the amir, Jabir al-Ahmad al-Jabir al-Sabah, in January 2006, many of these blogs picked up a campaign to reduce the number of electoral districts from twenty-five to five in order to cut back on notoriously corrupt electoral practices. When the amir called early parliamentary elections, bloggers jumped into the fray with a vengeance, highlighting corruption and driving the debate (with blog postings often showing up in newspapers). The Kuwaiti case is particularly interesting, as prior to 2006, most observers had seen the Kuwaiti blogosphere as relatively disengaged from politics and marginal to the public realm.

Conclusion

These clear indicators of change, together with the data in the annexed tables, demonstrate that seeming continuity/stagnation could be limited to the top of the political pyramid, especially when we "over-state the state" (Ayubi 1995). Conversely, the 'base,' or civil society and the regional landscape, are pregnant with change. Moreover, this discrepancy or 'contradiction' (as the Marxists call it) between the societal base and the political top cannot continue indefinitely, and its collapse could trigger further change. Thus the developmental state seems at present to be superseded by the predatory state and/or failed one—a steady process that could engender an impact as important as any 'big bang.'

As Chapter 1 made it amply clear, the framework for analyzing change/transformation emphasized the distinction between sudden noticeable triggers, the big bangs (for example, war, revolution, milestone events), and the steady, initially unnoticed but cumulative process of restructuring. Although both types could feed on each other, the emphasis in the different chapters has been rather on the steady process because it is the type that could be easily overlooked, even though some are talking now, for instance, of an "empire of bloggers " (al-Miligi 2009). Indeed the analysis of some of these blogs confirms the change in views and ideas that are taking place in an increasingly important (and youthful) segment of civil society (an aspect of the volcano underneath), in contrast to the fossilization at the top of political authority.

Although not clear at present, this existing discrepancy between the political top and the social base, between state authority and civil society, could be the occasion for another milestone event, and thus engender a new developmental birth, as many societies have experienced in history.

Appendix

Data and Comments on Middle East Transformations: 1989–2009

Data Sources

As those who have worked on data collection in many parts of the third world, and not only in the Arab Middle East, know this empirical process can be hazardous. Data are often unavailable, inconsistent, or contradictory. For some time, even population data for Saudi Arabia had a difference ratio of 30 percent, depending on the source. Even a relatively open state, such as Lebanon, is wary of revealing demographic statistics because these form the basis for the distribution of political posts and the functioning of the political system. Demographic data, then, becomes a component of national security. How much more difficult to collect are data about armed forces or decision-making.

The most important way out is never to be limited to one source. In addition to various national sources, the World Bank and the International Monetary Fund are essential. The *Economist Intelligence Unit* volumes about various countries of the region are also useful. Yearbooks coming from the region (in Arabic) such as *al-Ahram*'s, *al-Taqrir al-stratiji al-'arabi* (occasionally published in English translation as the *Arab Strategic Report*), the *Gulf Yearbook* by the Gulf Research Center, *Hal al-'umma al-'arabiya*, and the monthly *al-Mustaqbal al-'arabi*, issued by Beirut's Center for Arab Unity Studies, are helpful in locating the data and its interpretation. Since it began publishing yearly regional reports about the Arab world in 2002, the United Nations Development Programme (UNDP) includes sets of detailed data on developmental aspects of the region. The 1,202 pages of the five reports published to date include no fewer than 188 tables, including data from surveys and answers to questionnaires.

The data tables presented here are not to be compared, of course, to these huge enterprises with their massive resources. They attempt, however, to offer a quantitative panorama for quick referencing by the reader.

Demographics and the Population–Resource Gap

In general, there is population growth in the Middle East, but the rate of increase during the 1990s was higher than that after the year 2000. Sharp disparities among Arab countries notwithstanding, between 1960 and the start of the millennium, life expectancy increased by 23 years and infant mortality rates plummeted from 152 to 39 per thousand births. According to U.N. statistics in 1980, the population of the Arab Middle East was 172 million. It rose to 331 million in 2007 and is expected to grow by 2015 to 385 million. If an equivalent growth in resources does not follow to satisfy basic needs in education, employment, and nutrition, the region's 'youth bulge' could be detrimental rather than beneficial. In addition, given the arid nature of the region and the increasing water shortage, its countries could suffer from dependence on outside sources for food. About thirteen Arab countries at present depend on food imports for more than 40 percent of their needs.

Military conflicts and occupation make a bad situation worse. According to the 2009 *Arab Human Development Report*, "approximately half of all Palestinian households are dependent on food assistance provided by the international community. Some 33 percent (700,000 people) of what was formerly a middle-income society in the West Bank now relies on food aid. Worse still, the figure for Gaza stands at 80 percent of households, or 1.3 million people" (UNDP 2009, 162).

Urban Population Growth Rate

Along with the general increase in population figures, there is an evident increase in urban population growth in the Middle East. This acceleration was also greater during the 1990s, slowing down after 2000 in most of the countries in the region, with some exceptions, such as the United Arab Emirates, Israel, and Turkey. It is estimated that by 2020, the Arab Middle East will have 60 percent of its population in urban areas. Given the lack of necessary planning to cope with such an influx, overcrowding in urban areas could cause serious environmental, health, and social hazards.

GDP (Purchasing Power Parity)[1] and GDP (Per Capita-PPP)[2]
There has been a clear increase in the GDP of countries in the Middle East, with exceptions in conflict zones, such as the Occupied Palestinian Territories (the Gaza Strip and the West Bank), Sudan, and Iraq. There has been a particularly rapid increase in the GDP of the United Arab Emirates, Turkey, Israel, and Iran.

Average Annual Economic Growth Rate
Most states in the Middle East have experienced an increase in the average economic growth reate. Once again, conflict zones such as Iraq witness either lower or a slower growth rate.

External Debt
There has been a general increase in external debt in poor Arab Middle Eastern states, with exceptions such as Algeria and Egypt.

Public Debt Percentage of GDP
The public debt percentage of the GDP is influenced by both GDP growth and the amount of external debt. In general, it is decreasing in most MENA/Arab countries.

Budget and Development

Budget
In most MENA/Arab countries (with the exception of many oil-exporting countries, such as Bahrain, Kuwait, Libya, Qatar, and even Algeria) revenues are less than expenditure.

Military Budget
There was an increase in the military budget of the MENA/Arab countries during the 1990s, but since 2000 the military budget—in percentage terms—has either been decreasing or stabilizing.

Education Index, Human Development Index[3] and Gender Development Index[4]
The education, human development, and gender development indices of most of MENA/Arab countries have seen a general increase.

Government

Type of Political System
No significant changes have occurred in the political systems of Arab countries in the MENA region during the last five decades. It is at the top of the political pyramid where continuity mostly resides, in contrast—as the different chapters have shown—with the societal change that has taken place beneath, the 'volcano underneath' showing the discrepancy between 'social transformation' and the lack of political transition.

Heads of State in Power
Heads of states have changed little during the past five decades, and most of the changes that have taken place have been the result of the death of a head of state. Turkey, Israel, and Iran are exceptions because they have a democratic political system with elections.

Last Legislative Elections
Legislative elections are heavily controlled by the state (especially in Arab countries) and did not function properly until after 2000. Changes in the way elections are conducted and results are computed have started to take place slowly and irregularly in countries such as Egypt and Morocco.

Notes
1 Gross Domestic Product (GDP), or Gross Domestic Income (GDI), is the total value of all final goods and services produced in a particular economy, the dollar value of all goods and services produced within a country's borders in a given year.
2 Gross Domestic Product at Purchasing Power Parity per Capita (PPP) is the value of all final goods and services produced within a country in a given year divided by the average (or mid-year) population for the same year.
3 The Human Development Index is used to rank countries by level of "human development," indicating whether a country is developed, developing, or underdeveloped.
4 The Gender-related Development Index is an indication of the standard of living in a country used by the United Nations. It is one of the five indicators used by the United Nations Development Programme in its annual *Human Development Report*. It aims to show the inequalities between men and women in the following areas: long and healthy life, knowledge, and a decent standard of living.

Middle East Transformations: 1989–2008[1]

The tables below show statistics for twenty-six Middle Eastern states, of which three are non-Arab countries.

People and Economy

Country	Population	Urban Population Growth Rate (percent)	GDP (purchasing power parity) ($ billion)	GDP (per capita-PPP) ($)	Average Annual Growth Rate (percent)	External Debt ($ billion)	Public Debt Percentage of GDP (percent)
Algeria							
2009	34,178,188	1.196	235.5	7,100	3.4	2.913	13.8
2004	32,129,324	1.280	196.0	6,000	7.4	22.710	24.3
1999	31,133,486	2.100	140.2	4,600	3.2	31.400	25.6
1994	27,895,068	2.290	89.0	3,300	1.0	26.00	23.2
1989	24,946,073	3.000	59.0	2,645	2.0	32.100	27.8
Bahrain							
2009	753,000[2]	1.285	26.70	37,200	7.0	10.570	33.2
2004	677,886	1.560	11.29	16,900	4.9	4.682	35.4
1999	629,090	2.000	8.20	13,100	2.0	2.000	36.7
1994	585,683	2.960	6.80	12,000	4.0	2.600	38.5
1989	496,759	3.300	3.50	7,550	0	1.500	35.2
Comoros							
2009	752,438	2.766	0.741	1,100	1.0	0.232	25.4
2004	651,901	2.940	0.441	700	2.0	0.232	28.3
1999	562,723	3.110	0.400	700	3.5	0.219	30.5
1994	530,136	3.550	0.360	700	5.0	0.160	34.4
1989	444,484	3.500	0.163	390	2.1	0.238	40.6
Djibouti							
2009	516,055	1.903	1.889	3,800	6.0	0.428	27.5
2004	466,900	2.100	0.619	1,300	3.5	0.366	30.5
1999	447,439	1.510	0.530	1,200	0.6	0.276	33.4
1994	412,599	2.710	0.500	1,200	-1.0	0.355	34.4
1989	328,758	2.600	0.333	1,070	- 0.7	0.250	37.3

Country	Population	Urban Population Growth Rate (percent)	GDP (purchasing power parity) ($ billion)	GDP (per capita-PPP) ($)	Average Annual Growth Rate (percent)	External Debt ($ billion)	Public Debt Percentage of GDP (percent)
Egypt							
2009	83,082,869	1.642	442.6	5,500	7.0	28.84	84.7
2004	76,117,421	1.830	295.2	4,000	3.1	30.34	85.5
1999	67,273,906	1.820	188.0	2,850	5.0	28.00	87.3
1994	60,765,028	1.950	139.0	2,400	0.3	32.00	87.6
1989	54,777,615	2.600	25.6	490	0.5	40.40	88.2
Gaza Strip							
2009	1,551,859	3.349	11.950	2,900	0.8	...	...
2004	1,324,991	3.830	0.768	600	4.5	...	...
1999	1,112,654[3]	4.440	1.100	1,000	2.2	...	...
1994	731,296[4]	3.530	0.840	1,275	1.0	...	...
1989	596,261[5]	3.200	0.560	1,035	...	...	...
Iraq							
2009	28,945,657	2.507	112.80	4,000	9.8	40.40	54.3
2004	25,374,691	2.740	37.92	1,500	-21.8	93.95	55.5
1999	22,427,150	3.190	52.30	2,400	10.0	...[6]	...
1994	19,889,666	3.730	38.00	2,000	...	45.00[7]	60.7
1989	18,073,963	3.800	34.00	1,950	0	40.00[8]	61.4
Jordan							
2009	6,342,948	2.264	30.76	5,000	4.5	6.597	58.3
2004	5,611,202	2.670	23.64	4,300	3.1	7.683	58.1
1999	4,561,147	3.050	15.50	3,500	2.2	7.500	57.3
1994	3,961,194	3.500	11.50	3,000	5.0	6.800	56.0
1989	2,955,660	3.600	4.90	1,780	2.1	5.600	54.8
Kuwait							
2009	2,691,158[9]	3.547[10]	149.10	60,800	8.1	38.82	7.2
2004	2,257,549	3.360	41.46	19,000	4.6	12.18	29.5
1999	1,991,115	3.880	43.70	22,700	5.0	7.30	29.7
1994	1,819,322	5.240	25.70	15,100	15.0	7.20	30.3
1989	2,008,053	3.600	19.10	10,410	4.0	10.40	33.5

Country	Population	Urban Population Growth Rate (percent)	GDP (purchasing power parity) ($ billion)	GDP (per capita- PPP) ($)	Average Annual Growth Rate (percent)	External Debt ($ billion)	Public Debt Percentage of GDP (percent)
Lebanon							
2009	4,017,095	1.107	44.07	11,100	7.0	21.200	163.5
2004	3,777,218	1.300	17.82	4,800	3.0	20.790	145.4
1999	3,562,699	1.610	15.80	4,500	3.0	3.000	120.7
1994	1,819,322	5.240	25.70	15,100	3.0	7.200	122.4
1989	3,300,802	1.100	1.80	690	2.0	0.935	150.5
Libya							
2009	6,310,434[11]	2.17	88.86	14,900	7.3	5.521	3.6
2004	5,631,585	2.37	35.00	6,400	3.2	4.194	16.6
1999	4,992,838	2.40	38.00	6,700	1.0	4.000	16.4
1994	5,057,392	3.72	32.00	6,600	1.0	3.500[12]	15.3
1989			20.00	5,410	0	2.100[13]	13.2
Mauritania							
2009	3,129,486	2.399	6.310	1,900	4.0	2.4	89.0
2004	2,998,563	2.910	5.195	1,800	4.5	2.5	90.5
1999	2,581,738	2.990	4.700	1,890	4.2	2.5	93.2
1994	2,192,777	3.160	2.200	1,050	3.3	1.9	94.5
1989	1,977,466	3.000	0.843	440	2.7	2.2	95.3
Morocco							
2009	34,859,364	1.479	137.3	4,000	5.3	21.11	60.2
2004	32,209,101	1.610	128.3	4,000	6.0	17.32	76.2
1999	29,661,636	1.840	107.0	3,200	6.8	20.90	77.4
1994	28,558,635	2.120	70.3	2,500	2.0	21.30	78.4
1989	25,605,579	2.500	18.0	740	1.5	19.80	75.3
Oman							
2009	2,595,000	3.138	67.0	21,300	6.7	6.120	2.4
2004	2,903,165[14]	3.350	36.7	13,100	1.1	5.973	15.6
1999	2,446,645	3.450	18.6	7,900	-8.5	3.000	12.5
1994	1,701,470	3.460	16.4	10,000	6.1	3.000	12.5
1989	1,304,882	3.100	7.5	6,110	3.6	3.500	14.3

Country	Population	Urban Population Growth Rate (percent)	GDP (purchasing power parity) ($ billion)	GDP (per capita-PPP) ($)	Average Annual Growth Rate (percent)	External Debt ($ billion)	Public Debt Percentage of GDP (percent)
Qatar							
2009	833,285	0.957	67.00	101,000	11.8	48.91	6.0
2004	840,290	2.740	17.54	21,500	8.5	17.50	72.7
1999	723,542	3.620	12.00	17,100	-3.0	11.00	64.2
1994	512,779	2.560	8.80	17,500	-0.5	1.50	33.5
1989	468,632	6.300	5.40	17,070	9.0	1.00	46.3
Saudi Arabia							
2009	28,686,63	1.848	582.8	21,300	4.2	63.20	13.5
2004	25,795,938[15]	2.440	287.8	11,800	5.3	39.16	94.6
1999	21,504,613[16]	3.390	186.0	9,000	-10.8	...	...
1994	18,196,783	3.240	194.0	11,000	1.0	18.90	75.4
1989	16,108,539	4.000	74.0	5,480	5.2	15.70	64.9
Somalia							
2009	9,832,017[17]	2.815	5.524	600	2.6	3.0	98.4
2004	8,304,601	3.410	4.361	500	2.1	2.6	140.3
1999	7,140,643	4.130	4.000	600	...	2.6	145.6
1994	6,666,873	3.240	3.400	500	...	1.9	120.7
1989	8,248,133	3.200	1.500	190	1.5	2.0	159.4
Sudan							
2009	41,087,825	2.143	87.27	2,200	5.3	30.48	86.1
2004	39,148,162	2.640	70.95	1,900	5.9	16.09	87.0
1999	34,475,690	2.710	31.20	930	6.1	20.30	89.5
1994	29,419,798	2.360	21.50	750	7.0	17.00	84.9
1989	24,476,290	2.700	8.50	340	6.0	8.60	95.3
Syria							
2009	20,178,485[18]	2.129	95.36	4,900	2.4	6.72	41.2
2004	18,016,874[19]	2.400	58.01	3,300	0.9	21.55	89.0
1999	17,213,871	3.150	41.7	2,500	2.0	22.0	74.3
1994	14,886,672	3.740	81.7	5,700	7.6	19.4	84.7
1989	12,010,564[20]	3.800	20.3	1,962	5.6	4.86	70.6

Country	Population	Urban Population Growth Rate (percent)	GDP (purchasing power parity) ($ billion)	GDP (per capita-PPP) ($)	Average Annual Growth Rate (percent)	External Debt ($ billion)	Public Debt Percentage of GDP (percent)
Tunisia							
2009	10,486,339	0.980	81.88	8,000	4.7	19.33	53.1
2004	9,974,722	1.010	68.23	6,900	5.1	14.39	59.5
1999	9,513,603	1.390	49.00	5,200	5.0	12.10	65.3
1994	8,726,562	1.760	34.30	4,000	2.6	7.70	52.5
1989	7,916,104	2.300	9.60	1,270	5.8	6.80	50.4
United Arab Emirates							
2009	4,798,491[21]	3.689	184.6	40,400	8.5	73.71	22.4
2004	2,523,915[22]	1.570	57.7	23,200	5.2	20.71	18.1
1999	2,344,402[23]	1.780	40.0	17,400	5.0	14.00	13.4
1994	2,791,141	4.790	63.8	24,000	1.0	11.00	12.5
1989	2,115,109	6.400	22.0	11,900	3.0	9.30	11.4
West Bank							
2009	2,461,267[24]	2.178	11.95	2,900	0.8	...	...
2004	2,311,204	3.210	1.70	800	-22.0	...	...
1999	1,611,109	3.140	3.10	2,000	2.2	...	...
1994	1,443,790[25]	2.680	2.00	2,050	-7.0	...	...
1989	1,014,856[26]	2.300	1.50	1,550	9.0	...	...
Western Sahara							
2009	480,000[27]	2.200	0.900	...	...	...	...
2004	267,405	2.500	0.754	...	...	...	...
1999	239,333	2.400	0.240	...	...	...	...
1994	211,877	2.500	0.060	300	...	...	...
1989	186,488	2.800	0.045	...	...	...	...
Yemen							
2009	23,822,783	3.453	55.29	2,600	3.2	6.472	31.8
2004	20,024,867	3.440	15.09	800	2.8	6.044	39.5
1999	16,942,230	3.340	12.10	740	1.8	4.900	40.3
1994	11,105,202	3.340	9.00	800	3.1	7.000	42.3
1989	2,503,641	3.200	1.01	480	-6.6	2.230	45.7

Country	Population	Urban Population Growth Rate (percent)	GDP (purchasing power parity) ($ billion)	GDP (per capita-PPP) ($)	Average Annual Growth Rate (percent)	External Debt ($ billion)	Public Debt Percentage of GDP (percent)
Iran							
2009	66,429,284	0.883	842.0	13,100	6.4	21.77	25.0
2004	69,018,924	1.070	478.2	7,000	6.1	10.96	28.2
1999	65,179,752	1.070	339.7	5,000	2.1	21.90	29.4
1994	65,615,474	3.460	303.0	4,780	3.0	30.00	35.3
1989	53,866,523	3.400	93.5	1,800	2.0	4.30	36.4
Israel							
2009	7,233,701[28]	1.671	200.7	28,900	4.2	91.25	75.7
2004	6,199,008[29]	1.290	120.9	19,800	1.3	70.97	108.6
1999	5,749,760[30]	1.810	101.9	18,100	1.9	18.70	107.5
1994	5,050,850	2.220	65.7	13,350	3.5	24.80	108.8
1989	4,371,478	1.700	36.0	8,400	1.0	16.00	109.4
Turkey							
2009	76,805,524	1.312	906.5	12,900	4.5	294.3	37.1
2004	68,893,918	1.130	458.2	6,700	5.8	147.3	78.7
1999	65,599,206	1.570	425.4	6,600	2.8	93.4	65.4
1994	62,153,898	2.020	312.4	5,100	7.3	59.4	46.7
1989	55,355,831	2.100	62.6	1,180	7.4	40.3	49.4

1 The statistics and information provided here are compiled from the International Monetary Fund, the World Bank, the U.S. Central Intelligence Agency, and the United Nations *Human Development Reports*.
2 Includes 235,108 non-nationals.
3 In addition, there are some 6,000 Israeli settlers in the Gaza Strip.
4 In addition, there are 4,500 Israeli settlers in the Gaza Strip.
5 In addition, there are 2,500 Israeli settlers in the Gaza Strip.
6 Very heavy relative to GDP but the exact amount is unknown.
7 Excluding debt of about $35 billion owed to Arab Gulf states.
8 Excluding nominal debt to Gulf Arab states.
9 Includes 1,291,354 non-nationals.
10 This rate reflects a return to a pre-Gulf crisis rate of immigration of expatriates.
11 Includes 166,510 non-nationals.
12 Excluding military debt.
13 Excluding military debt.
14 Includes 577,293 non-nationals.
15 Includes 5,576,076 non-nationals.

16 Includes 5,321,938 non-nationals.
17 This estimate was derived from an official census taken in 1975 by the Somali government. Population counting in Somalia is complicated by the large number of nomads and by refugee movements in response to famine and clan warfare.
18 In addition, about 40,000 people live in the Israeli-occupied Golan Heights—20,000 Arabs (18,000 Druze and 2,000 Alawites) and about 20,000 Israeli settlers.
19 In addition, about 40,000 people live in the Israeli-occupied Golan Heights—20,000 Arabs (18,000 Druze and 2,000 Alawites) and about 20,000 Israeli settlers.
20 In addition, there are 10,500 Israeli settlers in the Golan Heights.
21 Estimate is based on the results of the 2005 census that included a significantly higher estimate of net immigration of noncitizens than previous estimates.
22 Includes an estimated 1,606,079 non-nationals. The 17 December 1995 census presents a total population figure of 2,377,453, and there are estimates of 3.44 million for 2002.
23 Includes 1,576,589 non-nationals.
24 In addition, there are about 187,000 Israeli settlers in the West Bank and fewer than 177,000 in East Jerusalem.
25 In addition, there are 110,500 Israeli settlers in the West Bank and 144,100 in East Jerusalem.
26 In addition, there are 65,000 Israeli settlers in the West Bank and 104,000 (estimated) in East Jerusalem.
27 Estimate is based on projections by age, sex, fertility, mortality, and migration. Fertility and mortality are based on data from neighboring countries.
28 Includes about 187,000 Israeli settlers in the West Bank, about 20,000 in the Israeli-occupied Golan Heights, and fewer than 177,000 in East Jerusalem.
29 Includes about 187,000 Israeli settlers in the West Bank, about 20,000 in the Israeli-occupied Golan Heights, more than 5,000 in the Gaza Strip, and fewer than 177,000 in East Jerusalem.
30 Includes about 166,000 Israeli settlers in the West Bank, about 19,000 in the Israeli-occupied Golan Heights, about 6,000 in the Gaza Strip, and about 176,000 in East Jerusalem.

Budget and Development

Country	Budget ($ billion)	Military Budget as percentage of GDP (figure in parentheses shows absolute sum spent in $ billion)	Education Index[1]	HDI[2]	GDI[3]
Algeria					
2009	Revenues 73.26 Expenditures 51.19	3.3 (1.860)	0.711	0.748	0.720
2004	Revenues 25.49 Expenditures 22.87	3.5 (2.197)	0.690	0.704	0.688
1999	Revenues 14.40 Expenditures 15.70	2.7 (1.300)	0.630	0.665	0.642
1994	Revenues 14.40 Expenditures 14.60	2.5 (1.360)	0.610	0.553	0.632
1989	Revenues 20.60 Expenditures 23.10	5.4 of central government budget (1.067)	0.560	0.453	0.625
Bahrain					
2009	Revenues 7.226 Expenditures 5.806	4.5 (2.860)	0.864	0.902	0.857
2004	Revenues 2.981 Expenditures 3.019	7.5 (0.618)	0.850	0.843	0.832
1999	Revenues 1.500 Expenditures 1.900	4.5 (0.277)	0.850	0.832	0.813
1994	Revenues 1.200 Expenditures 1.600	6 (0.245)	0.840	0.791	0.791

Country	Budget ($ billion)	Military Budget as percentage of GDP (figure in parentheses shows absolute sum spent in $ billion)	Education Index	HDI	GDI
1989	Revenues 1.136 Expenditures 1.210	11.4 of central government budget (0.149)	0.820	0.762	0.752
Comoros					
2009	Revenues 0.0276 Expenditures N/A	2.80 (0.005)	0.533	0.572	0.554
2004	Revenues 0.0276 Expenditures N/A	3.00 (0.006)	0.530	0.556	0.510
1999	Revenues 0.048 Expenditures 0.053	N/A (0.003)	0.500	0.506	0.500
1994	Revenues 0.096 Expenditures 0.088	...	0.490	0.331	0.495
1989	Revenues 0.067 Expenditures 0.07	12.06 of central government budget (0.002)	0.470	0.320	0.475
Djibouti					
2009	Revenues 0.135 Expenditures 0.182	3.8 (0.021)	0.553	0.513	0.507
2004	Revenues 0.135 Expenditures 0.182	4.4 (0.027)	0.520	0.494	0.495
1999	Revenues 0.156 Expenditures 0.175	4.5 (0.023)	0.390	0.412	0.482

Country	Budget ($ billion)	Military Budget as percentage of GDP (figure in parentheses shows absolute sum spent in $ billion)	Education Index	HDI	GDI
1994	Revenues 0.170 Expenditures 0.203	N/A (0.026)	0.430	0.226	0.453
1989	Revenues 0.117 Expenditures 0.163	23.0 of central government budget (0.030)	0.410	0.213	0.343
Egypt					
2009	Revenues 40.46 Expenditures 51.38	3.4 (3.250)	0.732	0.716	0.622
2004	Revenues 14.69 Expenditures 19.03	3.6 (2.440)	0.620	0.702	0.634
1999	Revenues 20.00 Expenditures 20.80	8.2 (3.280)	0.740	0.616	0.603
1994	Revenues 16.80 Expenditures 19.40	6.0 (2.050)	0.730	0.551	0.593
1989	Revenues 15.00 Expenditures 23.00	5.1 of central government budget (2.099)	0.710	0.540	0.573
Gaza Strip					
2009	Revenues 1.1490 Expenditures 2.3100[4]	...	...	0.731[5]	...
2004	Revenues 0.6770 Expenditures 1.1550	...	...	...	

Country	Budget ($ billion)	Military Budget as percentage of GDP (figure in parentheses shows absolute sum spent in $ billion)	Education Index	HDI	GDI
1999	Revenues 0.8160 Expenditures 0.8660	...	...	...	...
1994	Revenues 0.0336 Expenditures 0.0345	...	...	...	...
1989	...	...	...	...	...
Iraq					
2009	Revenues 42.4 Expenditures 49.9	8.6	0.530	0.583	0.621
2004	Revenues 12.80 Expenditures 13.40	1.3	0.520	0.586	0.634
1999	...	...	0.560	0.586	0.745
1994	...	...	0.580	0.614	
1989	Revenues 20.0 Expenditures 18.6	...	0.630	0.753	0.750
Jordan					
2009	Revenues 5.999 Expenditures 7.870	8.6	0.868	0.769	0.760
2004	Revenues 2.397 Expenditures 3.587	20.2 (2.043)	0.860	0.76	0.734
1999	Revenues 2.800 Expenditures 3.000	7.8 (0.609)	0.800	0.715	0.721

Country	Budget ($ billion)	Military Budget as percentage of GDP (figure in parentheses shows absolute sum spent in $ billion)	Education Index	HDI	GDI
1994	Revenues 1.700 Expenditures 1.900	7.9 (0.035)	0.730	0.628	0.710
1989	Revenues 1.200 Expenditures 2.300	19.4 of central government budget (0.593)	0.680	0.619	0.652
Kuwait					
2009	Revenues 113.30 Expenditures 63.55	5.3 (3.5600)	0.871	0.912	0.884
2004	Revenues 29.41 Expenditures 17.57	5.8 (2.5000)	0.827	0.871	0.810
1999	Revenues 8.10 Expenditures 14.50	7.9 (2.7035)	0.731	0.833	0.825
1994	Revenues 9.00 Expenditures 13.00	7.3 (2.5000)	0.722	0.809	0.800
1989	Revenues 7.1 Expenditures 10.5	10.5 of central government budget (1.1790)	0.641	0.734	0.793
Lebanon					
2009	Revenues 7.000 Expenditures 10.000	3.1 (0.731)	0.871	0.796	0.759
2004	Revenues 4.414 Expenditures 7.026	4.8 (0.541)	0.840	0.774	0.755

Country	Budget ($ billion)	Military Budget as percentage of GDP (figure in parentheses shows absolute sum spent in $ billion)	Education Index	HDI	GDI
1999	Revenues 4.900 Expenditures 7.900	5 (0.445)	0.820	0.749	0.734
1994	Revenues 9.000 Expenditures 13.000	7.3 (2.500)	0.800	0.600	0.722
1989	Revenues 0.050 Expenditures 0.650	...	0.780	0.597	0.717
Libya					
2009	Revenues 56.35 Expenditures 29.12	3.9 (1.3)	0.875	0.840	0.797
2004	Revenues 10.28 Expenditures 7.86	3.9 (1.3)	0.870	0.798	0.772
1999	Revenues 3.60 Expenditures 5.10	...	0.820	0.756	0.732
1994	Revenues 8.10 Expenditures 9.80	15 (3.3)	0.810	0.703	0.714
1989	Revenues 6.40 Expenditures 11.30, including capital expenditures of 3.60	...	0.790	0.680	0.711
Mauritania					
2009	Revenues 0.770 Expenditures 0.770	5.5 (0.421)	0.493	0.557	0.543

Country	Budget ($ billion)	Military Budget as percentage of GDP (figure in parentheses shows absolute sum spent in $ billion)	Education Index	HDI	GDI
2004	Revenues 0.421 Expenditures 0.378	3.7 (0.041)	0.420	0.486	0.456
1999	Revenues 0.329 Expenditures 0.265, including capital expenditures of 0.075	2.5 (0.030)	0.390	0.447	0.408
1994	Revenues 0.280 Expenditures 0.346, including capital expenditures of 0.061	4.2 (0.040)	...	0.254	0.398
1989	Revenues 0.265 Expenditures 0.273	25.0 of central government budget (0.043)	...	0.213	0.380
Morocco					
2009	Revenues 26.09 Expenditures 28.41	5.0 (0.421)	0.544	0.646	0.621
2004	Revenues 13.80 Expenditures 14.00, including capital expenditures of 2.10	4.8 (2.297)	0.530	0.64	0.604
1999	Revenues 8.40 Expenditures 10.00, including capital expenditures of 1.80	3.8 (1.361)	0.470	0.582	0.565

Country	Budget ($ billion)	Military Budget as percentage of GDP (figure in parentheses shows absolute sum spent in $ billion)	Education Index	HDI	GDI
1994	Revenues 7.50 Expenditures 7.70, including capital expenditures of 1.90	3.8 (1.100)	0.400	0.549	0.531
1989	Revenues 4.00 Expenditures 5.00, including capital expenditures of 1.20	...	0.320	0.530	0.520
Oman					
2009	Revenus 14.600 Expenditures 16.700	11.4 (0.445)	0.766	0.839	0.788
2004	Revenues 8.218 Expenditures 7.766	11.4 (0.242)	0.880	0.81	0.775
1999	Revenues 4.000 Expenditures 5.600	11.1 (1.672)	0.760	0.725	0.686
1994	Revenues 4.400 Expenditures 5.200, including capital expenditures of 1.000	16.0 (1.600)	0.730	0.654	0.652
1989	Revenues 3.100; Expenditures 4.200, including capital expenditures of 1.000	33 of central government budget (1.385)	0.680	0.530	0.610

Country	Budget ($ billion)	Military Budget as percentage of GDP (figure in parentheses shows absolute sum spent in $ billion)	Education Index	HDI	GDI
Qatar					
2009	Revenues 40.360 Expenditures 28.080	10.0 (1.230)	0.852	0.899	0.863
2004	Revenues 8.202 Expenditures 6.981, including capital expenditures of 2.200	10.0 (0.723)	0.830	0.844	0.850
1999	Revenues 3.400 Expenditures 4.300, including capital expenditures of 0.700	9.6 (0.940)	0.770	0.814	0.796
1994	Revenues 2.500 Expenditures 3.000, including capital expenditures of 0.440	...	0.740	0.795	0.752
1989	Revenues 1.700 Expenditures 3.400	...	0.720	0.740	0.732
Saudi Arabia					
2009	Revenues 293.00 Expenditures 136.00	10 (19.7)	0.787	0.835	0.783
2004	Revenues 78.77 Expenditures 66.76	10 (18.0)	0.710	0.777	0.739
1999	Revenues 32.30 Expenditures 44.00	12 (18.1)	0.670	0.740	0.703

Country	Budget ($ billion)	Military Budget as percentage of GDP (figure in parentheses shows absolute sum spent in $ billion)	Education Index	HDI	GDI
1994	Revenues 39.00 Expenditures 50.00, including capital expenditures of 7.50	13 (16.5)	0.640	0.742	0.689
1989	Revenues 24.00 Expenditures 37.90	35.5 of central government budget (13.3)	0.610	0.702	0.650
Somalia					
2009	...	0.9	...	0.284	...
2004	...	0.9	...	...	...
1999	...	...	...	...	...
1994	...	...	...	0.217	...
1989	Revenues 0.0747 Expenditurse 0.4776, including capital expenditures of 0.2807	...	...	...	...
Sudan					
2009	Revenues 11.840 Expenditures 12.950	3.00 (0.732)	0.693	0.526	0.502
2004	Revenues 2.402 Expenditures 2.546, including capital expenditures of 0.304	2.50 (0.581)	0.485	0.516	0.520
1999	Revenues 0.482 Expenditures 1.500, including capital expenditures of 0.030	0.55 (0.423)	0.470	0.475	0.453

Country	Budget ($ billion)	Military Budget as percentage of GDP (figure in parentheses shows absolute sum spent in $ billion)	Education Index	HDI	GDI
1994	Revenues 0.374 Expenditures 1.200, including capital expenditures of 0.214	2.20 (0.339)	0.420	0.276	0.410
1989	Revenues 0.867 Expenditures 1.500, including capital expenditures of 0.331	5.50 of central government budget (0.134)	0.402	0.231	0.398
Syria					
2009	Revenues 10.900 Expenditures 13.770	5.9 (0.993)	0.755	0.736	0.710
2004	Revenues 6.106 Expenditures 7.397, including capital expenditures of 3.600	5.9 (0.858)	0.750	0.716	0.689
1999	Revenues 3.500 Expenditures 4.200	8.0 (0.800–1.000)	0.680	0.663	0.640
1994	Revenues 7.130 Expenditures 9.500, including capital expenditures of 4.000	6.0 (2.200)	0.630	0.727	0.621
1989	Revenues N/A; Expenditures 4.600, including capital expenditures of 1.950	25.8 of central government budget (1.187)	0.610	0.698	0.592

Country	Budget ($ billion)	Military Budget as percentage of GDP (figure in parentheses shows absolute sum spent in $ billion)	Education Index	HDI	GDI
Tunisia					
2009	Revenues 9.652 Expenditures 11.03	1.4 (0.430)	0.750	0.762	0.750
2004	Revenues 6.101 Expenditures 6.855, including capital expenditures of 1.600	1.5 (0.356)	0.740	0.76	0.734
1999	Revenues 5.800 Expenditures 6.500, including capital expenditures to 1.400	1.5 (0.356)	0.680	0.695	0.681
1994	Revenues 4.300 Expenditures 5.500	3.7 (0.618)	0.620	0.690	0.620
1989	Revenues 3.080 Expenditures 3.420, including capital expenditures of 1.000	7.7 of central government budget (0.269)	0.590	0.627	0.598
United Arab Emirates					
2009	Revenues 83.15 Expenditure 48.30	3.1 (2.731)	0.791	0.903	0.855
2004	Revenues 17.35 Expenditure 23.85, including capital expenditures of 3.40	3.1 (1.600)	0.740	0.839	0.821

Country	Budget ($ billion)	Military Budget as percentage of GDP (figure in parentheses shows absolute sum spent in $ billion)	Education Index	HDI	GDI
1999	Revenues 5.40 Expenditures 5.80, including capital expenditures of 0.35	5.0 (2.118)	0.730	0.812	0.790
1994	Revenues 4.30 Expenditures 4.80	5.3 (1.470)	0.690	0.771	0.752
1989	Revenue 3.00 Expenditures 3.90, including capital expenditures of 0.27	40.0 of central government budget (1.590)	0.620	0.736	0.682
West Bank					
2009	Revenues 1.1490 Expenditures 2.3100[6]	...	...	0.731[7]	...
2004	Revenues 0.6766 Expenditures 1.1550	...	...	...	...
1999	Revenues 0.8160 Expenditures 0.8660	...	...	...	...
1994	Revenues 0.0434 Expenditures 0.0437	...	...	...	...
1989	Revenues 0.0474 Expenditures 0.0457	...	...	...	...
Western Sahara					
2009	...	...	...	...	...
2004	...	...	...	...	...

Country	Budget ($ billion)	Military Budget as percentage of GDP (figure in parentheses shows absolute sum spent in $ billion)	Education Index	HDI	GDI
1999	...	...	...	...	...
1994	...	...	...	...	...
1989	...	...	...	...	...
Yemen					
2009	Revenues 9.097 Expenditures 10.550	6.6 (0.126)	0.545	0.567	0.472
2004	Revenues 3.729 Expenditures 4.107	7.9 (0.886)	0.500	0.492	0.462
1999	Revenues 2.300 Expenditures 2.600	7.6 (0.414)	0.450	0.449	0.408
1994	...	14.0 (0.762)	0.420	0.323	0.384
1989	Revenues 0.474 Expenditures 0.848, including capital expenditures of 0.323	...	0.390	0.310	0.359
Iran					
2009	Revenues 51.00 Expenditure 103.00	2.5 (5.620)	0.792	0.777	0.750
2004	Revenues 40.38 Expenditures 40.29, including capital expenditures of 7.60	3.3 (4.300)	0.740	0.746	0.713
1999	Revenues 34.60 Expenditures 34.90, including capital expenditures of 11.80	2.9 (5.787)	0.730	0.715	0.696

Country	Budget ($ billion)	Military Budget as percentage of GDP (figure in parentheses shows absolute sum spent in $ billion)	Education Index	HDI	GDI
1994	...	According to official Iranian data, Iran spent 1,785 billion rials, including 0.808 billion in hard currency in 1992 and budgeted 2,507 billion rials, including 0.850 billion in hard currency for 1993.	0.710	0.672	0.672
1989	Revenue N/A Expenditures 55.10, including capital expenditures of 11.50	...	0.640	0.598	0.620
Israel					
2009	Revenues 68.44 Expenditures 70.06	7.3 (10.23)	0.946	0.930	0.927
2004	Revenues 44.98 Expenditures 51.07	8.7 (9.11)	0.906	0.927	0.940
1999	Revenues 55.00 Expenditures 58.00	9.5 (8.70)	0.900	0.883	0.879
1994	Revenues 33.40 Expenditures 36.30, including capital expenditures of 9.40	18 (12.50)	0.850	0.900	0.842
1989	Revenues 23.50 Expenditures 23.30	17.7 of central government budget (5.20)	0.720	0.852	0.756
Turkey					
2009	Revenues 164.60 Expenditures 176.30	5.3 (13.142)	0.812	0.798	0.763

Country	Budget ($ billion)	Military Budget as percentage of GDP (figure in parentheses shows absolute sum spent in $ billion)	Education Index	HDI	GDI
2004	Revenues 66.79 Expenditures 93.31	5.3 (12.155)	0.800	0.757	0.746
1999	Revenues 44.40 Expenditures 58.50, including capital expenditures of 3.70	4.3 (6.737)	0.760	0.728	0.722
1994	Revenues 36.50 Expenditures 47.60	5.6 (14.000)	0.730	0.739	0.698
1989	Revenues 10.16 Expenditures 12.01, including capital expenditures of 2.17	18.2 of central government budget (3.100)	0.580	0.671	0.651

1   The Education Index is measured by the adult literacy rate (with two-thirds weighting) and the combined primary, secondary, and tertiary gross enrollment ratio (with one-third weighting). The adult literacy rate gives an indication of the ability to read and write, while the gross enrollment ratio gives an indication of the level of education from kindergarten to postgraduate education.

2   The Human Development Index (HDI) is used to rank countries by level of "human development," also used to determine whether a country is developed, developing, or underdeveloped.

3   The Gender-related Development Index (GDI) is an indication of the standard of living in a country used by the United Nations. It is one of the five indicators used by the United Nations Development Programme in its annual *Human Development Report*. It aims to show the inequalities between men and women in the following areas: long and healthy life, knowledge, and a decent standard of living.

4   Includes the West Bank.

5   Includes the West Bank.

6   Includes the Gaza Strip.

7   Includes the Gaza Strip.

Government

Country	Type of Political System	Head of State in Power	Last Legislative Elections
Algeria			
2009	Republic	President Abdul-Aziz Bouteflika (since 28 April 1999)	National People's Assembly; last held 17 May 2007; next to be held in 2012. Council of Nations (Senate); last held 29 December 2009; next to be held December 2012.
2004		...	...
1999		President Liamine Zeroual (appointed president 31 January 1994; elected president 16 November 1995)	National People's Assembly; last held 5 June 1997; then held in 2001. Elections for two-thirds of the Council of Nations; last held 25 December 1997; then held in 2003.
1994		...	Elections—first round held 26 December 1991 (second round cancelled by the military after President Benjedid resigned on 11 January 1992, effectively suspending the assembly); the fundamentalist FIS won 188 of the 231 seats contested in the first round. Note: Elections (municipal and *wilaya*) held in June 1990, the first in Algerian history; results—FIS 55%, FLN 27.5%, other 17.5%, with 65% of voters participating.
1989		President Chadli Benjedid (since 7 February 1979)	Last held 26 February 1987.
Bahrain			
2009	Constitutional monarchy	King Hamad bin Isa al-Khalifa (since 6 March 1999)	Council of Representatives; last held November–December 2006; next to be held in 2010.
2004		...	House of Deputies; last held 31 October 2002; then held 2006. Note: First elections held since 7 December 1973; unicameral National Assembly dissolved 26 August 1975; National Action Charter created bicameral legislature 23 December 2000; approved by referendum 14 February 2001; first legislative session of parliament held 25 December 2002.

Country	Type of Political System	Head of State in Power	Last Legislative Elections
1999	...		
1994		Amir Isa bin Salman al-Khalifa (since 2 November 1961)	Unicameral National Assembly was dissolved 26 August 1975 and legislative powers were assumed by Cabinet; appointed Advisory Council established 16 December 1992.
1989		Amir Isa bin Salman al-Khalifa (since 2 November 1961)	...
Comoros			
2009	Republic	President Ahmed Abdullah Sambi (since 26 May 2006)	Held in April 2009.
2004		President Azali Assoumani (since 26 May 2002). Note: following a 1999 coup Azali was appointed president; in January 2002. He resigned his post to run in the 14 April 2002 presidential elections.	Unicameral Assembly of the Union (30 seats; half the deputies are selected by the individual islands' local assemblies and the other half by universal suffrage; deputies serve for five years). Note: Elections for the former legislature, the Federal Assembly (dissolved in 1999), were held 1 and 8 December 1996; the next elections for the Assembly of the Union were held 18 and 25 April 2004.
1999		Interim President Tadjddine Ben Said Massounde (since 6 November 1998). Note: President Mohamed Taki Abdulkarim died in office 6 November 1998 and was succeeded by Interim President Massoudne.	Federal Assembly; last held 1 and 8 December 1996.
1994		President Said Mohamed Djohar (since 11 March 1990)	Elections last held 12–20 December 1993; then held January 1998.

Country	Type of Political System	Head of State in Power	Last Legislative Elections
1989		President Ahmed Abdallah Abder-emane (since 22 October 1978)	Federal Assembly elected in March 1982.
Djibouti			
2009	Republic	President Ismail Omar Guelleh (since 8 May 1999)	Last held 8 February 2008; next to be held 2013.
2004		…	Last held 10 January 2003; then held in February 2008.
1999		President Hassan Gouled Aptidon (since 24 June 1977). Note: President Hassan Gouled announced early in the year that he would resign in April 1999.	At the time, last held 19 December 1997, and then held in 2003.
1994		…	Last held 18 December 1992; People's Progress Assembly (RPP) won 65 seats.
1989		…	Parliament and president elected April 1987— People's Progress Assembly (RPP) and Hassan Gouled Aptidon; sole legal party.
Egypt			
2009	Republic	President Muham-mad Hosni Mubarak (since 14 October 1981)	People's Assembly; three-phase voting; last held 7 and 20 November and 1 December 2005; next to be held November–December 2010. Advisory or Shura Council; last held June 2007; were due be held May–June 2010. Last presidential elections were held in 2005, and the next are due in 2011.
2004		…	People's Assembly; three-phase voting; last held 19 and 29 October, 8 November 2000; then held November–December 2005.

Country	Type of Political System	Head of State in Power	Last Legislative Elections
1999		...	People's Assembly; last held 29 November 1995; then held in 2000. Advisory Council; last held 7 June 1995.
1994		...	Last held 29 November 1990; then held in November 1995.
1989		...	Regular elections to People's Assembly every five years; next were due for April 1992. Two-thirds of Shura Council is elected for six-year term; next elections were to be held in October 1989, with remaining members appointed by president.

Presidential election every six years; last held October 1987. |

Gaza Strip and West Bank

2009	Occupied Territories[1]	Mahmoud Abbas[2]	Early presidential and parliamentary election to the Palestinian National Authority were to be held 25 January 2010, but did not take place because the split between the Hamas-controlled Gaza Strip under disputed Prime Minister Ismail Haniyeh and disputed President Aziz Duwaik and the Fatah-controlled West Bank under disputed Prime Minister Salam Fayyad and disputed President Mahmoud Abbas was not overcome.
2004			...
1999			...
1994			Under the Israel–PLO Declaration of Principles on Interim Self-Government Arrangements (DOP), Israel agreed to transfer certain powers and responsibilities to the Palestinian Authority, and subsequently to an elected Palestinian Council, as part of interim self-governing arrangements in the West Bank and Gaza Strip. A transfer of powers and responsibilities for the Gaza Strip and Jericho has taken place pursuant to the Israel–PLO 4 May 1994 Cairo Agreement on the Gaza Strip and the Jericho Area. The DOP provides that Israel will retain responsibility during the transitional period for external security and for internal security and public order of settlements and Israelis. Final status is to be determined through direct negotiation within five years.

Country	Type of Political System	Head of State in Power	Last Legislative Elections
1989			The Gaza Strip is governed by Israeli military authorities and Israeli civil administration. It is U.S. policy that the final status of the Gaza Strip will be determined by negotiations among the concerned parties. These negotiations will determine how this area is to be governed.
Iraq			
2009	Parliamentary democracy	President Jalal Talabani (since 6 April 2005)	Last held 15 December 2005 to elect a 275-member Council of Representatives; next were due to be held December 2009 but were in fact held 7 March 2010.
2004		Interim Iraqi Government (IG) President Ghazi al-Ujayl al-Yawr (since 1 June 2004); deputy presidents Ibrahim al-Jafari and Rowsch Shaways (since 1 June 2004). Note: The president and deputy presidents comprise the Presidency Council	Iraqi Interim National Council formed in July 2004.
1999		President Saddam Hussein (since 16 July 1979).	Last held 24 March 1996; then held in 2000.
1994		...	Last held 1 April 1989.
1989		...	National Assembly election held in October 1984. Legislative Council for the Autonomous Region election held September 1980.
Jordan			
2009	Constitutional monarchy	King Abdallah II (since 7 February 1999)	Chamber of Deputies; last held 20 November 2007; next to be held in 2011.
2004		...	House of Representatives; last held 17 June 2003; then to be held in 2007.

Country	Type of Political System	Head of State in Power	Last Legislative Elections
1999		...	House of Representatives; last held 4 November 1997; then to be held in November 2001.
1994		King Hussein bin Talal al-Hashimi (since 11 August 1952)	Last held 8 November 1993; then held in November 1997.

Note: House of Representatives has been convened and dissolved by the king several times since 1974, and in November 1989 the first parliamentary elections in 22 years were held. |
| 1989 | | ... | None scheduled. |
| **Kuwait** | | | |
| 2009 | Constitutional emirate | Amir Sabah al-Ahmad al-Jabir al-Sabah

(since 29 January 2006) | Last held 17 May 2008; next to be held in 2012. |
2004		Amir Jabir al-Ahmad al-Jabir al-Sabah (since 31 December 1977)	Last held 6 July 2003; then to be held in 2007.
1999		...	Last held 7 October 1996; then to be held around October 2000.
1994		...	Dissolved 3 July 1986; new elections were held 5 October 1992, with a second election in the 14th and 16th constituencies held in February 1993.
1989		...	National Assembly elected February 1985 (suspended July 1986).
Lebanon			
2009	Republic	President Michel Sulayman

(since 25 May 2008) | Last held in four rounds 29 May and 5, 12, and 19 June 2005; then held on 7 June 2009. |
| 2004 | | President Emile Lahud (since 24 November 1998) | Last held 27 August and 3 September 2000; then held in Spring 2005. |
| 1999 | | ... | Last held in the summer of 1996; then held in 2000. |

Country	Type of Political System	Head of State in Power	Last Legislative Elections
1994		President Elias Hrawi	National Assembly dissolved 3 July 1986; new elections held 5 October 1992 with a second election in the 14th and 16th constituencies held February 1993.
1989		Parliament failed to select a new president before President Amin Pierre Gemayel's term expired 23 September 1988. Acting Prime Minister Lt. Gen. Michel Aoun (since 23 September 1988); Acting Prime Minister Salim al-Huss (since 1 June 1987). Gemayel's last act as president was to appoint Gen. Michel Aoun as prime minister. However, the acting prime minister, Salim al-Huss refused to step down, resulting in two contending governments—one led by the Maronite Christian Aoun and the other by the Sunni Muslim Huss.	National Assembly election held every four years or within three months of dissolution of Parliament; security conditions have prevented parliamentary elections since April 1972.
Libya			
2009	Republic	Revolutionary Leader Col. Muammar Abu Minyar al-Qadhafi (since 1 September 1969)	Unicameral General People's Congress (760 seats; members elected indirectly through a hierarchy of people's committees).

Country	Type of Political System	Head of State in Power	Last Legislative Elections
2004			Unicameral General People's Congress (members elected indirectly through a hierarchy of people's committees).
1999		...	...
1994		...	...
1989		...	Representatives to the General People's Congress are drawn from popularly elected municipal committees.
Mauritania			
2009	Junta	Gen. Muhammad Ould Abdul Aziz, president of Military High Council of State (since 6 August 2008)	Senate; last held 21 January and 4 February 2007; then held in 2009. National Assembly; last held 19 November and 3 December 2006; next to be held in 2011.
2004		President Col. Maaouya Ould Sid Ahmed Taya (since 12 December 1984)	Senate; last held 12 April 2002; then held in April 2004. National Assembly; last held 19 and 26 October 2001; then held in 2006.
1999			Senate; last held 17 April 1998; then held in 2000. National Assembly; last held 11 and 18 October 1996; then held in 2001.
1994		...	Senate; last held 15 April 1994 (one-third of the seats up for reelection in 1996). National Assembly; last held 6 and 13 March 1992; then held in March 1997.
1989		...	Municipal election conducted in December 1986.
Morocco			
2009	Constitutional monarchy	King Mohammed VI (since 30 July 1999)	Chamber of Counselors; last held 8 September 2006; then held in 2009. Chamber of Representatives; last held 7 September 2007; next to be held in 2012.
2004		King Mohammed VI (since 30 July 1999)	Chamber of Counselors; last held 6 October 2003; then held in 2006. Chamber of Representatives; last held 27 September 2002; then held in 2007.

Country	Type of Political System	Head of State in Power	Last Legislative Elections
1999		King Hassan II (since 3 March 1961)	Chamber of Counselors; last held 5 December 1997; then held in December 2000. Chamber of Representatives; last held 14 November 1997; then held in November 2002.
1994		...	Chamber of Representatives; elections last held 15 June 1993 (direct popular vote) and 17 September 1993 (indirect special interest vote); next to be held 1997.
1989		...	Provincial elections held 10 June 1983. Elections for Chamber of Representatives held 14 September 1984.
Oman			
2009	Monarchy	Sultan and Prime Minister Qaboos bin Said al-Said (since 23 July 1970). Note: The monarch is both the chief of state and head of government.	Last held 27 October 2007; next to be held in 2011.
2004		...	Last held 4 October 2003; then held in 2007.
1999		...	
1994		...	...
1989		...	...
Qatar			
2009	Emirate	Amir Hamad bin Khalifa al-Thani (since 27 June 1995)	Unicameral Advisory Council (35 seats; members appointed). Note: No legislative elections have been held since 1970, when there were partial elections to the body; Council members have had their terms extended every year since the new constitution came into force on 9 June 2005.[3]
2004		...	...
1999		...	...

Country	Type of Political System	Head of State in Power	Last Legislative Elections
994		Amir and Prime Minister Khalifa bin Hamad al-Thani (since 22 February 1972)	...
989		...	Constitution calls for elections for part of State Advisory Council, a consultative body, but no elections have been held.
Saudi Arabia			
2009	Monarchy	King and Prime Minister Abdallah bin Abdul-Aziz al-Sa'ud (since 1 August 2005)	Consultative Council (150 members and a chairman appointed by the monarch for four-year terms).[4]
004		King and Prime Minister Fahd bin Abd al-Aziz al-Sa'ud (since 13 June 1982, but largely incapacitated since late 1995)	...
999		...	...
994		...	...
989		...	...
Somalia			
009	No permanent national government; transitional, parliamentary federal government	Transitional Federal President Sheikh Sharif Sheikh Ahmed (since 31 January 2009)	Unicameral National Assembly.[5]
004		Abdullahi Yusuf Ahmed (since 14 October 2004).	Fledgling parliament; a 275-member Transitional Federal Government in 2004 replaces the Transitional National Government created in 2000; the new parliament consists of 61 seats assigned to each of four large clan groups (Darod, Digil-Mirifle, Dir, and Hawiye) with the remaining 31 seats divided among minority clans.

Country	Type of Political System	Head of State in Power	Last Legislative Elections
1999		Somalia has no functioning government; the United Somali Congress (USC) ousted the regime of Major General Muhammad Siad Barre on 27 January 1991; the present political situation is one of anarchy, marked by interclan fighting and random banditry.	Unicameral People's Assembly; not functioning.
1994		Somalia has no functioning government; presidential elections last held 23 December 1986 and President Siad reelected without opposition.	Last held 31 December 1984.
1989		President and Commander-in-Chief of the Army Maj. Gen. Muhammad Siad Barre (since 21 October 1969).	Parliamentary election held 31 December 1984.
Sudan			
2009	Government of National Unity (GNU), National Congress Party (NCP), and Sudan People's Liberation Movement (SPLM) formed a power-sharing government under the 2005 Comprehensive Peace Agreement (CPA).[6]	President Umar Hassan Ahmad al-Bashir (since 16 October 1993)	Last held 13–22 December 2000; then held in 2009.

Country	Type of Political System	Head of State in Power	Last Legislative Elections
2004		...	Last held 13–22 December 2000; then held in December 2004.
1999		...	Last held 6–17 March 1996; then held in 2001.
1994		...	Appointed 300-member Transitional National Assembly officially assumes all legislative authority for Sudan until the eventual, unspecified resumption of national elections.
1989		...	...

Syria

2009	Republic under an authoritarian military-dominated regime	President Bashar al-Asad (since 17 July 2000)	Last held on 22–23 April 2007; next to be held in 2011.
2004		...	Last held 2–3 March 2003; then held in 2007.
1999		President Hafez al-Asad (since 22 February 1971)	Last held 30 November–1 December 1998; then held in 2003.
1994		...	Last held 22–23 May 1990; then held in May 1994.
1989		...	People's Council election held in February 1986.

Tunisia

2009	Republic	President Zine el-Abidine Ben Ali (since 7 November 1987)	Chamber of Deputies; last held on 24 October 2004; next was held in October 2009. Chamber of Advisors; last held on 3 July 2005; next to be held in July 2011.
2004		...	Last held 24 October 2004; then held in October 2009.
1999		...	Last held 20 March 1994; then held in 1999.
1994		...	Last held 2 April 1989; then held in March 1994.
1989		...	National election held 2 April 1989.

Country	Type of Political System	Head of State in Power	Last Legislative Elections
United Arab Emirates			
2009	Federation with specified powers delegated to the U.A.E. federal government and other powers reserved for member emirates	President Khalifa bin Zayid al-Nuhayyan (since 3 November 2004)	Elections for one half of the Federal National Council (the other half remains appointed) held 18–20 December 2006.[7]
2004		...	...
1999		President Zayid bin Sultan al-Nuhayyan (since 2 December 1971)	...
1994		...	...
1989		...	...
Western Sahara			
2009	Sovereignty unresolved[8]	Under *de facto* control of Morocco	...
2004		...	...
1999		...	...
1994		...	...
1989		...	...
Yemen			
2009	Republic	President Ali Abdullah Saleh (since 22 May 1990)	Last held April 2009.
2004		...	Last held 27 April 2003; then held in April 2009.

Country	Type of Political System	Head of State in Power	Last Legislative Elections
1999		...	In May 1997, the president created a Consultative Council, sometimes referred to as the upper house of parliament; its 59 members are all appointed by the president.
1994		...	Last held 27 April 1993.
1989		Haydar Abu Bakr al-Attas. (Before unification, al-Attas served as prime minister (1985–86) and chairman of the Presidium of the Supreme People's Council (1986–90) in the southern PDRY).	Elections for legislative body and Supreme People's Council are called for in the constitution, but none have been held.
Iran			
2009	Theocratic republic	Mahmoud Ahmadinejad (since 2005)	Last held 14 March 2008, with a runoff held 25 April 2008; next to be held in 2012.
2004		President (Ali) Muhammad Khatami-Ardakani (since 3 August 1997)	Last held 20 February 2004, with a runoff held 7 May 2004; then held in 2008.
1999		...	Last held 8 March and 19 April 1996; then held in 2000.
1994		President Ali Akbar Hashemi-Rafsanjani (since 3 August 1989)	Islamic Consultative Assembly elections last held 8 April 1992; then held in 1996.
1989		...	Parliamentary election held in April 1992. Assembly of Experts election will be held in 1989.
Israel			
2009	Parliamentary democracy	President Shimon Peres (since 15 July 2007)	Last held 10 February 2009; next to be held in 2013.

Country	Type of Political System	Head of State in Power	Last Legislative Elections
2004		President Moshe Katzav (since 31 July 2000)	Last held 28 January 2003; then held 2006.
1999		President Ezer Weizman (since 13 May 1993)	Last held 29 May 1996 (early elections were scheduled for 17 May 1999).
1994		...	Last held in June 1992; next held 1996.
1989		President Gen. Chaim Herzog (since 5 May 1983)	Held every four years unless required by dissolution of Knesset; last held in November 1988; then held June 1992.
Turkey			
2009	Republican parliamentary democracy	Abdullah Gul (since 2007)	Last held 22 July 2007; next to be held in November 2012.
2004		President Ahmet Necdet Sezer (since 16 May 2000)	Last held 3 November 2002; then held in 2007.
1999		President Suleyman Demirel (since 16 May 1993)	Last held 24 December 1995; then held 18 April 1999.
1994		...	Last held 20 October 1991; then held in May 1996.
1989		President Gen. Kenan Evren (since 1982)	According to the constitution, elections to the Grand National Assembly to be held every five years; last held 29 November 1987.

1   The West Bank and the Gaza Strip are Israeli-occupied, with their current status subject to the Israeli–Palestinian Interim Agreement. Permanent status will be determined through further negotiation. Israel continues its construction of a "seam line" separation barrier along parts of the Green Line and within the West Bank. It withdrew from four settlements in the northern West Bank, as well as settlers and military personnel from the Gaza Strip, in August 2005. Since 1948, about 350 peacekeepers from the UN Truce Supervision Organization (UNTSO), headquartered in Jerusalem, monitor ceasefires, supervise armistice agreements, prevent isolated incidents from escalating, and assist other UN personnel in the region. Israel removed settlers and military personnel from the Gaza Strip in August 2005.

2   Palestinian Prime Minister Mahmoud Abbas won the January 2005 poll to replace the late Palestinian leader Yasser Arafat.
3   The constitution provides for a new 45-member Advisory Council, or Majlis al-Shura. The public would elect two-thirds of the Majlis al-Shura, and the amir would appoint the remaining members. Preparations are underway to conduct elections to the Majlis al-Shura.
4   Although the Council of Ministers announced in October 2003 its intent to introduce elections for half of the members of local and provincial assemblies and a third of the members of the national Consultative Council, or Majlis al-Shura, incrementally over a period of four to five years, to date no such elections have been held or announced.
5   The Unicameral Transitional Federal Assembly (TFA) has 275 seats, with 244 members appointed by the four major clans (61 for each clan and 31 seats allocated to smaller clans and subclans).
6   The NCP, which came to power by military coup in 1989, is the majority partner. The agreement stipulates national elections in 2009.
7   The new electoral college—a body of 6,689 Emiratis (including 1,189 women) appointed by the rulers of the seven emirates—made up the only eligible voters and candidates. Four hundred and fifty-six candidates including 65 women ran for 20 contested FNC seats. One woman from Abu Dhabi won a seat, and 8 women were among the 20 appointed members.
8   Morocco claims and administers Western Sahara, whose sovereignty remains unresolved. A UN-administered ceasefire has remained in effect since September 1991, administered by the UN Mission for the Referendum in Western Sahara (MINURSO), but attempts to hold a referendum have failed and parties thus far have rejected all brokered proposals. Several states have extended diplomatic relations to the "Sahrawi Arab Democratic Republic," represented by the Polisario Front in exile in Algeria, while others recognize Moroccan sovereignty over Western Sahara. Most of the approximately 102,000 Sahrawi refugees are sheltered in camps in Tindouf, Algeria.

References

Abdul 'Ati, Muhammad. 2002. "Muhasilat al-sira'," 27 May 2002, http://www.aljazeera.net/in-depth/aljeria-election/2002/5/5-25-2.htm (accessed 25 November 2002).

Abdul Ghani, Najiba. 2007. *Taqrir iqlimi 'an al-dirasat al-mashiya li-l-mashru'at al-muwjjaha li-l-mar'a al-'arabiya fi majal al-sihha.* Cairo: Arab Women Organization.

Abdul Rahman, Hamdi, Nagih Ibrahim, and Ali al-Sharif. 2002. *Taslit al-adwa' 'ala ma waqa'a fi-l-jihad min akhta'.* Cairo: al-Turath al-Islami.

Abdulla, R. 2005a. "Taking the E-train: The Development of the Internet in Egypt." *Global Media and Communication* 1 (2): 149–65.

———. 2005b. *al-Intarnit fi Misr wa-l-'alam al-'arabi.* Cairo: Dar al-Afaq li-l-Nashr wa-l-Tawzi'.

———. 2005c. *Towards Believing What You See on the Egyptian News.... Well, at Least Most of It.* The Twelfth AUC Research Conference Proceedings, American University in Cairo, Egypt.

———. 2005d. "What They Post: Arabic-language Message Boards after the September 11 Attacks." In M. Salwen, B. Garrison, and P. Driscoll, eds. *Online News and the Public*, 279–302. Mahwah, NJ: Lawrence Erlbaum Associates.

———. 2006. "An Overview of Media Developments in Egypt: Does the Internet Make a Difference?" *Global Media Journal, Mediterranean Edition* 1 (1): 88–100.

———. 2007a. "Islam, Jihad, and Terrorism in Post 9/11 Arabic Discussion Boards." *Journal of Computer-Mediated Communication* 12 (3), http://jcmc.indiana.edu/vol12/issue3/abdulla.html (accessed 31 January 2010).

———. 2007b. *The Internet in the Arab World: Egypt and Beyond*. New York: Peter Lang.

———. 2008. "Arabic Language Use and Content on the Internet." Report presented to the Bibliotheca Alexandrina as part of the Access to Knowledge project, http://www.bibalex.org/a2k/attachments/references/rasha20en.pdf (accessed 22 December 2008).

———. 2009. "Policing the Internet: Online Freedom of Expression in the Arab World." *Emirates Occasional Papers* 68, Emirates Center for Strategic Studies and Research.

Abdulla, R.A. 1991. "The Effect of CNN on the Egyptian News during the Gulf War." Unpublished term paper, American University in Cairo.

Abdulla, R.A. 1995. "Welcome to the World of the Internet." *Brains Beyond Borders* 1 (1): 1–3.

AbouZeid, Ola. 1995. "al-Mar'a al-misriya fi-l-ahzab al-siyasiya." In Ola AbouZeid, ed. *al-Mar'a al-misriya wa-l-'amal al-'am*. Cairo: Centre for Political Research and Studies.

———. 2000. "Takhsis maqa'id li-l-mar'a fi-l-hayakil al-muntakhaba: dirasa fi-l-hala al-misriya." In Salwa Sharawi, ed. *Tamthil al-mar'a fi-l-majalis al-muntakhaba*, 167–95. Cairo: Public Administration Research and Consultation Centre.

———. 2001. "Taqyim al-musharaka al-siyasiya li-l-mar'a al-misriya: intikhabat 'am 2000." Lead paper for a roundtable organized by the Centre for Political Research and Studies, Cairo University, 28 April.

———. 2007. *Waqi' wa mustaqbal mashru'at nuhud al-mar'a al-'arabiya*. Cairo: Arab Women Organization.

Abu-Rabi', Ibrahim M. 2004. *Contemporary Arab Thought: Studies in Post-1967 Arab Intellectual History*. New York: Pluto Press.

Abu-Taleb, Hassan. 1994. "Egypt's Foreign Policy towards the Arab World 1970–1981." PhD thesis, Cairo University. (Later published in a slightly modified book form as *Egyptian-Arab Relations* by the Center of Arab Unity Studies, Beirut, 1996.)

Acharya, Amitai. 2007. "The Emerging Regional Architecture of World Politics." *World Politics* 59: 629–52.

Achou, Albert, and Peter Drucker. 2007. *The Clash of Barbarisms*. London: Saqi Books.

Adams, C. 1933. *Islam and Modernism in Egypt*. New York: Oxford University Press.

Ahmad, Makram A. 2002a. "al-Qawa'id tunaqish qiyadatiha fi liman Wadi al-Natrun." *al-Musawwar*, 28 June, 1, 12.

———. 2000b. "Ahmad yuhawir qiyadat al-Jama'a al-Islamiya kharij al-sujun." *al-Musawwar*, 5 July, 7–17.

Ajami, Fouad. 1981. *The Arab Predicament: Arab Political Thought and Practice since 1967*. Cambridge: Cambridge University Press.

Alagha, Joseph Elie. 2006. *The Shifts in Hizbollah's Ideology: Religious Ideology, Political Ideology and Political Program*. Amsterdam: Amsterdam University Press.

Alexander, Yonah. 2002. *Palestinian Religious Terrorism: Hamas and Islamic Jihad*. Ardsley, NY: Transnational Publishers.

"Algeria's Women Police Defy Danger and Stereotypes," Reuters, 6 August 2009.

Ali, Mohammed Hage. 2009. "Hezbollah's Political Evolution." *The Guardian*, 12 April.

Al Jazeera. 2008. "UN: Poverty Worsening in Gaza." 24 July, http://english. aljazeera.net/news/middleeast/2008/07/2008724105341256363.html (accessed 4 January 2010).

Amin, Galal. 1982. *'Awamil kharijiya aththarat fi tarikh Misr.* Beirut: Centre for Arab Unity Studies (CAUS).

Amin, H. 1996. "The Middle East and North Africa." In A. Wells, ed. *World Broadcasting: A Comparative View*, 121–44. New Jersey: Ablex.

———. 2001. "Mass Media in the Arab States." In K. Hafez, ed. *Mass Media, Politics, and Society in the Middle East*, 23–44. Cresskill, NJ: Hampton Press.

———. 2004. "Social Engineering: Transnational Broadcasting and Its Impact on Peace in the Middle East." *Global Media Journal* 2 (4), http://lass. calumet.purdue.edu/cca/gmj/OldSiteBackup/SubmittedDocuments/ archivedpapers/spring2004/refereed/amin.htm (accessed 5 January 2009).

Amin, H., and L. Gher. 2000. "Digital Communications in the Arab World Entering the 21st Century." In L. Gher and H. Amin, eds. *Civic Discourse and Digital Age Communications in the Middle East*, 109–40. Stanford, CT: Ablex.

Amin, Samir. 1977. *La nation arabe*. Paris, Minuit.

———. 2006. *Muzakkirati: madi li-hirasat al-mustaqbal*. London: Saqi Books.

———. 2007. "Political Islam in the Service of Imperialism." *Monthly Review*. http://monthlyreview.org/1207amin.htm#Volume, 1–16 (accessed 17 February 2010).

————. 2008. *The World We Wish to See: Revolutionary Objectives in the Twenty-first Century*. New York: Monthly Review Press.

Amiri, Rannie, "Time for Change? Understanding Lebanon's June Elections." *Counterpunch*, 1–3 May, http://www.counterpunch.org/amiri05012009.html (accessed 10 May 2010).

Arab Advisors Group (AAG) website. 2008, http://www.arabadvisors.com (accessed 5 January 2009).

Arab Network for NGOs and Arab Women Organization (AWO). 2005. *al-Taqrir al-sanawi al-rabi' li-l-munazamat al-ahliya al-'arabiya 2004: tamkin al-mar'a.*

Arab Radio and Television website. 2009, http://www.artonline.tv (accessed 7 January 2009).

Arab Women Organization (AWO). 2003. "al-Siyasat al-'amma." AWO document prepared by the AWO executive board, http://www.arabwomenorg.org/OrganizationGeneralPolicy.pdf (accessed 4 August 2010).

————. 2005. "Juhud Jami'at al-Duwal al-'Arabiya wa munazamatiha al-mutakhassisa min ajl taf'il al-hadaf al-thalith min ahdaf al-alfiya: ta'ziz al-musawah bayn al-jinsayn wa tamkin al-mar'a." Paper presented at the Sectorial Meeting of the League of Arab States and the United Nations, Cairo, 22–24 November.

Arkoun, Muhammad. 2002. *The Unthought in Contemporary Arab Thought*. London: Saqi Books.

Armstrong, David. 1993. *Revolution and World Order: The Revolutionary State in International Society*. Oxford: Clarendon Press.

Ashour, Omar. 2009. *The Deradicalization of Jihadists: Transforming Armed Islamist Movements*. New York and London: Routledge.

Assi, Hussein. 2009. "Who are Hezbollah's New Candidates for 2009 Elections?" *Al Manar*, 4 March, http://www.almanar.com.lb/newssite/NewsDetails.aspx?id=80317&language=en (accessed 10 May 2010).

al-'Awdah, Salman. 2007a. "Positive Alternatives," 18 November, http://en.islamtoday.net/artshow-413-526.htm (accessed 17 February 2010).

————. 2007b. "Taking Care of Things at Home," 28 June, http://en.islamtoday.net/artshow-239-519.htm (accessed 17 February 2010).

al-'Awwa, Salwa. 2006. *al-Jama'a al-Islamiya al-musallaha fi Misr*. Cairo: Dar al-Shuruq.

Ayubi, Nazih. 1982. "The Vulnerability of the Rich." In Malcolm H. Kerr and EI-Sayed Yassin, eds. *Rich and Poor States in the Middle East*, 349–414. Boulder, CO: Westview Press.

————. 1992. "Withered Socialism or Whether Socialism? The Radical Arab States as Populist-Corporatist Regimes." *Third World Quarterly* 13:89–105.

————. 1995. *Overstating the Arab State*. London: I.B. Tauris.

Al-Azmeh, Aziz, and Effie Fokas, eds. 2008. *Islam in Europe*. London and New York: Cambridge University Press.

Badran, Tony. 2009. "Hezbollah's Agenda in Lebanon." In *Current Trends in Islamist Ideology*, vol. 8. Washington, D.C.: Center on Islam, Democracy and the Future of the Muslim World, Hudson Institute.

al-Baghdadi, Ahmed. 2005. "Na'am, al-libiraliyyun wahdahum hum al-dimuqratiyyun." In Shukri al-Nabulsi, ed. *al-Libiraliyyun al-judud: jadal fikri*, 113–30. Cologne: al-Kamel Verlag.

Baker, Raymond Williams. 2003. *Islam without Fear: Egypt and the New Islamists*. Cambridge, MA: Harvard University Press.

Barakat, Halim. 1993. *The Arab World: Society, Culture, and State*. Berkeley, CA: University of California Press.

al-Barghouti, Tamim. 2008. *The Umma and Dawla*. London: Pluto Press.

Barraclough, Geoffrey, and Rachel F. Wall. *Survey of International Affairs*. 1955–56. Oxford: Oxford University Press for the Royal Institute of International Affairs.

Bayat, Assef. 2003. "The 'Street' and the Politics of Dissent in the Arab World." *Middle East Report*, no. 226:10–17.

————. 2007. *Making Islam Democratic: Social Movements and the Post-Islamist Turn*. Stanford, CA: Stanford University Press.

El-Beblawi, Hazem. 1982. "The Predicament of the Arab Gulf Oil States." In Malcolm H. Kerr and EI-Sayed Yassin, eds. *Rich and Poor States in the Middle East*, 165–224. Boulder, CO: Westview Press.

Beck, Ulrich. 2003. "The Silence of Words: On Terror and War." *Security Dialogue* 34(3): 255–67.

Bedjaoui, Youcef, Abbas Aroua, and Méziane Aït-Larbi. 1999. *An Inquiry into the Algerian Massacres*. Geneva: Hoggar.

Ben Aicha, Ahmad. 1996. "*al-Hayat* tuqabil Amir al-Gharb Ahmad Ben Aicha." Interview by Muhammad al-Muqaddim, *al-Hayat*, 8 June, 8.

————. 2000. "Ben Aicha: haqq al-'amal al-siyasi madmun fi ittifaq al-hudna." Interview by Muhammad al-Muqaddim, *al-Hayat*, 3 February, 8.

Ben Hajar, Ali. 2000. "Ali Ben Hajar yarwi li-l-*Hayat* tajribatuh dakhil al-Jama'a al-Musallaha wa-tafasil inshiqaquh 'anha." Interview by Muhammad al-Muqaddim, *al-Hayat*, 5 February, 8.

Benda, Julien. 2007. *The Treason of the Intellectuals*. New Brunswick, NJ: Transaction Publishers.

Benzine, Rachid. 2004. *Les nouveaux penseurs de l'Islam*. Paris: A. Michel.

Bermeo, Nancy. 1992. "Democracy and the Lessons of Dictatorship." *Comparative Politics* 24 (3): 273–91.

Binder, Leonard. 1958. "The Middle East Subordinate International System." *World Politics* 10:408–29.

———. 1964. *The Ideological Revolution in Middle East*. New York: John Wiley and Sons, Inc.

———. 1988. *Islamic Liberalism: A Critique of Development Ideologies*. Chicago, IL: Chicago University Press.

al-Bitar, Nadeem. 2002. *al-Muthaqqafun wa-l-thawra: suqut al-intalijantsiya al-'arabiya*. Beirut: Bisan Books.

Bou Abdullah, Awad. 2006. "Nar taht al-ramad fi balad al-milyun shahid." Interview by Ahmad Abdullah, *al-'Ayn al-Thalitha*, Al Arabiya, 10 November.

Bourdieu, Pierre. 2007. *Sketch for a Self-Analysis*. Chicago, IL: University of Chicago Press.

———. 2008. *Political Interventions: Social Science and Political Action*. New York: Verso.

Bouteflika, Abdelaziz. 2005. "Bouteflika yatlub 'al-'afuw' min 'al-ta'ibiyyin." Report by Muhammad al-Muqaddim, *al-Hayat*, 9 February, 8.

Boyd, D. 1975. Development of Egypt's Radio: 'Voice of the Arabs' under Nasser. *Journalism Quarterly* 52 (4): 645–53.

———. "Egyptian Radio: Tool of Political and National Development." *Journalism Monographs* 55 (3): 501–39.

———. "Saudi Arabia's International Media Strategy: Influence through Multinational Ownership." Paper presented at the Association for Education in Journalism and Mass Communication, Baltimore, MD, August 1998.

———. 1999. *Broadcasting in the Arab World: A Survey of the Electronic Media in the Middle East*, 3rd ed. Ames, IA: Iowa State University Press.

Brachman, Jarret. 2009. *Global Jihadism: Theory and Practice*. New York: Routledge.

Bröning, Michael. 2009. "Hamas 2.0: The Islamic Resistance Movement Grows Up." *Foreign Affairs*, 5 August, http://www.foreignaffairs.com/articles/65214/michael-brÄning/hamas-20 (accessed 10 January 2010).

Brown, L. Carl. 1984. *International Relations of the Middle East*. Princeton, NJ: Princeton University Press.

Brubaker, Roger. 1996. *Nationalism Reframed: Nationhood and the National Question in the New Europe*. New York: Cambridge University Press.

Bruckman, Jarret. 2009. *Global Jihadism*. London and New York: Routledge.

Camus, Michel. 1991. "Le Maghreb." In Maurice Flory, Bahgat Korany, P. Mantran and Michel Camus, *Regimes Politiques Arabes*. Paris: PUF, http://www.reuters.com/article/idUSTRE5754S42009080 (accessed 19 February 2010).

Carey, Sabine. 2002. "Uncovering the Dynamics of Domestic Conflict: A Time-Series Analysis of Protest and Repression in Latin America and Sub-Saharan Africa." Paper prepared for the ECPR Joint Sessions, "Workshop 9: The Systematic Study of Human Rights Violations," March.

Carter, Jimmy. 2006. "Punishing the Innocent Is a Crime." *New York Times*, 7 May, http://www.nytimes.com/2006/05/07/opinion/07iht-edcarter.html (accessed 10 January 2010).

Chatham House. 2009. *The Gulf Region: A New Hub of Global Financial Power*. London: Royal Institute of International Affairs.

Chehab, Zaki. 2007. *Inside Hamas: The Untold Story of Militants, Martyrs and Spies*. London: I.B. Tauris.

Choukri, Nazli. 1986. "The Hidden Enemy: A New View of Remittances in the Arab World." *World Development* 14 (6): 697–712.

Cobden, Richard. 1867. *Political Writings*, vol. 1. London: Ridgway.

Cordesman, Anthony. "Preliminary 'Lessons' of the Israeli–Hezbollah War." 2006. Draft working paper, http://csis.org/files/media/csis/pubs/060817_isr_hez_lessons.pdf (accessed 10 May 2009).

Cordesman, Anthony H., with George Sullivan, and William D. Sullivan. 2007. *Lessons of the 2006 Israeli–Hezbollah War*. Significant Issues Series, vol. 29, no. 4. Washington, D.C.: CSIS Press.

Cosantini, Faruq. 2005. "al-Jaza'ir: tahqiq hukumi yuhammil al-'amn mas'uliyyat ikhtifa' 6,146 madani." Interview by Bou Allam Ghimrasa, *al-Sharq al-awsat*, 1 April, 1.

———. 2006a. "al-Amn awqaf nisf milyun jaza'iri bi-tuhmat al-Irhab." interview by Ramadan Bil'amry, Al Arabiya, 24 January.

———. 2006b. "Huwar ma' ra'is al-lajna al-istishariya li-himayat huquq al-insan." Interview by Omar Taha, *al-Zaman*, 11 November, 19.

Davenport, Christian. 2000. *Human Rights Violations and Contentious Politics*. Lanham: Rowman and Littlefield.

Davidson, Christopher. 2008. *Dubai: The Vulnerability of Success*. London: Hurst.

Dawisha, Adeed. 2003. *Arab Nationalism in the Twentieth Century: From Triumph to Despair*. Princeton, NJ: Princeton University Press.

Dessouki, Ali E. Hillal. 1982. The New Arab Political Order: Implications for the 1980s." In Malcolm H. Kerr and EI-Sayed Yassin, eds. *Rich and Poor States in the Middle East*, 319–47. Boulder, CO: Westview Press.

Easton, David. 1953. *The Political System*. New York: Knopf.

———. 1965. *A Systems Analysis of Political Life*. New York: Wiley.

Economic and Social Commission for Western Asia (ESCWA). 2004. "Where Do Arab Women Stand in the Development Process: A Gender-based Statistical Analysis." 12 January, http://www.escwa.un.org/information/publications/edit/upload/SDD04E1.pdf (accessed 12 May 2010).

———. 2005. "Women's Empowerment in the Arab Region: Achievements, Challenges and Futures Actions." Paper presented at the Sectorial Meeting of the League of Arab States and the United Nations, Cairo, 22–24 November.

"Egypt Court Cancels Jail Terms for News Editors." 2009. *Reuters*, http://af.reuters.com/article/topNews/idAFJOE50U07F20090131 (accessed 31 January 2009).

Ehteshami, Anoushiraven. 2007. *Globalization and Geo-Politics in the Middle East: Old Games, New Rules*. London and New York: Routledge.

———. 2008. *Competing Power Brokers of the Middle East: Iran and Saudi Arabia*. Abu Dhabi: Emirates Centre for Strategic Studies and Research, Occasional Papers.

Erlanger, Steve. 2009. "Egypt Pressed on Gaza's from Without and Within." *New York Times*, 2 January, http://www.nytimes.com/2009/01/03/world/middleeast/03egypt.html (accessed 10 January 2010).

Esposito, John, and John Voll. 2001. *The Makers of Contemporary Islam*. New York: Oxford University Press.

Eyerman, Ron. 1994. *Between Culture and Politics: Intellectuals in Modern Societies*. London: Polity Press.

Fandi, Mamun. 2001. *Saudi Arabia and the Politics of Dissent*. New York: St. Martin's Press.

Fandy, M. 2007. *(Un)Civil War of Words: Media and Politics in the Arab World*. Westport, CT and London: Praeger Security International.

Fawcett, Louise, ed. 2005. *International Relations of the Middle East*. Oxford: Oxford University Press.

Feldman, Shai. 2006. "The Hezbollah–Israel War: A Preliminary Assessment." *Middle East Brief*, no. 10. Crown Center for Middle Eastern Studies, Brandeis University, http://www.brandeis.edu/crown/ publications/meb/MEB10.pdf (accessed 11 May 2010).

Fero, Marc. 1986. *Comment on racont l'histoire aux enfants dans le monde entier.* Paris: Payot.

Flory, Maurice, Bahgat Korany, and Michel Camus. 1991. *Regimes politiques arabes.* Paris: Presses universitaires de France.

Fontana, Benedetto. 2009. "Power and democracy: Gramsci and Hegemony in America." In Jospeh Francese, ed. *Perspectives on Gramsci: Politics, Culture, and Social Theory*. New York: Routledge.

Foucault, Michel. 2000. *Power*. New York: New Press.

Fromkin, David. 2000. *Peace to End All Peace: Creating the Middle East, 1914–1922*. London: Penguin.

Fukuyama, Francis. 1992. *The End of History and the Last Man*. Glencoe, IL: Free Press.

Fuller, Graham E. 2006–2007 "The Hezbollah-Iran Connection: Model for Sunni Resistance." *Washington Quarterly* 30 (1): 139–50.

Gabriel, Kemal. 2005. "al-Libiraliyya al-jadida wa fada' yatashakkal." In Shukri al-Nabulsi, ed. *al-Libiraliyyun al-judud: jadal fikri*, 75–88. Cologne: Al-Kamel Verlag.

Gambill, Gary C. 2003. "The Syrian Occupation of Lebanon." *Middle East Forum*, 13 March, http://www.meforum.org/article/546 (accessed 31 January 2010).

Gause, F. Gregory, III. 1994. "The Illogic of Dual Containment." *Foreign Affairs* 73 (2): 22–44.

Gerges, Fawaz. 2005. *The Distant Enemy*. London and New York: Cambridge University Press.

Ghalioun, Burhan. 1997. *Etat contre nation*. Paris: Maspero.

Ghazoul, Ferial J., ed. 2007. *Edward Said and Critical Decolonization*. Cairo: American University in Cairo Press.

Gibb, H. 1947. *Modern Trends in Islam*. Chicago, IL: Chicago University Press.

Gilpin, Robert. 1981. *War and Change in World Politics*. Cambridge: Cambridge University Press.

Goldstone, Jack. 1989. *Revolution and Rebellion in the Early Modern World.* Berkeley, CA: University of California Press.

Gramsci, Antonio. 1971. *Selections from the Prison Notebooks*. New York: International Publishers.

Gruber, Shai. 2007. "Hamas: Pragmatic Ideology." *Fletcher School Journal for Studies of Southwest Asia and Islamic Civilization*, Spring, http://www.ciaonet.org/olj/aln/aln_spring07/aln_spring07e.pdf (accessed 31 January 2010).

Gunning, Jeroen. 2008. *Hamas in Politics: Democracy, Religion, Violence*. New York: Columbia University Press.

Haas, Ernest. 1953. "The Balance of Power: Prescription, Concept and Propaganda." *World Politics* 5 (4): 442–77.

Hafez, Kai. 2005. "Arab Satelite Broadcasting: Democracy Without Political Parties." *Transnational Broadcasting Studies*, no. 15, http://www.tbsjournal.com/Archives/Fall05/Hafez.html (accessed 6 January 2009).

Haffadh, Nada. 2008. "Women's Security and Health Issues." Paper presented at the second Arab Women Organization conference, "Women in the Concept and Issues of Human Security: Arab and International Perspectives," Abu Dhabi, 11–13 November.

Hafiz, Usama, and Asim Abdul Majid. 2002. *Mubadarat qaqf al-'unf: ru'ya waqi'iya wa nazra shar'iya*. Cairo: al-Turath al-Islami.

Hall, John, and Ralph Schroeder. 2006. *The Anatomy of Power: The Social Theory of Michael Mann*. New York: Cambridge University Press.

Hamzeh, Ahmed Nizar. 2004. *In the Path of Hezbollah*. Syracuse, NY: Syracuse University Press.

Harik, Judith Palmer. 2004. *Hezbollah: The Changing Face of Terrorism*. London: I.B. Tauris.

Hefner, Robert, ed. 2005. *Remaking Muslim Politics: Pluralism, Contestation, Democratization*. Princeton, NJ: Princeton University Press.

Heikal, Mohamed. 1978a. "Egypt's Foreign Policy." *Foreign Affairs* 56:714–27.

———. 1978b. *The Sphinx and the Commissar*. New York: Harper and Row.

Heydemann, Steven. 2007. "Upgrading Authoritarianism in the Arab World." Analysis Paper, no. 13. Saban Center for Middle East Policy at the Brookings Institute.

Heydemann, Steven, ed. 2000. *War, Institutions and Social Change in the Middle East*. Berkeley and London: University of California Press.

Hilal, Ali, and Gamil Mattar. 1980. *al-Nizam al-iqlimi al-'arabi*. Beirut: Centre for Arab Unity Studies.

Hilton, I. 2005. "'Al-Jazeera': And Now, the Other News." *New York Times*, 6 March, http://tv.nytimes.com/2005/03/06/books/review/006HILTON. html?pagewanted=print&position (accessed 7 March 2010).

Hiro, Dilip. 1993. *Lebanon Fire and Ember*. New York: St. Martins Press.

El-Hokayem, Emile. 2007. "Hezbollah and Syria Outgrowing the Proxy Relationship." *Washington Quarterly* 30 (2): 35–52.

Hourani, Albert. 1970. *Arabic Thought in the Liberal Age, 1789–1939*. Cambridge: Cambridge University Press.

———. 1991. *A History of the Arab Peoples*. New York: MJF Books.

Hroub, Khaled. 2008. "Hamas In and Out of Power." In "Domestic Change and Conflict in the Mediterranean: The Cases of Hamas and Hezbollah." *EuroMeSCo Paper 65*, January.

Hudson, Michael C. 1994. "Democracy and Foreign Policy in the Arab World." In David Garnham and Mark Tessler, eds. *Democracy, War and Peace in the Middle East*, 195–221. Bloomington: Indiana University Press.

Hudson, Michael, ed. 1999. *Middle East Dilemmas*. New York: Columbia University Press.

Humphreys, Stephen. 2005. *Between Memory and Desire: The Middle East in a Troubled Age*. Berkeley, CA: University of California Press.

Ibrahim, Nagih. 1990. *Hatmiyyat al-muwajaha*. Cairo: n.p.

———. 2005a. *Hatmiyyat al-muwajaha wa-fiqh al-nata'ij*. Cairo: al-Abikan.

———. 2005b. *Tajdid al-khitab al-dini*. Cairo: al-Abikan.

———. 2007. "Ibrahim yakshif al-sitar 'an ahdath akhbar al-mubadara." Interview by Usama Abdul Azim, http://egyig.com/Public/chapters/ interview/6/83640472.html (accessed 10 May 2010).

Ibrahim, Nagih, Asim Abd al-Majid, and Essam Dirbala. 1984. *Mithaq al-'amal al-islami*. Cairo: n.p.

Ibrahim, Nagih, and Karam Zuhdi. 2005. *Hidayat al-khala'iq bayna al-ghayat wa-l-wasa'il*. Cairo: al-Abikan.

Ibrahim, Saad Eddin. 1982. "Oil, Migration, and the New Arab Social Order." In Malcolm Kerr and El-Sayed Yassin, eds. *Rich and Poor States in the Middle East*, 17–70. Boulder, CO: Westview Press.

———. 1999. "The Changing Face of Egypt's Islamic Activism." In P. Marr, ed. *Egypt at the Crossroads: Domestic Stability and Regional Role*, 29–46. Washington, D.C: National Defense University Press.

———. 2004. "Challenges for Islam and Democracy." Lecture delivered at the Law Faculty, McGill University, Montreal, Canada, 19 February.

Idris, Mohamed. 2001. *Tahlil al-anzima al-iqlimiya al-far'iya.* Cairo: al-Ahram.

Indyk, Martin, G. Fuller, A. Cordesman, and P. Marr. 1994. "Dual Containment." *Middle East Policy* 3:1–26.

Information and Decision Support Center (IDSC). 2008. "Egyptian Blogs: A New Social Cyberspace." Informatics Reports, no. 17 (May).

Inter-Parliamentary Union (IPU). 2008a. *Equality in Politics: A Survey of Women and Men in Parliaments.* Reports and documents, no. 54. Geneva: IPU. http://www.ipu.org/PDF/publications/equality08-e.pdf (accessed 12 May 2010).

———. 2008b. *Women in National Parliaments: Situation as of 31 October 2008.* http://www.ipu.org/PDF/publications/equality08-e.pdf (accessed 3 June 2010).

International Center for Journalists (ICJ) website. 2008. http://knight.icfj.org/Awards/KnightAwardsPastWinners/WaelAbbas/tabid/807/Default.asp (accessed 12 November 2008).

International Labor Organization (ILO). 2004. *World Empowerment Report 2004–05: Employment, Productivity and Poverty Reduction,* http://www.un.org/special-rep/ohrlls/ohrlls/Global-reports.htm (accessed 3 June 2010).

International Telecommunication Union (ITU). 2001. *Internet on the Nile: Egypt Case Study.* http://www.itu.int/itudoc/gs/promo/bdt/cast_int/80621.pdf (accessed 1 November 2009).

Izel, B., J.S. Wafa, and W. Isaac. 1999. "What is the GIA?" In Youcef Bedjaoui, Abbas Aroua, Méziane Aït-Larbi, eds. *An Inquiry into the Algerian Massacres,* 373–459. Geneva: Hoggar.

Jaber, Hala. 1997. *Hezbollah: Born with a Vengeance.* New York: Columbia University Press.

Jacoby, Russel. 2000. *The Last Intellectuals: American Culture in the Age of Academe.* New York: Basic Books.

Jahin, Salih. 2007. "al-Muttahham al-12 fi qadiyyat ightiyal al-Sadat." Interview by Ahmad al-Khatib, *al-Jarida,* 2 December, 12.

Jensen, Michael Irving. *The Political Ideology of Hamas: A Grassroots Perspective.* London: I.B. Tauris.

Jerbawi, Ali. 2008. "International Conflicts and Women." Unpublished paper submitted to the 2nd Summit of the Arab Woman Organization, Abu Dhabi.

Kabir, Mustafa. 2002. "Amir mantiqatt al-Sharq al-Jaza'iri li-Jaysh al-Inqadh: 'awdat al-inqadh mas'alat waqt," *al-Zaman,* 2 February, 8.

Kandil, Amani. 1995. *The Arab Civil Society.* Cairo and Washington: World Alliance for Citizen Participation (CIVICUS).

———. 1997. "Religious Nonprofit Organizations in Egypt." Paper presented to members of the Johns Hopkins Comparative Nonprofit Sector Project.

———, ed. 2005. *al-Taqrir al-sanawi al-rabi' li-l-munazzamat al-ahliya al-'arabiya: tamkin al-mar'a.* Cairo: Arab Network for NGOs.

———. 2006a. *Promoting the Role of Egyptian NGOs Concerned with Youth* (in Arabic and English). Cairo: UNFPA.

———, ed. 2006b. *al-Tatawwur al-'alami wa-l-iqlimi li-mafhum huquq al-insan wa in'ikasatih 'ala al-munzzamat al-ahliya.* Cairo: Arab Network for NGOs in cooperation with UNDP.

———, ed. 2007. *al-Taqrir al-sanawi al-sadis li-l-munazzamat al-ahliya al-'arabiya: al-shabab fi manzumat al-mujtama' al-madani al-'arabi.* Cairo: Arab Network for NGOs.

———. 2008a. *Kharitat al-mujtama' al-madani al-'arabi.* Cairo: al-Shabaka al-Arabiya li-l-Munazzamat al-Ahliya.

———. 2008b. *al-Sharaka al-ijtima'iya wa mas'uliyat al-jam'iyat al-ahliya fi-l-tanmiya bi-duwal al-khalij al-'arabi.* Series of Social and Labor Studies no. 46. Bahrain: Executive Bureau of the Council of Ministers of Labor and Social Affairs for the Council of Cooperation between Arab Gulf Countries.

———, ed. 2008c. *al-Taqrir al-sanawi al-sabi' li-l-munazzamat al-ahliya al-'arabiya: al-atfal fi manzumat al-mujtama' al-madani al-'arabi.* Cairo: Arab Network for NGOs.

———. 2009a. *Social Responsibility in Gulf Countries.* Series of Social and Labor Studies, no. 56. Bahrain: Executive Bureau of the Council of Ministers of Labor and Social Affairs for the Council of Cooperation between Arab Gulf Countries.

———. 2009b. "Enhancing Civil Society in Egypt: An Opinion Poll." Unpublished report, National Council of Human Rights, Egypt.

———. 2010. *Mu'ashshirat fa'iliyat munazzamat al-mujtama' al-madani al-'arabi (Misr, Lubnan, al-Maghrib).* Cairo: Arab Network for NGOs.

Kandil, Amani, Abdullah Al-Khatib, Ayman Abdel-Wahab, Hashim Al-Husseini, and Fathia El-Saidi. 1998. *al-Isham al-iqtisadi wa-l-ijtima'i li-l-munazzamat al-ahliya fi-l-duwal al-'arabiya.* Cairo: Arab Network for NGOs.

Kandil, Amani, Emad Adly, Amina Lemriny, Rabia El-Naciri, Ibrahim Mohammed Ibrahim, and Seham Negm. 2003. *al-Shabakat al-'arabiya li-l-munazzamat ghayr al-hukumiya*. Cairo: Arab Network of NGOs.

Kandil Amani, Ilham Fateem, Amna Khalifa, Afaf al-Hemi, Naimaa ben el-Khatib, Hayim Sujud. 2010. *Indicators of Effectiveness in Arab Civil Society*. Cairo: Arab Network for NGOs.

Karpat, Kemal. 1982. *Political and Social Thought in the Contemporary Middle East*. New York: Praeger Press.

Kennedy, Paul. 1988. *The Rise and Fall of the Great Powers*. New York: Random House.

Keohane, Robert O., and Joseph S. Nye, Jr. 1977. *Power and Interdependence*. Boston: Little & Brown.

Kepel, Gilles. 2000. "Islamism Reconsidered." *Harvard International Review*, no. 22.

———. 2002. *Jihad: The Trial of Political Islam*. Cambridge, MA: Harvard University Press.

Kerr, Malcom. 1966. *Islamic Reform: The Political and Legal Theories of Muhammad 'Abduh and Rashid Rida*. Berkeley, CA: University of California Press.

Kerr, Malcolm H., and EI-Sayed Yassin, eds. 1982. *Rich and Poor States in the Middle East*. Boulder, CO: Westview Press.

Khalil, Abdallah. 2006. *al-Dalil al-tashri'i al-'arabi li-l-munazzamat al-ahliya*. Cairo: Arab Network for NGOs,.

Khalil', Azza. 2006. *al-Harakat al-ijtima'iya fi-l-'alam al-'arabi*. Cairo: Matbu'at Madbuli.

Khan, A. 2006. "The War Crime Machine: Defeating the IDF." *Counterpunch*, July 29/30. http://ssrn.com/abstract=946311 (accessed 24 July 2010).

Kissinger, Henry. 1994. "Reflections on Containment." *Foreign Affairs* 73(3): 113–30.

Kiwan, Fadia. 2007. *Taqrir iqlimi 'an al-dirasat al-mashiya li-l-mashru'at al-muwajjaha li-l-mar'a al-'arabiya fi majal al-siyasa*. Cairo: Arab Women Organization.

Kolakowski, Leszek. 1981. *Main Currents of Marxism: Its Origin, Growth and Dissolution: The Breakdown*. New York: Oxford University Press.

Koonings, Kees, and Dirk Kruijt. 2002. *Political Armies: The Military and Nation Building in the Age of Democracy*. New York: Zed Books.

Korany, Bahgat. 1976. *Social Change, Charisma and International Behavior*. Leiden: Sijthoff.

———. 1986. "Hierarchy within the South: In Search of Theory." In *Third World Affairs Yearbook, 1986*, 85–101. London: Third World Foundation for Social and Economic Studies.

———. 1988. "The Dialectics of Inter-Arab Relations 1967–1987." In Y. Lukacs and A. Batta, eds. The *Arab–Israeli Conflict*, 164–78. Boulder, CO: Westview Press.

———. 1997. "The Old/New Middle East." In Laura Guazzone, ed. *The Middle East in Global Change*. New York: St. Martin's.

———. 1999. "The Arab World and the New Balance of Power in the Middle East." In Michael Hudson, ed. *Middle East Dilemma: The Politics and Economics of Arab Integration*. New York: Columbia University Press.

———. 2005. "The Middle East since the Cold War." In Louise Fawcett, ed. *International Relations of the Middle East*, 59–77. Oxford: Oxford University Press.

———. 2008. "The World's Visions of Safety and Security: How Far Have Women Been Taken into Consideration?" Paper presented at the second Arab Women Organization conference, "Women in the Concept and Issues of Human Security: Arab and International Perspectives," Abu Dhabi, 11–13 November.

Korany, Bahgat, and Ali E.H. Dessouki, eds. 2008. *The Foreign Policies of Arab States*, 3rd ed. Cairo and New York: American University in Cairo Press.

Korany, B., R. Brynen, and P. Noble, eds. 1995. *Political Liberalization and Democratization in the Arab World: Theoretical Perspectives*. London: Lynne Rienner Publications.

———. 1998. *Political Liberalization and Democratization in the Arab World: Comparative Experiences*. Boulder, CO: Lynne Rienner.

Korany, Bahgat, Timothy M. Shaw, Juan Lindau, Cyril K. Daddieh, and Jorge I. Dominquez. 1986. *How Foreign Policy Decisions are Made in the Third World*. Boulder, CO: Westview Press.

Kramer, Martin. 2008. "1967 and Memory." *National Security Studies Program at the Weatherhead Center for International Affairs*. Middle East Strategy at Harvard, 13 November. http://blogs.law.harvard.edu/mesh/2008/11/1967-and-memory/ (accessed 11 May 2010).

Kristiansen, Wendy. 1999. "Challenge and Counterchallenge: Hamas' Response to Oslo." *Journal of Palestinian Studies* 28 (3): 19–36.

Kuhn, Thomas. 1970. *The Structure of Scientific Revolutions.* 2nd ed. Chicago: Chicago University Press. First published in 1962.

Kurzman, Charles. 1998. *Liberal Islam: A Sourcebook.* New York: Oxford University Press.

Kurzman, Charles, and Lynn Owens. 2002. "The Sociology of Intellectuals." *Annual Review of Sociology* 28:63–90.

Kuttab, D. 2008. "Satellite Censorship Arab League Style. *Arab Media and Society*, March. http://www.arabmediasociety.com/?article=651 (accessed 6 January 2009).

Laroui, Abdallah. 1976. *The Crisis of the Arab Intelligentsia: Traditionalism or Historicism?* Berkeley, CA: University of California Press.

Leelah, Ali. 2007. *Taqrir iqlimi 'an al-dirasat al-mashiya li-l-mashru'at al-muwajjaha li-l-mar'a al-'arabiya fi majal al-ta'lim.* Cairo: Arab Women Organization.

Legrenzi, Matteo. 2008. "Did the GGC Make a Difference?" In C. Harders and M. Legrenzi, eds. *Beyond Regionalism*, 107–24. Aldershot, UK, and Burlington, U.S.: Ashgate.

Leila, Ali, and Kandil, Amani, eds. 2007. *al-Idara al-rashida fi-l-mujtama' al-madani al-'arabi.* Cairo: Arab Network for NGOs.

Levitt, Matthew. 2004. "Hamas from Cradle to Grave." *Middle Eastern Quarterly* 11 (1): 3–15, http://www.meforum.org/582/hamas-from-cradle-to-grave (accessed 11 May 2010).

———. 2006. *Hamas: Politics, Charity in the Service of Jihad.* New Haven, CT: Yale University Press.

Lotfi, Wael. 2005. *Zahirat al-du'at al-judud.* Cairo: Maktabat al-Usra.

Louer, Laurence. 2009. *Transnational Shia Politics.* New York: Columbia University Press.

Love, K. 1969. *Suez: The Twice-fought War.* New York: McGraw-Hill.

Maddi, Shukri. 1978. *Hazimat yunyu 1967 fi-l-riwaya al-'arabiya.* Beirut: al-Mu'assasa al-'Arabiya li-l-Dirasat wa-l-Nashr.

Makiya, Kanan. 1993. *Cruelty and Silence: War, Tyranny, Uprising, and the Arab World.* New York: W.W. Norton Press.

Maniruzzaman, Talukder. 1987. *Military Withdrawal from Politics: A Comparative Study.* Cambridge, MA: Ballinger Publishing.

Mann, Michael. 1993. *The Sources of Social Power.* Vol. 2: *The Rise of Classes and Nation-states, 1760–1914.* New York: Cambridge University Press.

Mann, Michael. 2003. *Incoherent Empire.* New York: Verso.

Mannes, Aaron, Mary Michael, Amy Pate, Amy Silva, V.S. Subrahmanian, and Jonathan Wilkenfeld. 2008. "Stochastic Opponent Modeling Agents: A Case Study with Hezbollah." In Huan Liu, John J. Salerno, and Michael J. Young, eds. *Social Computing, Behavioral Modeling, and Prediction*, 37–45. London: Springer.

Marghalani, K., P. Palmgreen, and D. Boyd. 1998. "The Utilization of Direct Satellite Broadcasting (DBS) in Saudi Arabia." *Journal of Broadcasting and Electronic Media* 42 (3): 297–314.

al-Masri, Munther Wassef. 2008. "Education: The Effective Route for Women's Security." Paper presented at the second Arab Women Organization conference, "Women in the Concept and Issues of Human Security: Arab and International Perspectives," Abu Dhabi, 11–13 November.

Mathison, Sandra, ed. 2005. *Encyclopedia of Evaluation*. London: Sage Publications.

McAdam, Doug, John D. McCarthy, and Mayer Zald. 1996. *Comparative Perspectives on Social Movements: Political Opportunities, Mobilizing Structures, and Cultural Framings*. Cambridge: Cambridge University Press.

McGregor, Andrew. 2006. "Hezbollah's Tactics and Capabilities in Southern Lebanon." *Terrorism Focus* 3 (30), http://www.jamestown.org/single/?no_cache=1&tx_ttnews%5Btt_news%5D=860 (accessed 11 May 2010).

"Media Production City: A Colossal Media Complex," http://www.tour-egypt.net/mpc.htm (accessed 27 October 2002).

Meyer, David. 2002. "Opportunities and Identities: Bridge Building in the Study of Social Movements." In David S. Meyer, Nancy Whittier, and Belinda Robnett, eds. *Social Movements: Identity, Culture and the State*, 2–21. Oxford and New York: Oxford University Press.

———. 2004. "Protest and Political Opportunities". *Annual Review of Sociology* 30:125–45.

Meyer, David, and Debra C. Minkoff. 2004. "Conceptualizing Political Opportunity." *Social Forces* 8 (4): 1457–92.

Mezraq, Madani. 2004. "Liqa' ma' Madani Mezraq: al-amir al-watani li-jaysh al-inqadh al-islami." Interview by Maysoon Azzam. *Mashahid wa Ara'*, Al Arabiya, 18 October, 2004.

———. 2005. "Mezraq li-*l-Hayat*: jihat fi-l-hukum kanat tuharrik al-ahdath." Interview by Muhammad al-Muqaddim, *al-Hayat*, 8 March, 8.

Miles, H. 2005. *Al Jazeera: The Inside Story of the Arab News Channel that Is Challenging the West*. New York: Grove Press.

al-Miligi, Hassan. 2009. "Imbaraturiyat al-mudawunat: hurras al-maslaha al-'amma wa ruqaba' al-siyasiyin wa wasa'il al-i'lam." *Al Masry Al Youm*, 5 November.

Mishal, Shaul, and Avraham Sela. 2000. *The Palestinian Hamas: Vision, Violence and Coexistence*. New York: Columbia University Press.

Moghadam, Assaf. 2008/2009. "Motives for Martyrdom." *International Security* 33 (Winter): 46–78.

Moore, Barrington, Jr. 1966. *The Social Origins of Dictatorship and Democracy: Lord and Peasant in the Making of the Modern World*. Boston: Beacon Press.

Morgenthau, Hans. 1948. *Politics among Nations*. New York: Knopf.

Morris, Benny. 2001. *Righteous Victims: A History of the Zionist–Arab Conflict, 1881–1999*. New York: Vintage.

Mosaad, Nevine. 2008. *al-Musharka al-siyasiya li-l-mar'a al-'arabiya*. Cairo: Friedrich Ebert Stiftung.

Moul, W. 1989. "Measuring the Balance of Power: A Look at Some Numbers." *Review of International Studies* 15:101–21.

Mounayer, M. 2001. *Hezbollah Unveiled* (Video Recording). Princeton, NJ: Films for the Humanities and Sciences.

Muhanna, Elias. 2009. "Deconstructing the Popular Vote in Lebanon's Election." *Middle East Monitor* 4 (1), http://www.mideastmonitor.org/issues/0907/0907_3.htm (accessed 11 May 2010).

Muqaddim, Muhammad. 1999. "Madani fi janazit Hachani," *al-Hayat*, 24 November 1999, 6.

———. 2005. "Bouteflika yatlub al-'afw 'an 'al-ta'ibin'," *al-Hayat*, 2 September 2005, 6.

al-Nabulsi, Shukri, ed. 2005. *al-Libiraliyyun al-judud: Jadal Fikri*. Cologne: Al-Kamel Verlag.

Nasser, Gamal Abdel. 1960. *Khutab 1959*. Cairo: State Department of Information.

Nelson, A. 2004. "Reality Television." *The Guardian*, 21 April, http://www.guardian.co.uk/media/2004/apr/21/Iraqandthemedia.broadcasting (accessed 7 March 2010).

———. 2008. "Arab Media: The Web 2.0 Revolution." *Carnegie Report* 5 (1), http://www.carnegie.org/reporter/17/amedia2/index.html (accessed 6 January 2009).

"Netanyahu Warns Lebanon over Hezbollah Power-Share." 2009. *Reuters*, 10 August, http://www.reuters.com/article/idUSTRE5794WT20090810 (accessed 11 May 2010).

Noble, Paul. 1991. "The Arab System: Pressures, Constraints, and Opportunities." In Bahgat Korany and Ali E. Hilal Dessouki, eds. The *Foreign Policies of Arab States*, 2nd. ed. 67–167. Boulder, CO: Westview Press.

———. 2008. "From Arab System to Middle Eastern System." In Bahgat Korany and Ali E.H. Dessouki, eds. *The Foreign Policies of Arab States*, 3rd ed. 67–166. Cairo and New York: American University in Cairo Press.

Norton, Augustus Richard. 2007a. *Hezbollah: A Short History*. Princeton, NJ: Princeton University Press.

———. 2007b. "The Role of Hezbollah in Lebanese Domestic Politics." *International Spectator* 42 (4): 475–91.

Nye, Joseph S., Jr. 1989. *Bound to Lead: The Changing Nature of American Power*. New York: Basic Books.

Oakley, Cory. 2007. "Hezbollah's Victory Shatters Israeli 'Invincibility.'" *Socialist Alternative*, 26 April. http://www.sa.org.au/mag-archive-from-old-website/84-edition-107/405-hezbollahs-victory-shatters-israeli-invincibility (accessed 11 May 2010).

Orbit website. 2009. http://www.orbit.net (accessed 7 January 2009).

Ottaway, Marina, Amr Hamzawy, and Robert Dunn. 2009. *Limited Pluralism*. Washington, D.C.: Carnegie Endowment for International Peace.

Ottaway, Marina, and Julia Choucair-Vizoso, eds. 2008. *Beyond the Façade: Political Reform in the Arab World*. Cairo: American University in Cairo Press.

Ould Mohammedou, Mohamed M. 2007. *Understanding Al Qaeda: The Transformation of War*. London: Pluto Press.

Owen, Roger. 2000. "The Cumulative Impact of Middle Eastern Wars." In Steven Heydemann, ed. *War, Institutions and Social Change in the Middle East*, 325–34. Berkeley and London: University of California Press.

Oyahia, Ahmad. 2007. "al-Jaza'ir tu'lin maqtal 17 alf musallah mundhu bidayat al-'unf." Interview by Bou Allam Ghimrasa, *al-Hayat*, 22 March, 1, 6.

Palestinian Central Bureau of Statistics for the Palestinian National Authority. 2007. "Palestine in Figures, 2007," http://www.paltrade.org/en/about-palestine/Figures.pdf (accessed 31 January 2010).

Peres, Shimon, with Arye Noar. 1993. *The New Middle East.* New York: Henry Holt.

Pintak, L. 2006. *America, Islam, and the War of Ideas: Reflections in a Bloodshot Lens.* Cairo: American University in Cairo Press.

PLO Negotiations Affairs Department. "Palestinian Refugees," http://www.bad-plo.org/news-updates/PalestinianRefugees.pdf.

Price, M. 2008. "A Charter of Contradictions." *Arab Media and Society,* March, http://www.arabmediasociety.com/?article=650 (accessed 6 January 2009).

Qaradawi, Yusuf. 1998. "al-Mas'uliya al-shar'iya 'an ahdath al-Jaza'ir." *al-Shari'a wa-l-hayah*, Al Jazeera, 1 February.

Quandt, William. 1986. *Camp David: Peace-making and Politics.* Washington, D.C.: Brookings Institution.

———, ed. 1988. *The Middle East: Ten Years after Camp David.* Washington, D.C.: Brookings Institutions.

Reporters Sans Frontières (RSF). 2006. "Handbook for Bloggers and Cyber Dissidents." http://www.rsf.org (accessed 14 December 2008).

———. 2010. World Day Against Cyber Censorship. http://www.rsf.org (accessed 13 March 2010).

Ritzer, George, ed. 2007. *The Blackwell Companion to Globalization.* London, Blackwell.

Rivlin, Richard. 2007. *Desert Capitalists.* London: Blatonmore Media Ltd.

Riyad, Mahmud. 1982. *Mudhakkirat Mahmud Riyad*, vol. 2. Cairo: Dar al-Mustaqbal a1-'Arabi.

Roberts, Hugh. 2001. "France and the Lost Honor of Algeria's Army." *Times Literary Supplement*, 12 October, 3.

Rogan, Eugene. 2005. "The Emergence of the Middle East into the Modern State System." In Louise Fawcett, ed. *International Relations of the Middle East*, 17–46. Oxford: Oxford University Press.

Roy, Oliver. 1996. *The Failure of Political Islam.* Cambridge, MA: Harvard University Press.

———. 2008. *The Politics of Chaos in the Middle East.* New York: Columbia University Press.

Rugh, W. 1979. *The Arab Press: News Media and Political Processes in the Arab World.* Syracuse, NY: Syracuse University Press.

———. 2004. *Arab Mass Media: Newspapers, Radio, and Television in Arab Politics.* Westport, CT and London: Praeger Security International.

Saad, Reem. 2000. "War in the Social Memory of Egyptian Peasants." In Steven Heydemann, ed. *War, Institutions and Social Change in the Middle East*, 240–57. Berkeley and London: University of California Press.

Saghieh, Hazem. 2005. *Ma'zaq al-fard fi-l-Sharq al-Awsat*. London: Saqi Books.

Said, Edward. 1994. *Representations of the Intellectual*. New York: Vintage Books.

———. 1995. *The Politics of Dispossession: The Struggle for Palestinian Self-Determination, 1969–1994*. New York: Vintage Books.

———. 2001. *Power, Politics, and Culture*. New York: Vintage Books.

———. 2003. *Culture and Resistance: Conversations with Edward Said*. Cambridge, MA: South End Press.

———. 2006. *Conversations with Edward Said*. New York: Seagull Books.

Sa'id, Muhammad al-Sayyid. 1994. *Mustaqbal al-nizam al-'arabi ba'd azmat al-khalij*. Kuwait: 'Alam al-Ma'rifa.

Sakr, N. 1999. "Satellite Television and Development in the Middle East." *Middle East Report*, http://www.merip.org/mer/mer210/sakr.html (accessed 6 January 2009).

———. 2001. *Satellite Realms: Transnational Television, Globalization and the Middle East*. London: I.B. Tauris.

———, ed. 2007. *Arab Media and Political Renewal*. London: I.B. Tauris.

Salah, Mohammed. 2003. "al-Sulutat al-Misriya tutliq ithnan min qadat al-Jama'a al-Islamiya." *al-Hayat*, 3 October, 1.

———. 2006. "al-Qahira tuqir bi-itlaq a'da' al-Jama'a al-Islamiya 'ala duf'at." *al-Hayat*, 13 April, 6.

Salame, Ghassan, ed. 1988. "Inter-Arab Politics: The Return of Geography." In William Quandt, ed. *The Middle East: Ten Years after Camp David*, 319–53. Washington, D.C.: Brookings Institution.

———. 1994. *Democratie sans democrates*. Paris: Fayard.

Salamon, Lester M. 2004. *Global Civil Society*, vol. 2. Sterling, VA: Kumarian Press.

Salamon, Lester M., and Helmut Anheier. 1997. *Defining the Nonprofit Sector*. Manchester: Manchester University Press.

Salvatore, A. 1997. *Islam and the Political Discourse of Modernity*. London: Ithaca.

Samroui, Mohamed. 2003. *Chronique des années de sang: Algérie, comment les services secrets ont manipulé les groupes islamistes*. Paris: Denoël.

Sartre, Jean Paul. [1947] 2001. *What Is Literature?* London: Routledge.

Al-Sayed, Mustafa. 1999. "The UAR Experience." In Michael Hudson, ed,. *Middle East Dilemmas*. New York: Columbia University Press.

Sayegh, Yezid. 2000. "War as Leveler, War as Midwife: Palestinian Political Institutions, Nationalism and Society since 1948." In Steven Heydemann, ed. *War, Institutions and Social Change in the Middle East*, 200–39. Berkeley and London: University of California Press.

Schleifer, A. 1998. "Media Explosion in the Arab World: The Pan-Arab Satellite Broadcasters." *Transnational Broadcasting Studies*, no. 1, http://www.tbsjournal.com/Archives/Fall98/Articles1/Pan-Arab_bcasters/pan-arab_bcasters.html (accessed 6 January 2009).

———. 2001. "The Sweet and Sour Success of Al Jazeera." *Transnational Broadcasting Studies*, no. 7, http://www.tbsjournal.com/Archives/Fall01/Jazeera_sas.html (accessed 6 January 2009).

———. 2005. "The Impact of Arab Satellite Television on the Prospects for Democracy in the Arab World." *Foreign Policy Research Institute*, http://www.fpri.org/enotes/20050512.middleeast.schleifer.arabsatel-litetvdemocracy.html (accessed 6 January 2009).

Schlumberger, Oliver. 2007. *Debating Arab Authoritarianism: Dynamics and Durability in Nondemocratic Regimes*. Stanford, CA: Stanford University Press.

Schulz, Michael. 2008. "Hamas between Sharia Rule and Demo-Islam." In Ashok Swain, Ramses Amer, and Joakirn Ojendal, eds. *Globalization and Challenges to Building Peace*, 195–212. London: Anthem Press.

Seib, P. 2007. *New Media and the New Middle East*. New York: Palgrave Macmillan.

Sengupta, Kim, and Ben Lynfield. 2009. "Tunnels—The Secret Weapon for Hamas." *The Independent*, 6 January, http://www.independent.co.uk/news/world/middle-east/tunnels-ndash-the-secret-weapon-for-hamas-1228140.html (accessed 11 May 2010).

Shahin, Emad. 1997. *Political Ascent: Contemporary Islamic Movements in North Africa*. Oxford: Westview Press.

al-Shamsi, Fatma, and Hassan Y. Ali. 2008. "Globalization and Women's Status in the Middle East: A Blessing or a Curse?" Paper presented at the second Arab Women Organization conference, "Women in the Concept and Issues of Human Security: Arab and International Perspectives," Abu Dhabi, 11–13 November.

Shanahan, Rodger. 2005. *The Shia of Lebanon: Clan, Parties and Clerics*. London: I.B. Tauris.

Sharabi, Hisham. 1967. "The Crisis of the Intelligentsia in the Middle East." *The Muslim World* 4(3): 187–93.

Shawkat, Khaled. 2005. "al-Libiraliyyun al-judud aw al-libiraliya kama afhamuha." In Shukri al-Nabulsi, ed. *al-Libiraliyyun al-judud: jadal fikri*, 99–113. Cologne: Al-Kamel Verlag.

Shay, Shaul. 2007. *The Shahids.* London: Transactions Publishers.

Shils, Edward. 1972. *The Intellectual and the Power and Other Essays.* Chicago: Chicago University Press.

Shukri, Ghali. 1970. *Zahirat al-muqawama fi-l-adab al-'arabi.* Cairo: Dar aı-Ma'arif.

Sørensen, Georg. 2006. "Liberalism of Restraints and Liberalism of Imposition: Liberal Values and World Order in the New Millennium." *International Relations* 20 (3): 251–72.

Souidia, Habib. 2002. *al-Harb al-qadhira*, translated from the French by Rose Makhlouf. Damascus: Ward Publications.

Staten, Cliff. 2008. "From Terrorism to Legitimacy: Political Opportunity Structures and the Case of Hezbollah." *Online Journal of Peace and Conflict Resolution* 8 (1): 32–49, http://www.trinstitute.org/ojpcr/8_1staten.pdf (accessed 31 January 2010).

Stephens, Robert. 1971. *Nasser.* London: Penguin.

Sternberg, Fritz. 1950. *Capitalism and Socialism on Trial.* New York: John Day.

Taher, Bahaa. 2009. "al-Thaqafa lam ta'ud laha qima . . . wa 'rigal al-amn' yudirun kul shay'." *Al Masry Al Youm.* Issue no. 1689, 27 January.

Taher, Tahra. 2008. "al-Atfal fi manzumat al-mujtama' al-madani al-'iraqi." In Amani Kandil, ed., *al-Taqrir al-sanawi al-sabi' li-l-munazzamat al-ahliya al-'arabiya: al-atfal fi manzumat al-mujtama' al-madani al-'arabi*, 227–53. Cairo: Arab Network for NGOs.

Tamimi, Azzam. 2001. *Rachid Ghannouci: A Democrat Within Islamism.* New York: Oxford University Press.

———. 2007. *Hamas: A History from Within.* Northampton, MA: Olive Branch Press.

Telhami, Shibley. 1999. "Power, Legitimacy, and Peace-Making in Arab Coalitions: The New Arabism." In Leonard Binder, ed. *Ethnic Conflict and International Politics in the Middle East.* Gainesville, FL: University Press of Florida.

Thomas, Clive T. 1984. *The Rise of the Authoritarian State in Peripheral Societies.* New York: Monthly Review Press.

Thompson, William. 1973. "The Regional Sub-System." *International Studies Quarterly* 16:89–119.

Tilly, Charles, ed. 1975. *The Formation of National States in Western Europe.* Princeton, NJ: Princeton University Press.

Tripp, Charles. 2006. *Islam and the Moral Economy: The Challenges of Capitalism.* New York: Cambridge University Press.

Tucker, Robert C., ed. *The Marx-Engels Reader*, 2nd ed. New York: W.W. Norton Press.

"UN: Gaza Unemployment Rises to 49 Percent." 2008. *Associated Press,* 18 December, http://lists.mcgill.ca/scripts/wa.exe?A2=indo812c&L=palde v&D=1&P=1680 (accessed 24 July 2010).

United Nations Conciliation Commission for Palestine (UNCCP). 1961. *Historical Survey of Efforts of the United Nations Conciliation Commission for Palestine to Secure the Implementation of Paragraph 11 of General Assembly Resolution 194* (III), U.N. Doc. A/AC.25/W.81/Rev.2.

United Nations Development Fund For Women (UNIFEM). 2004. *Progress of Arab Women.* Amman: UNIFEM, Arab States Regional Office.

United Nations Development Programme (UNDP). 2002–2009. *Arab Human Development Reports.* New York: UNDP.

———. 2006. *The Arab Human Development Report: Towards the Rise of Women in the Arab World.* New York: UNDP, Regional Bureau for Arab States.

United Nations Relief and Works Agency (UNRWA). 2008. *Prolonged Crisis in the Occupied Palestinian Territory: Socio-Economic Developments in 2007.* Report no. 3, 51.

United Nations University. 1999. *Codes of Conduct for Partnership in Governance.* New York: United Nations University.

Urwa, Abbas. 2001. "al-Madhabih fi-l-Jaza'ir: huwar ma' al-Profisur Abbas Urwa." *Bila Hudud*, Al Jazeera, 19 February.

"Waking from Its Sleep: A Special Report on the Arab World." 2009. *The Economist*, 25 July, 1–16.

Warschawski, Michel, and Gilbert Achcar. 2006. *The 33 Day War: Israel's War on Hezbollah in Lebanon and its Aftermath.* London: Saqi Books

World Economic Forum. 2007. *The Global Gender Gap Report 2007.* Geneva: World Economic Forum.

Yassine, Sayed, and Kandil, Amani. 2008. "al-Mujtama' al-madani fi itar al-kharita al-ma'rifiya li-l-'alam." In Amani Kandil, ed. *al-Mawsu'a al-arabiya li-l-mujtama' al-madani*, 22–38. Cairo: Arab Network for NGOs.

Yavuz, Hakan M. 2003. *Islamic Political Identity in Turkey*. Oxford: Oxford University Press.

Yous, Nasurllah. 2007. *Qui a Tué à Bentalha?* Paris: La Découverte.

al-Za'aneen, Jamal. 2007. *Taqrir iqlimi 'an al-dirasat al-mashiya li-l-mashru'at al-muwajjaha li-l-mar'a al-'arabiya fi majal al-ittisal*. Cairo: Arab Women Organization.

Zayani, M. 2005. "Introduction: Al Jazeera and the Vicissitudes of the New Arab Mediascape." In M. Zayani, ed. *The Al Jazeera Phenomenon*, 1–46. Boulder, CO: Paradigm.

al-Zayat, Muntasir. 2005. "Muhami al-usuliyyin: mawqifi sa'b fi Bulaq al-Dakrur." *al-Sharq al-awsat*, 9 November, 5.

al-Zu'bai, Basheer. 2007. *Taqrir iqlimi 'an al-dirasat al-mashiya li-l-mashru'at al-muwajjaha li-l-mar'a al-'arabiya fi majal al-iqtisad*. Cairo: Arab Women Organization.

Zubaida, Sami. 2001. *Islam, the People and the State: Political Ideas and Movements in the Middle East*. New York: I.B. Tauris.

Zuhdi, Karam, and Najih Ibrahim. 2002a. *Istratijiyyat wa tafjirat al-Qa'ida: al-akhta' wa-l-akhtar*. Cairo: al-Turath al-Islami.

———. 2002b. *Nahr al-zikrayat*. Cairo: al-Turath al-Islami.

———. 2003. *Tafjirat al-Riyadh: al-ahkam wa-l-athar*. Cairo: al-Turath al-Islami.

Other Sources

al-Ahram

Al Jazeera

Al Masry Al Youm

Arabawy Blog

Al Arabiya

al-Hayat

Internet World States

al-Nahar

al-Taqrir al-stratiji al-'arabi al-sanawi. Cairo: Al-Ahram Center for Political and Strategic Studies, various years.

Index

dialogue 45, 52, 55
Diana 16
donors 53
Dubai 100

E
Economic and Social Commission for
    Western Asia 122
economic reform 44
education 49, 50, 52, 55
Egypt 44, 47, 48, 50, 51, 52, 54, 55, 59, 61,
    63, 64, 65, 69, 71, 72, 74, 75, 78, 81,
    87, 95, 100, 103, 107, 139–60
Egyptian Communist Party 104
Egyptian Network for Child's Rights 51
Egyptian Space Channel 67
El Mehwar 74
elections 79, 185
electronic media 60
elite 23, 44, 48, 92, 94, 95, 96
Emergency Law 54
employment 97
enlightenment 97
entrepreneurship 96, 97, 111
ethics 56
Europe 9, 10, 67, 69, 73, 95
Ezra, Gideon 71

F
Facebook 76, 78–79
Fadlallah, Sheikh Muhammad Hassan
    184
Fahd, Prince 33
al-Farhan, Fouad 81
Farouk, Kind 15
Fatah 194
Fayyad, Ali 186
female empowerment 48, 50, 52, 55

feminism 107
feudalism 96
foreign pressures 44
France 9
Frankfurt School 107
Free Officers 14, 22
freedom 44, 48, 51, 53, 60, 96, 98, 100
freedom of expression 59, 61, 66, 67,
    70, 80, 81

G
Gabriel, Kemal 101
Gaza 71
Gender Parity Indices 122
al-Ghannushi, Rashid 112
al-Ghazzali, Muhammad 112
global financial crisis 57
globalization 8, 44, 48, 94, 98, 100, 101,
    110
good governance 44
Gramsci, Antonio 107
Gulf 49, 50, 53, 54, 57, 59, 63, 67, 73, 77,
    90, 100
Gulf Cooperation Council 23
Gulf War 12, 36, 37, 65, 66, 67, 68, 69

H
Hamas 12, 16, 20, 167–95
al-Hariri, Rafiq 77
Hashem, Jawal 100
Hashemite 17, 24
Hawa, Said 111
Al Hayat 74
al-Husari, Sati' 103
health 48, 49, 50
healthcare 52
Heikal, Muhammad Hassanein 9, 106,
    201

Hezbollah 12, 20, 167–95
Hilal, Ali al-Din 100
Holy Land Foundation for Relief and
    Development 173
households 51
human development 44
human rights 43–44, 46, 48, 50, 51, 52,
    53, 54, 55, 202
Hussein, Saddam 19

I
Ibn Khaldun 95
Ibrahim, Khalid 145
illiteracy 55
imperialism 21, 91, 93
information technology 47
inheritance 51
Initiative for Ceasing Violence 139,
    146
intellectual 85–117
International Center for Journalism 77
International Labor Organization 199
Inter-Parliamentary Union 127
Intifada 176
Iran 9, 59, 60
Iraq 8, 52, 63, 64, 65, 66, 67, 69, 100,
    103, 107
Islam 16, 77, 90, 95, 105
al-Islam Charitable Society 173
Islamic Association 51, 52
Islamic Association for Palestine 173
Islamic Group 139, 140, 144–46, 192
Islamic Salvation Army 140, 146–8
Islamic Salvation Front 140
Islamic Society 173
Islamism 110–15
Islamist 85, 88, 90, 94, 99, 101, 102, 110,
    139–60

Israel 9, 10, 12, 13, 59, 60, 71
Israeli Defense Forces 13, 20
Italy 68
Izz al-Din al-Qassam Brigades 179–80

J
al-Jama's al-Islamiya see Islamic Group
Al Jazeera 61, 65, 69–73, 80, 106
Jerusalem Post 71
Jews 13
Jihadi 140
Jihadism 19
al-Jihad Organization 140
Johns Hopkins University 47
Jordan 48, 50, 52, 64, 69, 73, 75, 81, 87,
    90, 95, 97, 100, 103
Judeh, Nasser 73

K
Kamel, Sheikh Saleh 68
Kaplan, Morton 8
Kennedy, Paul 12
Kharitat al-mujtama' al-madani al-'arabi
    45
Khashoggi, Adnan 33
Khatibi, Abd al-Kebir 109
al-Khawaja, Abdulhadi 202
al-Khazin 106
Khomeini, Ayatollah 15
Knight International Journalism
    Award 77
Kuttab, Daoud 81–82
Kuwait 28, 44, 50, 54, 64, 66, 67, 69,
    87, 95

L
Laroui, Abdallah 109, 110
League of Arab States 10, 18, 23, 28, 119

278 Index

Nile TV International 68, 73
Nilesat 73
Nixon, Richard 27
Nobel Peace Prize 18
nonstate actors 20, 167–95
North Africa 67
North America 73

O
Occupied Palestinian Territories 167,
    171, 172
October War 12, 13, 19, 27, 91
oil 30, 33
Oman 54, 69
Orbit 68, 69, 74, 80
Organization of the Petroleum
    Exporting Countries 27
organizations 43–44, 46, 49, 51, 52, 54,
    55, 56, 67
Orthodox Association 51
Oslo Accords 18, 174–75
Ottoman Empire 12, 16

P
Pahlavi dynasty 15
Pakistan 9
Palestine 13, 50, 90, 95, 106, 107
Palestine Liberation Organization 174
Palestinian issue 71, 72
Palestinian Territories 63
Pan-Arab 24, 27–33, 63, 106
philanthropic 52–53
political discourse 48
political parties 44
political reform 44
political science 46
Popular Front for the Liberation of
    Palestine 104

poverty 44, 48, 50, 52
preaching 52
print journalism 60
private sector 94, 123, 131, 132
privatization 11, 98
professional habilitation 52
progressive 91, 99
protest movements 44
public opinion 56

Q
Qadhafi, Mu'ammar 26, 197
al-Qaeda 38, 139, 140, 141, 146
al-Qahira al-yawm 69
al-Qaradawi, Youssef 112
Qatar 50, 54, 64, 69, 71, 72, 80, 81
al-Qusi, Khalid Ibrahim 144

R
Rabat 44
radicalization 192
Radio Monte Carlo 66
Rajjam, Abd al-Razzaq 147
refugees 169
registration 53, 54
religious discourse 46
Reuters 76
revolution 11, 14, 15, 60, 62
Rhodes armistice agreement 10
Rida, Rashid 110
Rugh, William 62

S
al-Sabah, Jabir al-Ahmad al-Jabir 202
Sadat, Anwar 28, 34, 62, 140
al-Sadr, Imam Musa 193
Saghieh, Hazem 99
Said, Abd al-Mon'iem 100